CU00960993

THE RIDGES OF
ENGLAND, WALES AND IRELAND

SCRAMBLING, MOUNTAINEERING AND CLIMBING

About the Author

Outdoor journalist and author Dan Bailey has a passion for the world's wild steep places. When he's not out researching guidebooks he photographs and writes about mountain sports for travel and outdoor magazines, Sunday newspapers and online media. He has hiked, climbed and occasionally hobbled in mountains across five continents, although he still maintains that the hills of home are tops. Dan and his wonderful wife live on the Fife Riviera, within easy reach of rocks, water and the superb Scottish Highlands.

Dan Bailey is also the author of *Scotland's Mountain Ridges* (Cicerone) and *West Highland Way* (Pocket Mountains).

THE RIDGES OF
ENGLAND, WALES AND IRELAND

SCRAMBLING, MOUNTAINEERING AND CLIMBING

by
Dan Bailey

2 POLICE SQUARE, MILNTHORPE, CUMBRIA LA7 7PY
www.cicerone.co.uk

© Dan Bailey 2009
First edition 2009
ISBN: 978 1 85284 539 1

A catalogue record for this book is available from the British Library.

Photographs by the author unless otherwise stated.

oS Ordnance Survey® This product includes mapping data licensed from Ordnance Survey® with the permission of the Controller of Her Majesty's Stationery Office. © Crown copyright 2009. All rights reserved. Licence number PU100012932.

Maps for routes 42 to 48 include Ordnance Survey Ireland data reproduced under Ordnance Survey Ireland Permit number 8559. © Ordnance Survey Ireland/Government of Ireland.

Printed by KHL Printing Co Pte Ltd, Singapore.

Warning

Mountaineering can be a dangerous activity carrying a risk of personal injury or death. It should be undertaken only by those with a full understanding of the risks and with the training and experience to evaluate them. While every care and effort has been taken in the preparation of this guide, the user should be aware that conditions, especially in winter, can be highly variable and can change quickly. Holds may become loose or fall off, rockfall can affect the character of a route, snow and avalanche conditions must be carefully considered. These can materially affect the seriousness of a climb, tour or expedition.

Therefore, except for any liability which cannot be excluded by law, neither Cicerone nor the author accepts liability for damage of any nature (including damage to property, personal injury or death) arising directly or indirectly from the information in this book.

Advice to Readers

Readers are advised that, while every effort is made by our authors to ensure the accuracy of our guidebooks as they go to print, changes can occur during the lifetime of a particular edition. Please check the Cicerone website (www.cicerone.co.uk) for any updates before planning your trip. It is also advisable to check information on such things as transport, accommodation and shops locally. Even rights of way can be altered over time. We are always grateful for information about any discrepancies between a guidebook and the facts on the ground, sent by email to info@cicerone. co.uk or by post to 2 Police Square, Milnthorpe LA7 7PY.

Front cover (main picture): The pinnacle on pitch 8 of Amphitheatre Buttress (Route 21).
Inset top: Sunset on the pinnacles on Howling Ridge (Route 44) *Inset bottom:* The knife edge, pitch 4 of Commando Ridge (Route 20) *Back cover:* The Glaciated Slab on Intake Ridge (Route 15)

CONTENTS

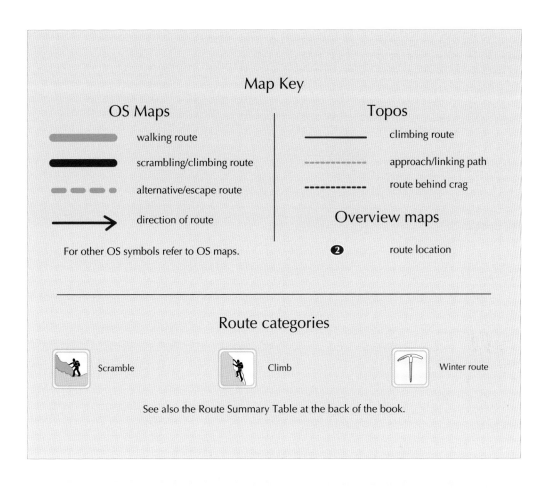

Map Key

OS Maps

———————— walking route

———————— scrambling/climbing route

– – – – • alternative/escape route

——————▶ direction of route

For other OS symbols refer to OS maps.

Topos

———————— climbing route

·-·-·-·-·-·- approach/linking path

– – – – – – – route behind crag

Overview maps

❷ route location

Route categories

Scramble

Climb

Winter route

See also the Route Summary Table at the back of the book.

Thanks and Acknowledgements

A project of this scale couldn't be completed without plenty of advice and assistance. Many people deserve my thanks: David George of Outdoor Elements and Stephanie Briggs of Spring PR for providing Raichle footwear – it was a long rocky road. Pauline Hand at Ordnance Survey for all those maps. Juliet Hutton of Harvey Maps for her own cartographical contributions. John Appleby for his wisdom on 'lost' Welsh ridges. Terry Cheek for sharing his extensive knowledge of the Exmoor Coast. Graham Adcock for his thoughts on Skeleton Ridge. Patrick Doyle and Paddy Dillon for mountains of Irish hill info. Glenda Davies of Visitwales and Charlene Boyle and Johanna King of Tourism Ireland for helping field trips run smoothly. I'd also like to thank all the friends with whom I shared climbs in this book, for going far beyond the call of duty, shrugging off the showers and still coming out smiling (usually) – Gemma Bayliss, Mark Beaumont, Jan Coggins, Andrew Guckian, Chris Harrison, Nathan Kingerlee, Ross Kinghorn, Lorraine McCall, Steve Perry, Lizzie Pinard, Derek Queenan, Tom Rimmington, Martina Sykorova, Alan Walker, Ben Whiteley, Clare Wilkie and Joe Williams. I'm grateful too to the Cicerone team for all their support and patience; we got there eventually. Finally, love and admiration are due as ever to my wife Pegs for making it all worthwhile.

Location of routes

ATLANTIC
OCEAN

NORTH
SEA

○ Inverness

○ Fort William

Edinburgh ○

Carlisle ○

1–16

LAKE
DISTRICT

Belfast ○

IRISH
SEA

47–48
CONNEMARA

Galway ○

Dublin ○

Manchester ○

○ Sheffield

17

PEAK
DISTRICT

21–39

40

41 SNOWDONIA

45–46
KERRY

Cork ○

42–44

Cardiff ○

London ○

19

EXMOOR

Southampton ○

18 ISLE OF WIGHT

○ Plymouth

20

ENGLISH
CHANNEL

Climbers on Napes Needle and Needle Ridge (Route 13)

INTRODUCTION

THERE IS SOMETHING SPECIAL about ridges. When rock, sky and climber meet a sort of spell is woven, an experience that blends vastness with detail, mind-cleansing space with up-close climbing intricacy. Mountaineers with an eye for bold forms and beautiful backdrops are drawn to the edges, where some of the most rewarding routes in the British Isles are waiting. The strength of the pull is in the line. Seen from a distance the compelling simplicity of an arete unfailingly draws the attention. You can't help scaling it in your mind's eye before even leaving the valley, picturing yourself grappling with pinnacles and tiptoeing along knife edges. The irresistibility of mountain ridges was felt too by climbing's pioneers; the most prominent of our ridges were explored in the sport's infant days, and have a rich traditional heritage built over decades of ascents.

On such venerable classics old fashioned mountaineering challenges like route finding, exposure and weather – rather than technical prowess – come to the fore. In contrast to cragging or sport climbing the moves matter rather less than the overall feel, the sense that we're having an adventure in a high, wild place. Since the scale and beauty of the surroundings are integral to the endeavour, climbing ridges is as much an aesthetic experience as a physical exercise. As we trace a skyline route it's almost as if we are enacting a sort of topographical metaphor for determinism. The land's twists and turns are laid out ahead. There's no turning aside; we can only go on, following where our ridge leads. But that's not to say we're not free to enjoy ourselves along the way – in fact, that's the whole point!

As did its sister volume, *Scotland's Mountain Ridges*, this book aims to be a practical blow-by-blow guide but also a collection to browse at home, drawing inspiration for future trips or fondly reliving past exploits. Rejecting the arbitrary convention that divides climbing from

The strength of the pull is in the line – Tryfan and Bristly Ridge (Route 31), East Gully Arete (Route 30) and Dolmen Ridge (Route 29) from the Gribin Ridge

(Left) Mounting the crest on the unique pitch 6, Skeleton Ridge (Route 18)

scrambling has allowed route selection to rely purely on merit rather than difficulty. The featured ridges span the grade spectrum from the simplest of scrambles to mid-level rock climbs, aiming to please mountaineers of all stripes. The hope is that less hands-on hillwalkers will view the harder routes as goals to work towards, while even the most seasoned climber ought to recognise that the easier classics are hugely worthwhile. To reject routes of low technicality on the basis of grade alone would just be to deny oneself a fully rounded appreciation of the hills.

Although many chapters incorporate a ridge into a longer day of hillwalking, the adventurous atmosphere of even the simplest scrambles puts them on a different level from everyday walking. The inclusive ethos only goes so far; this is definitely a book for mountaineers, both aspiring and accomplished. Because ridge climbing is a perennial pastime there's a seasonal element too, with only a small number of graded winter climbs (I wish there were more). From gentle to gnarly, the common thread binding these routes is that they are all ridges – and all rewarding.

Scotland is the undisputed acme of British Isles mountain ridge climbing; but while there's nothing further south to equal the Cuillin's scale or the majesty of An Teallach, the routes detailed here have plenty of variety and quality. The rugged post-glacial ranges of Cumbria, Snowdonia and Kerry naturally offer most scope to ridge enthusiasts. But superb adventures can be found elsewhere too, even a few in surprisingly unmountainous seaside locations – proof that there's climbing gold *beyond* them thar hills. From the rolling Derbyshire dales to the sunkissed south coast of England the settings are as diverse as they are dispersed. Chalk, limestone, sandstone, gritstone, quartzite, rhyolite, granite and grass – the broad range of terrain featured here reflects both the geological richness of mountaineering in these islands and the wonderful variety of landscapes that we have at our disposal.

SO WHAT IS A RIDGE ANYWAY?

Some span the empty air between summits; others buttress the flanks of craggy cwms or sea cliffs. Wherever it may be, if it's longer than it is wide, with a defined crest and steep sides, then it is unquestionably a ridge. So far, so unambiguous. But in order to accommodate some otherwise

very worthwhile borderline cases this book has relaxed the selection criteria slightly. While they do incorporate sharp-edged sections into their length, a handful of the chosen routes could more honestly be described as hybrids – part ridge, part something else; the climbs on Dove Crag (route 5) and Grey Crag (route 16) are two such. Other non-rigorous grounds to cover a route include simply what it's called. Cam Crag Ridge (route 15) is really more of a rambling buttress if we're splitting hairs, but since it's an excellent scramble then who cares? Arete my case.

GEOGRAPHICAL SPREAD

Three nations feature in this book. It's a slightly quirky grouping, but the reasoning is that no single country south of Scotland has enough ridge climbing scope to warrant a volume to itself. The ties that bind in this case are coils of rope, the common ground the routes themselves – and if climbing can't unite us all for a while then what hope is there? Among the areas covered Northern Ireland is conspicuous by its absence. Taking a lead from Monty Python this book accepts the fact that Ulster has no decent ridges, which is no one's fault – not even the English – but it does support Northern Ireland's *right* to ridges.

GRADES AND DIFFICULTY

When is a 'scramble' really a 'climb'? How long is a piece of rope? Trying to draw a firm line between scrambling and rock climbing, as if they were essentially distinct activities, would be futile. Yet convention suggests we do just that. Perhaps this is because two independent grading systems have evolved, one for hillwalking scramblers and the other for climbers. The fuzzy area in which these grades merge is a place of confusion.

But really, what's the difference? Both scrambling and climbing involve using your hands (feet, chin, dogged determination and the rest) to move over steep ground from which it would be undesirable to fall. Both can be incorporated into a long day in the hills. You might think that scrambles don't require a rope, but some certainly do. And although climbing is generally seen as something that's done with strings attached, climber are often happy to go rope-free. The key difference lies in the degree of difficulty, which is surely a matter for each individual, and

So when does a 'scramble' become a 'climb'?
Blurring the boundaries on the East Ridge of Brandon Peak (Route 46)

so this book makes no fundamental distinction between scrambles and climbs.

Nevertheless it's helpful to abide by the conventional grades. With a little fine tuning the confusing mess can be incorporated into one complete system. In this book the obsolete climbing grade Easy has been superceded and subdivided into scrambling grades 1 to 3. After this come the conventional climbing grades Moderate, Difficult and so on. The weird and confusing 3S classification sometimes employed in scrambling guidebooks has been abandoned, because it overlaps with the climbing grade Moderate.

- *Grade 1* is where hillwalking becomes really interesting. Classic examples include the traverse of Crib Goch and Blencathra's Sharp Edge, routes that walkers with little relevant experience but a head for heights would find achievable – if exciting – in benign conditions. Although they can be very exposed the hands-on passages are generally

short and sometimes even avoidable. Route finding is intuitive.

- *Grade 2* routes include longer sections on steeper rock, generally a little more technical and not so easily downclimbed or escaped from. The safest line may not be immediately obvious and competence is required.

- *Grade 3* routes are committing and serious, with at least one (sometimes more) significant pitch of exposed thought-provoking ground that may include moves of Moderate or even Difficult standard climbing.

- *Moderate* is like grade 3, only more so; and things just get more exciting from there...

A mountain simply *is*. Neither the routes up it nor the grades they are given would exist without climbers, and a ridge is only a climb because we choose to use it as such. Grading is an abstract and

CLIMBING GRADES				
UK Adjectival	**UK Technical**	**UIAA**	**France (sport)**	**US**
1 scramble				5.1
2 scramble		I	1	
3 scramble				5.2
Moderate				
Difficult 'Diff'		II	2	5.3
Very Difficult 'V Diff'		III	3	5.4
Severe 'S'		IV		5.5
			4	
	4a	V-		5.6
Hard Severe 'HS'	4b		5	
		V		
Very Severe 'VS'	4c			5.7
		V+		
				5.8
			5+	
Hard Very Severe 'HVS'	5a	VI-		
				5.9
		VI	6a	
Extremely Severe 1 'E1'	5b			5.10a
		VI+	6a+	5.10b
etc				

imperfect attempt to calibrate the experience, a sort of language in a limited sense; it doesn't have meaning *out there*, but only in use. Whether we find a route hard or easy is entirely down to us. The scales we measure it against say plenty about climbers and rather less about the rock; they are objective only insofar as they represent a consensus. Grades convey a very limited set of data, and fail to capture most of *how it feels to you* to climb a certain route on a given day: the rock's rough warmth; the percussive chink of climbing gear on a heathery breeze; the greys and greens of the mountain backdrop; the banter. Difficulty really isn't proportional to quality, so don't get hung up on the numbers – they only mean what we let them.

Grade table

Collating and comparing international grading systems isn't an exact science, but the table opposite should at least give overseas visitors, or those new to climbing, a rough field translation between different schemes. The common abbreviation of each adjectival grade is listed on the table (Difficult is usually referred to as Diff, Very Severe as VS and so on).

LEARNING THE ROPES?

By their nature the ridges detailed in this book tend to have a strong mountaineering flavour – even the seaside ones. Beginners might find the relative remoteness and the sense of scale daunting, but these aspects are integral to the experience. Reading a route on paper is a very different exercise from climbing up it. What might in advance look like an easy romp could well hold a few surprises on the day – awkward gear placements or perplexing route finding. Spiced with difficulty of escape and occasional looseness, dampness, dirt and botany, the weatherbeaten adventurous atmosphere of the big traditional crags puts even the easiest ridge into a different league from the balmy bolted clip-ups of Portland or Sella. Those more accustomed to the join-the-dots gymnastics of sport or indoor climbing will need to adopt a new approach in the hills; this is an entirely different game, as close to sport climbing as fell running is to sprinting. But that's not to say it is exclusive or inaccessible. Ridge climbs are not the preserve of grizzled beardies with secret

Compared to the Alps our hills lack only scale – Yr Wyddfa and Garnedd Ugain from the Crib Goch pinnacles (Route 33)

Moving together can be a handy skill on easy ridges – racing the sunset on Howling Ridge (Route 44)

handshakes and an encyclopaedic knowledge of arcane knots. Given that grade 1 scrambles are just hands-on walks with added exposure there's a good old-fashioned classic for even the greenest beginner.

On these routes all-round hill fitness trumps a chicken-legged boulderer's physique, and the solid attributes of a hillwalking and scrambling generalist are of far more use than an ability to 'heel hook', 'thumb sprag' and 'crank like a disease'. The cobwebby term *hill sense* captures it nicely. Requisites for the average ridge include an aptitude with map and compass, sound basic rope work, cool route finding judgement on complex and occasionally serious terrain, the ability to take loose rock and vegetation in one's stride, stamina for the long walk-ins and a sense of humour when you get rained off yet again. Even in southerly hills weather conditions can be harsh – stormy whiteouts in the Carneddau for instance can be almost Cairngorm-like in their ferocity, and life-threatening for the unwary or underprepared.

Assimilating all this by making a gradual progression through the grades from the easiest scrambles upwards is a traditional route into mountaineering and an immensely satisfying way to learn the ropes. (See Appendix 1 for a list of the routes in this book, in ascending order of difficulty.) Many ridges are suited to this DIY approach. Nevertheless it would be remiss of any guidebook author not to suggest that it is safer – if less adventurous – to practise techniques under the expert supervision of an experienced friend or qualified instructor. Since the sport began, British and Irish climbers looking to progress into the Alpine arena have honed their skills on the classic ridges closer to home. But while there are few better places to build the necessary confidence and competence, these routes are so much more than just a stepping stone to higher things. Only in terms of sheer scale are the hills of home a second-best option. If the days of affordable long weekends in the Alps are numbered, we've plenty to fall back on.

Whether or not you're practising for the Matterhorn, ridges with discontinuous hard scrambling or easy climbing can be good places to employ the 'Alpine' technique of moving together (what our transatlantic cousins call *simulclimbing*). Since its utility is generally confined to scrambly ground, and in particular ridge routes, climbers more attuned to outcrops or walls might regard this as a dark art. Although the principles are simple, the technique frequently seems to be badly bodged, and its misuse can have disastrous consequences – one off, all off. Ideally moving together should be both safer than soloing and quicker than pitching. But for this to be so it is essential to have minimal slack and decent protection between the climbers at all times, either leader-placed or natural runners; all members of a party need to be climbing comfortably within their limit, to be

working as a smooth intuitive team, and to be alert to the situations in which taking a quick belay might actually be more sensible. Handled right, moving together is a trusty weapon in your ridge climbing armoury – but it needs to be learned through careful practice, and should never be employed casually.

STAYING SAFE

Although serious climbers are occasionally snobbish about low-grade 'bimbles', unroped scrambling can be as psychologically testing as any 'climb' and is often rather riskier. On any route of any difficulty there are places where an unprotected slip could be unpleasant or even terminal; gravity respects no grade distinctions after all. Classics like Crib Goch can be as mobbed as a high street in the sales, but despite the carefree atmosphere the frequency of serious accidents on such low-grade routes is high. Even the easiest ridges are far from trivial, and need to be treated with respect.

There's grim enjoyment in battling hostile elements – snow turns to downpour on Great Gable (Route 14)

The key to a full appreciation of the outdoors (to say nothing of a long healthy life) is remaining flexible in the face of changing conditions. When it rains experienced climbers might sensibly set their sights a bit lower than they'd planned, settling for a scramble when harder things don't appeal. There is a grim enjoyment to be had in battling hostile elements and winning through to achieve something substantial, but bear in mind that ridge scrambles can be particularly precarious in wet or windy weather. In these conditions walkers for whom the routes are a challenge at the best of times ought to think twice, particularly if the party is of mixed abilities. Whether or not it is responsible to bring children on a scramble, for instance, is a matter for personal judgement on the day. Suffice to say, none of the routes in this book should be treated lightly. Enjoy them but always have an eye for the possible consequences, and never be embarrassed to retreat.

WHAT GEAR?

Ropes

Since one person's gripping epic is another's inconsequential solo it's not helpful to dictate when, where or how to use safety gear here. Confidence can vary with mood and with the weather and the decision whether to solo, move together or resort to pitches can only be made on-route. However, for readers new to this game, I can offer some general guidance. Scramblers on a grade 1 route can sensibly expect not to need a rope. On grade 2 and 3 scrambles it is wise to carry one – also a harness and a minimal rack consisting of a few nuts, slings and runners. Ideally it'll stay in the bag all day; but then who knows when you'll encounter an unexpected tricky bit, a slimy seep, a cloudburst or a simple loss of nerve? Gear choice for Moderates and Difficults is a grey area even for accomplished climbers, but as a general rule once the route is hard enough that you're consciously holding on and planning the next moves with care then it's usually time to crack out the kit. Climbs of around Diff/VDiff and upwards tend to be tackled with conventional fixed pitches and a full rack.

Footwear

In days of yore leather boots were *de rigueur*. Anyone training for the Alps could choose to follow in the pioneers' clumpy footsteps on even the hardest routes detailed in this book, although there's no need to do so. If you've got reasonably supportive and grippy soles then either summer walking boots and or approach shoes will suffice on the long stretches of bottom-end climbing that tend to characterise routes from grade 1 to about Difficult – they're better than climbing shoes in the rain and rough, and who wants to carry extra unnecessary footwear? Not being a fan of wet toes and sprained ankles I favour boots, while fellrunning lightweights tend to go for trainers. Moving further up the grade scale people generally feel happier in rock shoes. As if consumer choice weren't already baffling enough, there is another footwear option to consider – the walking/scrambling/climbing hybrid – but in general these are designed for drier climes, and fall down on waterproofing.

Winter gear

Picking the right gear to suit a given winter climb can be the subject of much deliberation and even public disagreement in magazines and web forums. Since the winter content of this book is minimal there's no need here to wade into debates about how long an axe should be. As a rough rule of thumb for beginners, the minimum gear for a grade I ridge in winter is: suitably stiff 4-season crampon-compatible boots; 10 or 12-point crampons designed for general mountaineering use and a single mountaineering or walking axe. A rope is optional, though there may be times you'll wish you'd brought one. Climbs of grade II, III and upwards tend to feel safer with 12-point (or even 14-point) crampons, two technical tools and a full winter rack.

Headgear

Head protection is another source of controversy in the climbing media. When to don a helmet is a decision for each individual, although wherever there's loose rock waiting to be kicked down onto your head – and that's pretty much any route in this book – it might save you a serious injury. A prevalent misapprehension is that easy ground means low risk, but once the air is thick with whirring missiles of death it's irrelevant whether you're scrambling Tryfan with the kids in tow or teetering up a crumbling South Coast chalk horror. Arguably the busier the route, the more chance there is of stonefall.

Despite climate change it's still possible to get lucky: winter grips Helvellyn (Route 2)
... and the crowds come flocking

Traditionally climbers were penny pinching scruffbags, fanatical freeloaders who thought nothing of hitching to the Himalaya and wouldn't have been seen dead in a brand new softshell. It would be a shame if that noble heritage were advertised into oblivion. Fashion has as much to answer for on the hills as on the catwalk. Take the current marketing mantra 'light = right' (a sceptical translation might be 'spend more, get less'). While going unencumbered is nice for backpackers and runners, and genuinely important on big serious alpine routes where speed increases safety, it need not be the first priority for domestic climbs and scrambles. Rough rock soon takes its toll on less durable lightweight gear. Besides, are the weight savings even noticeable on your average British hill day in any case? Why pay for a trendy tissue paper rucksack if you're then going to stuff it brim full of heavy chocks and chocolate, cams and cameras? If your battered old kit still does the job then surely it's better to make do for another year and save money for petrol and pub?

WINTER ROUTES

Winter climbing might be possible from October to May on higher Scottish hills, but the window of opportunity is generally narrower further south. For those parts of the British Isles that aren't fortunate enough to call themselves Caledonian, conditions have always been notoriously fickle and fleeting – especially so in recent years. Contemporary climbers could be forgiven for thinking that there are really only two seasons – dry and wet – the latter holding sway for 11 months. The irony is that this is happening at a time when winter mountaineering is enjoying an unprecedented boom in popularity. Those who find the climate disheartening are in the company of guidebook writers and the long-suffering friends that they drag on rainy research trips. Many of the climbs described here as summer trips would be fantastic under snow, and where possible the route notes give a little appropriate information. However poor conditions during the preparation period for this book meant that only a handful of ridges could be climbed and photographed in good winter conditions.

Of the regions covered in this book the Lake District offers the best chance of axe-wielding action, while significant freezes are rather less common in North Wales. Travel further south-west again and there's a snowball's chance in Hell (although the vertical vegetated slopes of Kerry and Connemara would be superb in any future ice age). However, névé say never. Ignore the jaded pessimists, nurture a flickering flame of faith in a secret corner of your heart, and you might just get lucky some time. As with all the best things in life, the right conditions don't last long, so you need to be prepared to drop everything at short notice to take advantage of them. Opportunism is the name of the game; forward planning (beyond having your gear ready by the front door) is generally fruitless.

Winter climbing isn't defined by the season so much as the state of the route – and this is where ethics come in. Climate change-driven desperation might have fostered a tendency to regard any light dusting of snow as suitable, but climbing out-of-condition routes is just environmental vandalism dressed up as dry (or rather, wet) tooling. It's best to avoid technical winter routes unless the turf is solid, rocks rimed and snow cover is more than a cosmetic patina; those who don't play by these rules could be damaging rare plants and spoiling things for everyone else. Arguably the point needs labouring more south of the border, where the pressure of numbers is greater and the hordes are concentrated in just a few key venues for one or two weekends annually. We all dream of névé gleaming under a blue sky, but given the more likely event of unconsolidated powder or slush, teams with their hearts set on a ridge might consider a classic easy scrambling traverse such as Striding Edge or the Snowdon Horseshoe. Such routes don't rely on turf or ice, and can be done with a clear conscience in most conditions. No turf was harmed in the making of this book.

Winter routes are graded numerically using Roman numerals (to distinguish them from the Arabic numerals of scrambling grades). Starting from a fairly basic I the numbers run up to around X, with the scale left open-ended at the top to accommodate future rises in climbing standards. Climbs are graded for good conditions; but if the state of the ground changes daily as a result of the weather then so too can the difficulty. On a route climbed after fresh snowfall you could be excavating holds and protection from precarious mounds of powder; return to the same spot once freeze-thaw has firmed things up and axes might be swung confidently into polystyrene névé. These are dramatically different experiences – yet on paper it's the same route. So long as grades are taken with a healthy pinch of salt this variability is one of the great attractions of winter mountaineering.

Winter grades

Grade I
Where hillwalking turns into mountaineering. This covers easy snow gullies up to about 45° and ridges that would get a low scrambling grade in summer, such as Crib Goch or Striding Edge. Care and basic competence is required, although in good conditions experienced climbers may happily solo.

Grade II
Notably steeper, with short ice pitches in gullies or sections of basic technical mixed climbing on ridges. Ropes are a very sensible precaution.

Grade III
Appreciable technical pitches requiring a full range of winter climbing skills and equipment; can be very tricky in imperfect conditions.

Grade IV
More serious and sustained again… and so on.

AVALANCHE!

Snowfall can bring with it the dangers of cornices and avalanches. Those who assume that these are only worth worrying about north of the border might note that the worst avalanche disaster in British history took place not in the Cairngorms but in the South Downs. On 27 December 1836 a row of houses in the Sussex town of Lewes was obliterated by a huge mass of snow shed from the steep hillside above. About 15 people were buried, eight of whom perished. Back then of course, winters really were winters. In these less snowy times the Highlands tend to have the most frequent and the biggest avalanches, but even in the relatively benign mountain environments of North Wales and Cumbria slides do occasionally happen, and people have been caught out with tragic consequences.

Climbers are perhaps less likely to be buried alive than simply knocked off their feet and carried over a crag, but either scenario is undesirable. At times of high avalanche risk a ridge may well be a safer option than the gullies on either side of it, but don't count on it uncritically. A well-known avalanche black spot in the Lake District, for instance, is the scarp slope leading from Striding Edge to the Helvellyn plateau; there are many others. It pays to be alert throughout the approach and walk-off, since these will tend to cross slopes at an ideal angle for a slide.

Because of the rarity of the necessary conditions England, Wales and Ireland are not graced with avalanche forecasting services of the calibre of Scotland's SAIS. With the exception of the very useful felltop conditions reports from Helvellyn climbers have to fall back on their own

judgement. It's sensible to study the weather patterns for a few days prior to heading out, noting how much snow may be falling on the hills and the aspects on which untrustworthy windborne accumulations might be expected. When out keep tabs on the stability of the snowpack, and don't be shy about changing plans if there's a reasonable doubt. Consider booking on an avalanche awareness course or, at the very least, read a decent textbook, such as *Avalanche!* by Robert Bolognesi (Cicerone 2007). Don't die of ignorance, as they say.

WILD NIGHTS OUT

Seen through a time lapse camera the evening exodus of walkers from the hills might look almost a natural rhythm, a diurnal mass migration in step with the music of the spheres. As darkness approaches people tend to hurry downwards, as if fearing monsters in the gloom. But with a head torch and an open mind there's no reason for hill days to end at sunset. Why not climb high in the last rays of sunshine, savouring evening's pyrotechnic colours from a summit and saving the walkout for the hush of dusk? Indeed, why go home at all? Night walking can be eye-opening,

The advantage of a late finish – evening pyrotechnics over Pillar

Wild campsites are everywhere, and they're not all as busy as this one at Styhead Tarn

darkness cloaking daytime's familiar contours in mysterious murk. Bathed in a milky moonlight strong enough to cast shadows, ridge scrambles take on a novel and dream-like charm.

Those for whom comfort and convenience are high priorities might be pleased to learn that there is no practical need to stay out overnight on any of the routes described in this book. However there is much to be gained from doing so. The camp/climb combination is a deeply rewarding aspect of mountaineering, a way to get closer to nature for longer, absorbing the silence and solitude in unhurried contemplation long after the daylight hordes have melted away. You will feel more connected to the land when you're not sharing it with gangs of fellow walkers. More prosaically, setting up a base below a remote crag can give you several days of mountain climbs for the price of only one walk-in. Wild camping in the warmer months can be a rare treat, but in winter it is unlikely to save much time or leave you in a better state to climb in the morning than might a slightly longer walk-in from a warm bed in the valley.

Outside peak daylight hours even the most-visited cwms can be deserted, and suitable for a dusk-til-dawn camp. With their rugged cirques, sheltered turfy hollows and scattered tarns the mountains of the British Isles offer a profusion of superb camp and bivvy sites. In this book only the more obvious overnight options are explicitly mentioned; there will generally be many others for those prepared to exercise both legs and imagination.

Despite its life-enhancing nature wild camping is not a statutory right in Ireland, England or Wales, without the express permission of the landowner, and potential sites mentioned in this book are no exception. Permission ought to be sought if at all possible. In practice it is often hard to find out just who owns what, especially if the site in question has been chosen on the hoof. Discreet camping without prior approval may often be tolerated in isolated open hill country far from farms and habitation, but in these cases responsible behaviour is particularly important. This is a privilege, not a right. As a rule it is worth travelling only in small groups and dismantling tents during the day. Light no fires, dispose of toilet waste fastidiously and leave no trace of your presence. Just remember, it's not strictly legal; if you're asked to move on then comply without complaint.

Unlike in Scotland bothies are rare in the hills of England, Wales and Ireland. Fewer still are well placed to be used as accommodation while climbing routes in this book.

ENVIRONMENTAL CONSIDERATIONS

Although tending to go hand in glove with an appreciation of unspoilt landscapes, climbing and hillwalking are not environmentally neutral pastimes. If the hill environment is to be preserved in as healthy a state as possible then we each need to do our bit as individuals, adopting the 'leave no trace' philosophy popularised in America. Every step we take has an impact of sorts; the trick is to minimise it.

The old adage 'take only memories, leave nothing but footprints' doesn't tackle the most visible negative effect of mass access, namely path erosion, the net result of thousands of those footprints.

As the surface of a heavily used path deteriorates into a stony mess walkers naturally gravitate towards the verges, so that the busiest routes eventually spread over the hillside into broad rubbly highways. Vegetation is denuded and surface run-off carves deep scars. In popular locations the best long-term solution – and an expensive one – is to surface the busy routes with stone flags and steps. Although it may be necessary there's still something over-manicured about it, snaking pavements sent into the hills like the tentacles of a creeping urbanisation. Where this hasn't yet happened the responsible course is to stick to the middle of paths to prevent the dreaded spread, not to cut corners where routes zigzag, and to avoid scree running or running down loose path surfaces.

Rubbish is an unsightly and ecologically damaging presence in the busiest locations. The solution is to pack out everything that you've carried in, including fruit peel which does not readily biodegrade in the mountain environment. Better still would be to pick up any other food packaging found lying discarded by others; sadly there's always some.

Wild land has the power to enrich our lives – Crib Goch (Route 33) looms over Llanberis Pass

Human waste is another issue to consider, an unsanitary and anti-social problem that may become worse as more people flock to the hills. If you've got to go make it far from any water sources, paths and crag bases – 30 metres at the very least (more would be considerate). Ledges on climbing routes are not suitable places and hiding the evidence isn't as simple as building a pile of stones since solid waste does not break down rapidly and animals may unearth whatever's been left. The least that can be done is to bury it in the soil and burn any toilet paper, leaving no glowing embers. Better still in our crowded national parks is to take everything home in a ziplock bag, an approach that has become compulsory in parts of the United States and may well be coming to a hill near you soon. Tampons and sanitary towels do not readily decompose and should always be packed out.

Even getting to and from the mountains has become an environmental hot potato. Keen climbers can notch up an unenviable carbon count just zipping around the country every weekend by car in search of dry rock or snowy hills. For all their costs cars are too comfortable, convenient and flexible for many of us to give them up willingly and there are often no realistic alternatives. Have you tried following fleeting dry weather around Ireland with a mountain of gear in tow, using only public transport? I wouldn't. Responsible drivers will arrange lift (and cost) sharing wherever possible. Public transport is a guilt-free option and perfectly practical in populous parts of the Lake District and Snowdonia.

Our vanishing landscapes

Regardless of whose names are on the title deeds the open spaces of these islands are in a sense common property. These are our green lungs, places of refuge with the power to enrich all our lives. Nevertheless, landscapes that ought to be preserved for future generations are being steadily compromised by commercial development, public space encroached on by private interests. In recent years most hill regions have undergone rapid industrialisation, sprouting gleaming forests of metal windmills, hundreds of miles of access roads and power lines. Even significant landscape protection designations such as national park status cannot guard against long-range visual intrusion inflicted from beyond park boundaries.

Windfarms are being built so widely that it seems we will soon see monumental spinning blades on every horizon, a dispiriting nationwide uniformity where once there were unspoilt and distinctive landscapes on a human scale.

Whatever its climatic benefits, renewable energy technology poorly planned and insensitively sited carries enormous environmental costs. In a landmass as tiny and densely populated as the British Isles the fact that we still have so much scenic and ostensibly wild country should be a source of collective joy; yet power companies, the 'green' lobby and the governments they influence seem to regard empty windswept spaces as nothing but an under-used resource. Ironically this attitude stems from the same exploitative mindset that has brought the world to the brink of global meltdown.

GETTING AROUND

England and Wales

Giving the flexibility to respond to changing weather, and offering convenient load carrying, driving is naturally the preferred choice for many walkers and climbers. However at busy times of year roads and car parks in popular parts of our national parks can get pretty congested. As a result, pay and display car parks have now proliferated in the Lake District, and are seen at a few key locations elsewhere. These tend to be expensive, and over the course of a holiday parking costs soon add up. The obvious alternative is public transport. Decent rail and bus links make this a feasible option for those travelling long distance to the Lake District and, slightly less conveniently, Snowdonia. Getting around within these two national parks can also be managed very well by bus thanks to extensive local networks; the more these services are used the more likely they are to be maintained. However, even in the Lake District and Snowdonia public transport black holes do exist, notably in western Lakeland dales such as Wasdale and Ennerdale and the quieter backwaters of Snowdonia such as Cwm Pennant. Perhaps the most obvious drawback of relying on public transport is that it ties you to the timetables.

Irish visitors to Snowdonia can make good use of sea links from Dublin to Holyhead. The Lake District will take slightly longer to get to by sea;

Dublin to Liverpool would be the best maritime route and Larne to Fleetwood would be another option for climbers based in the north. Flights from Ireland are not likely to be particularly time saving as neither Snowdonia nor the Lake District is close to a major airport.

Ireland

Accessing hills by public transport can be a time-consuming affair in rural Ireland; long walks or optimistic hitch hikes are sometimes needed to get from the nearest bus stop to the start of the intended route. It's possible, but it just takes some commitment. Travelling the back roads of Kerry and sparsely populated Connemara is far easier by car. Motorised visitors from mainland Britain have two options – a car ferry (from Holyhead to Dublin) or a flight and hire car combination. Cork is the nearest 'major' airport to Kerry, while Galway serves Connemara. Ryanair and Aer Arann are the two main operators.

ACCOMMODATION

England and Wales

In the national parks there's generally a wide range of accommodation from youth hostels, independent backpacker hostels, club huts and camp sites to B&Bs, inns and smart hotels. Self-catering holiday cottages may look expensive but for a group of friends staying a week they can often work out cheaper than hostels on a per-person-per-night basis. Accommodation options are listed in each route chapter.

Ireland

The three distinct Irish mountain areas described in this book happen to be on well-beaten tourist trails, each centred around its own little town: MacGillycuddy's Reeks (routes 42 to 44) are on the doorstep of Killarney; Mount Brandon (routes 45 and 46) is reasonably close to Dingle; and the 12 Bens and Mweelrea (routes 47 and 48) aren't too far from Clifden. Accommodation options are many and varied in each area, especially in these tourist towns, where you'll find the usual selection of backpacker hostels and youth hostels, B&Bs, hotels, self-catering cottages and camp sites. For UK visitors the basic cost of living in Ireland tends to seem very high, although exchange rates do vary.

ACCESS

England and Wales

From 19th-century stirrings of an embryonic access movement via the Kinder Trespass of the 1930s to today's rather more mundane collaborative solutions, there is a long history of disputed access to open hill country. The issue is part of a wider culture clash between rural landowners and the landless urban majority, private and public.

In Scotland ambitious access legislation has established a universal right to roam more or less at will, provided the interests of land managers and workers are respected. By comparison the reforms of recent years in England and Wales remain rather more piecemeal and half-baked, covering only some defined and delineated areas. Even these concessions were hard won, the result of decades of lobbying by walkers' and climbers' representative bodies. The Countryside and Rights of Way Act (CROW) 2000 has guaranteed a right to pedestrian access to over 865,000 hectares of officially designated open moor and mountain country in England and roughly 450,000 hectares in Wales – now known as 'access land', and highlighted on Ordnance Survey maps. In addition to the longstanding statutory right to use thousands of public rights of way throughout the country climbers and walkers are now legally entitled to go off path in CROW areas; unless, that is, landowners see fit to say otherwise.

In contrast to Scotland, the grounds on which landowners south of the border are still able to impose restrictions are arguably rather too liberal, but at least steps have been taken in the right direction. Most of the English and Welsh routes in this book are on access land, with the exception of the sea cliff climbs; CROW as it stands covers hills but not coasts, although there are now official moves to close this access loophole by establishing a legal right to pedestrian access all along England's coastline.

The most significant single landowner in upland areas is the National Trust, an organisation that generally operates an enlightened policy towards access issues. The National Trust subscribes to the idea of public access as a legitimate land use in its own right, a force for good in the countryside. Where their presence doesn't conflict with habitat conservation walkers and climbers are generally welcomed. The Trust has pledged to continue to provide access to hill land in its care, although the

It's not only them thar hills that have gold – Commando Ridge, a Cornish treasure (Route 20)

policy of charging for car parking in these areas means public access is unfettered but not always 'free'. Despite the efforts of various interested parties there is still no legal right to wild camp in England and Wales.

Ireland

When it comes to public access in the countryside Ireland lags far behind most of Western Europe. Protected rights of way are few, and the freedom to wander off path is still regarded a privilege not a right. Irish hill land tends to be privately owned, often by innumerable small farmers, and although there is a loose tradition of tolerance towards roaming on unenclosed uplands, this is not guaranteed by law. Technically, countryside access may be restricted at any time, and it is not unknown for walkers to be turned away or even intimidated by irate landowners. Many Irish farmers seem to think free access just means the

public tramping about causing random havoc – an attitude that may stem from ignorance about the generally successful regimes that have been established in neighbouring countries.

Climbers' and walkers' organisations such as the Mountaineering Council of Ireland (MCI) are working towards eventually establishing a legal right to reasonable access, although it seems an uphill struggle. Until such legislative reforms are made – as they surely must be one day – it is important to tread sensitively in Ireland, being especially circumspect around farmyards and enclosed fields, parking without compromising access for farm vehicles, and where practical (it usually isn't!) seeking landowners' permission before wild camping. The MCI publish guidelines for responsible behaviour in the hills; it's all commonsense courtesy really, but doubly worth adhering to if relations with landowners are to improve in the future.

USING THIS GUIDEBOOK

Each route chapter starts with an information box giving a breakdown of the route statistics – grade, distance, ascent, time – and other useful information such as maps needed, nearby accommodation suggestions and any options for arriving by public transport. Each route also carries one of three symbols in the margin to allow the reader to spot at a glance whether the route description treats it primarily as a scramble, a rock climb or a winter climb (see the key on page 7). These symbols are meant as rough guides only. After all, there is no essential difference between harder scrambles and easier climbs and most summer routes can also double as winter climbs given the requisite snow and ice. For brief notes on **seasonal variations**, check the last entry in the information box.

Distance and **ascent** figures are given for the day as a whole – that's the sum of the approach, the climb and the return home. Where there is a choice of approach, descent or continuation these figures refer to the variation given precedence in the text. There's generally more than one way to tackle a hill; the described routes tend to include a walk over a summit or two as well as the ridge climb itself, so if pushed for time it's usually possible to shorten the walking stage. It's always difficult to give a **route time** without knowing the abilities of the people involved. The quoted times are pretty generous, and ought to reflect times achievable by averagely able walkers and climbers in good conditions. Whippets could probably knock hours off some routes, but they might miss out on the odd photo opportunity. Poor visibility, wet rock or deep snow tend to significantly increase the time it takes to complete any hill day.

Route grades refer only to the climb itself; no attempt has been made to grade walk-ins. Their difficulty should be clear from the **route description**. Where possible the overall length of each technical climb is listed, although in some cases this is just a best guess. The figures refer to the distance covered on rock rather than vertical height gain. Individual pitch lengths and detailed pitch descriptions are only given where such close coverage seems helpful. If the ground offers a variety of possible lines and places to belay, the route description will be less painstaking, and may only explicitly mention the most salient features. Compass directions are abbreviated (W, NW) and are approximate. 'Left' and 'right' are relative to the direction of travel. (See the box below or Appendix 4: Glossary of Climbing Jargon if any of the terminology used is unclear.)

Each route is accompanied by an extract from the 1:50000 OS (or OSI) map to show its location, although some features mentioned in the information boxes and route descriptions only appear on the 1:25000 maps. (In Ireland, the spellings used on the Harvey maps have been followed as the OSI maps are inconsistent, but place names should be easy to recognise.) Some of the climbs are also illustrated by topos, which show the routes described and any key rock features mentioned in the descriptions.

MOUNTAIN LANGUAGE GLOSSARY

- Cumbrian *tarn* (small lake)
  = Welsh *llyn*
  = Irish Gaelic *lough*

- Cumbrian *cove* (cirque, corrie)
  = Welsh *cwm*
  = Irish Gaelic *coum*

- Cumbrian *beck* (stream)
  = Welsh *afon*
  = Irish Gaelic *abhainn*

- Cumbrian *hause* (pass, col)
  = Welsh *bwlch*
  = Irish Gaelic *bealach, mam, bearna*

See Appendix 4 for a Glossary of climbing jargon.

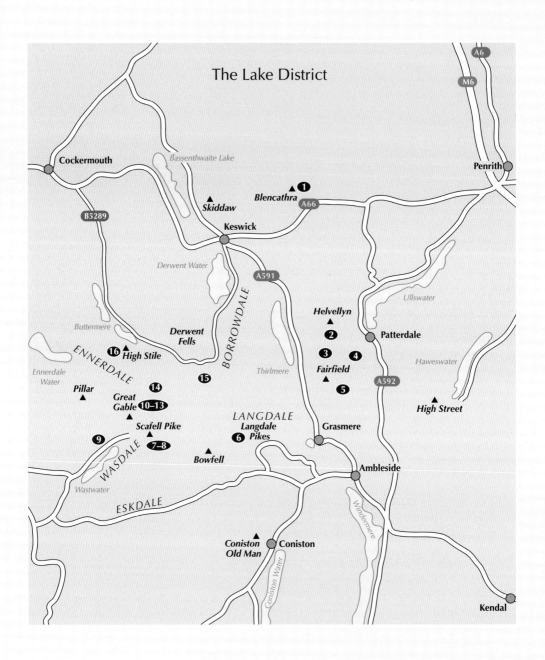

The Lake District

A6

M6

Cockermouth

Bassenthwaite Lake

Penrith

Blencathra ▲ ❶

▲ Skiddaw

A66

B5289

Keswick

Derwent Water

A591

Ullswater

Helvellyn
▲

Buttermere

Derwent
Fells

❷

❸   ❹   Patterdale

❶❻ High Stile

ENNERDALE

Ennerdale
Water

BORROWDALE

Thirlmere

Fairfield
▲

❺

Haweswater

A592

❶❺

Pillar
▲

❶❹

High Street
▲

Great
Gable
▲   ❶⓪–❶❸

Scafell Pike
▲

❼–❽

LANGDALE

Langdale
Pikes

❾

WASDALE

❻

Grasmere

Bowfell
▲

Wastwater

Ambleside

ESKDALE

Windermere

Coniston
Old Man ▲

Coniston

Coniston Water

Kendal

THE LAKE DISTRICT

A source of inspiration for generations of poets and romantics, the Lake District is the most picturesque and user friendly of our upland areas. The stone-walled fields, woods and meres of the dales create a soft pastoral feel, a tameness that contrasts with the wrinkled skyline of the high fells. This upper world has the raw ruggedness of true mountain country.

With a rich horde of classic routes on unimpeachable rock it's no wonder that the Lakes has a long and thriving climbing heritage; this is, after all, the cradle of the sport. Soaring Alpine-style aretes may be thinner on the ground here than in other mountain areas, but there are notable exceptions. Lakeland's ridges span the grade range to give a collection of scrambles and climbs of the highest quality.

Transport links around the national park are quick and convenient; nowhere's very far from anywhere else and it's often as quick to walk between adjacent valleys as to drive the long way round on twisting mountain roads. And after hours? Cumbria's characterful climbers' pubs and local beers are second to none.

Beautiful Borrowdale from the top of Intake Ridge

Route 1 – Sharp Edge and Hallsfell Ridge, Blencathra

Grade	1
Distance	7km
Ascent	680m
Time	4½ hours
Start/finish	Layby on the A66 250m west of the White Horse Inn at Scales (NY340267)
Maps	OS Landranger (1:50000) 90; OS Explorer (1:25000) OL5; Harvey British Mountain Map (1:40000) Lake District
Accommodation	Campsites east of Scales; B&Bs in Threlkeld; youth hostel in Keswick (0870 770 5894)
Sleeping out	Sheltered in a craggy bowl, Scales Tarn is a superb place to pitch a tent on short-cropped turf – however it's not secluded enough to leave a tent all day. An early start from a high camp here could see you on top of Blencathra via Sharp Edge in well under an hour; you'd be back at your tent packing up before the day's first walkers arrived.
Public transport	Scales is on the main bus route between Penrith (mainline rail link) and Keswick/ Workington.
Seasonal notes	The illustrations here show a cosmetic wintry dusting rather than full winter climbing conditions; given more substantial snow cover Sharp Edge is a fairly challenging I/II climb on which a rope might prove welcome. It doesn't seem to hold snow well. Hallsfell Ridge is easier, but still at least grade I. On rainy days bear in mind that the Skiddaw slate of the area is slippery when wet.

The slabby wall at the end of Sharp Edge

Y ANY STANDARD Blencathra is an imposing
and charismatic mountain. Scored by deep
gullies and buttressed with ridges, its precipitous
southern wall dominates the wide rolling valley
at its foot. Under snow there are few more
Alpine views in the district. Tucked
away around the back – only
clearly seen from the east – is the
hill's real star attraction, perhaps
the best and certainly the most
famous easy ridge scramble in
England. It is indeed a 'sharp
edge' – knife keen, even.
Despite its fearsome profile
the summertime difficulties are
modest, the main one being an
exhilarating sense of exposure.
It seems that a slip from this
slate rooftop might land you in
the tarn far below. Completing
the loop with Hallsfell Ridge gives
more of the same, top-quality easy
scrambling in a magnificent location.

Blencathra from St John's in the Vale; Hallsfell Ridge drops steeply from the right summit

31

APPROACH	CLIMB

If the layby is full limited alternative parking is available just east along the minor road behind the White Horse Inn, in the mouth of Mousthwaite Comb. From the main road layby take the path north onto the fellside. This follows the field boundary on a rising line behind Scales, before climbing quite steeply into Mousthwaite Comb. Here the noise of the busy A-road begins to recede. The path crosses the craggy little west wall, a spot that can gather plenty of drifted snow in winter despite its lowly elevation. Above the comb is a broad shoulder and a path junction. Take the well trodden WNW route above the River Glenderamackin. The great two-tiered wedge of Sharp Edge is now visible ahead, a sight that should quicken your pace; less confident scramblers can be reassured that it's not as edgy as it looks. Cross Scales Beck and follow a steep path up its N bank to reach the perfect little pool of Scales Tarn, hard against the foot of Sharp Edge. The path now zigzags to reach the crest.

Sharp Edge, grade 1

The rock of the crest offers many reassuring sharp edges (!), although it has been buffed to a sheen in key places. Scrappy flanking paths on the right side avoid the point entirely, and are much less enjoyable than the direct assault. Easy angled rocks are followed by a level arete, pleasantly airy but not at all hard. As you proceed you could almost fancy that the ridge is gathering itself, getting ready to put up a fight. Abruptly it narrows into a serrated knife edge, with a tricky and very exposed step down from a pinnacle into a little gap. Polish shows the way, but in ice or wet you'll wish it didn't. Clamber over the next rock mass to reach another gap, with gullies cutting away on either side below. This is the point at which the level ridge runs up against the parent mountain. A sting in the tail awaits – a sloping wall above the gap. It is easier than it looks – an abiding theme on this route; a fall from here would be nasty, but the holds are positive. If in doubt move right into

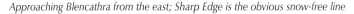

Approaching Blencathra from the east; Sharp Edge is the obvious snow-free line

The distant North Pennines from the tricky step on Sharp Edge

a clear-cut groove line. Beyond this first tier the ground gets steadily easier, and too soon you're up on the plateau. A path follows the edge S for a few hundred metres before turning hard right to reach the main summit, a perch overlooking the full sweep of the south face.

DESCENT

Hallsfell Ridge, grade 1

Fittingly, the ridge starts just beneath the summit cairn. It is a narrow chiselled gangway, quite interesting in descent. A succession of rock tiers drops steeply downhill, calling for fun but modest scrambling at several points; though some of the difficulties can be avoided on a lower flanking path, the ridge is best appreciated by sticking to the crest. It's neither as sustained nor as ferocious looking as the ascent route, but Hallsfell Ridge is longer than one might imagine and would be much more popular if Sharp Edge hadn't taken the limelight. The difficulties gradually ease as heather replaces rock and a clear path then continues down the steep lower shoulder to reach the foot of the fell near Gategill farm.

Now turn left onto a path that bounds the base of the mountain. At Doddick Gill a signed detour splits from the more logical direct route and in the interests of future access it's best to follow it. After this brief climb the path continues beneath Doddick Fell to reach the gorge of Scaley Beck. Reaching the stream involves descending a little polished rock step, surprisingly awkward in the wet. The parking layby is five minutes beyond the gorge.

Route 2 – Striding Edge and Swirral Edge, Helvellyn

Grade	I
Distance	10km
Ascent	840m (not counting a detour to Catstye Cam)
Time	6 hours
Start/finish	Once the done thing, roadside parking on the double yellow lines at the entrance to the Grisedale turnoff may now incur the wrath of the authorities. Further east along the A592 there is a private pay and display car park opposite the Patterdale Hotel (NY396159); alternatively, park in Glenridding.
Maps	OS Landranger (1:50000) 90; OS Explorer (1:25000) OL5; Harvey British Mountain Map (1:40000) Lake District
Accommodation	Patterdale Youth Hostel 0845 3719337; Helvellyn Youth Hostel 0845 3719742; Sykeside campsite near Brotherswater 017684 82239; Gillside campsite and bunkhouse in Glenridding 017684 82346
Sleeping out	The Red Tarn bowl is an obvious wild camp location, but hardly secluded.
Public transport	Infrequent bus from Penrith (mainline rail link) to Patterdale – limited service in winter

Seasonal notes

Without snow this is a simple scrambly hillwalk, too easy to be described in this guide. In full winter conditions the route may be just a low-end grade I, yet it is frequently underestimated and avoidable mishaps occasionally befall the underequipped. Note: unless you're particularly keen to meet the Patterdale Mountain Rescue Team, crampons and an axe are strongly recommended. Be aware of any avalanche risk on the exit slopes after Striding Edge, and watch out for cornices here and on the descent to Swirral Edge. Helvellyn's Red Tarn Face is one of the most 'reliable' winter climbing venues in the Lakes, and Striding Edge makes a particularly satisfying end-of-day descent after a day on the steeper routes.

OVERWHELMING POPULARITY cannot diminish the spectacular class of England's finest winter horseshoe. With aesthetic swooping curves and chiselled crests, these look like archetypal mountaineering ridges. The impression is particularly striking under sunshine and snow. On such days Striding Edge seems an apt name as you lope along its airy spine, with a backdrop of gleaming hills rippling off to the distant white line of the high North Pennines. Though it's at the most inclusive end of the climbing spectrum the positions are exhilarating throughout; if any route can disprove the idea that quality is proportional to difficulty, it is this. Don't come expecting a technical tussle, just a memorable and deeply rewarding day. To beat the crowds avoid weekends and bank holidays at all costs; true misanthropes might prefer a lonely dawn start.

APPROACH

From the A592 in Patterdale follow the minor Grisedale road up a steep hill, passing a house and a wooded dell – a good place to spot red squirrels. Just beyond the trees turn right on a side track, crossing a bridge to reach a gate on the edge of a field. Take the path through the field. Beyond a stone wall this swings left to make a long rising traverse up Grisedale's northern slope, a bit of a trudge if there's soft snow. At about the 710m contour cross a stile in the drystone wall. Visible ahead is the Red Tarn face of Helvellyn, while to the south the ridges and rugged coves of Nethermost and Dollywagon Pikes beckon (see route 3). Now pick up a path WSW along the broad crest. The slopes on each side soon pinch together to form Striding Edge.

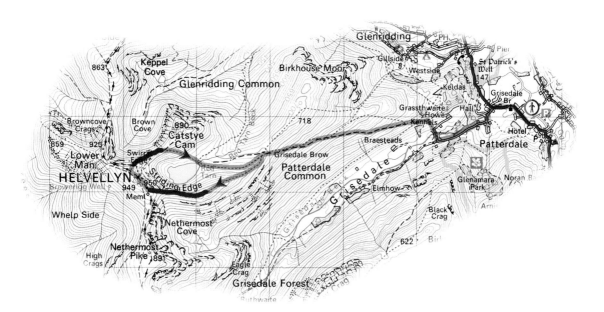

St Sunday Crag (Route 4) from Striding Edge

Striding Edge, I

From a mini-summit the crest ahead looks particularly enticing, a gently serrated curving knife edge that draws the eye towards the flat topped bulk of Helvellyn. It is as good as it looks. Although it only demands very basic scrambling, and perhaps the occasional axe placement if you're lucky with conditions, Striding Edge has a superbly airy feel; a leap to either side would be ill advised. For the timid a cheating path slinks along the N flank, missing out the ridge crest exposure and thus much of the enjoyment; if it is banked with deep snow the arete will be easier in any case. Cross a level rock 'pavement',

Approaching Helvellyn – it's as good as it looks

then continue over the bumps to reach a 'bad step' just before Striding Edge meets the main mountainside. Negotiate this by downclimbing a short broken groove on the left – polish shows the way. Beyond a little gap is a final rocky barrier, which can be skirted on the right or taken direct. Steep snow slopes now lead to the summit plateau. Beware: Avalanches are not unheard of here.

From the memorial cairn at the top of this slope follow the plateau rim to the crossed walls of the summit windbreak. On a clear day the views from England's third highest point are everything you'd expect, ranging from pretty much every major Cumbrian summit to Morecambe Bay, the Yorkshire Dales and the hills of southern Scotland.

DESCENT

Continue N parallel to, but well back from, the curving edge of the Red Tarn face, which is often substantially corniced. Pass a trig point to reach a marker cairn above the drop-off point (metaphorically speaking!) for Swirral Edge.

Swirral Edge, I

The amusing mispronunciation *Squirrel Edge* might give a false impression of the difficulty. You don't need the lightning reflexes of a tree rat, but careful footing is still a must. Though shorter, this is a worthy twin to Striding Edge. The initial descent is fairly steep and needs to be treated with caution, especially if it's icy or there is a cornice. Unless snow has drifted overnight, a line of bucket steps should show the way. From this point it's possible to fall an impressive distance, as a random walker once demonstrated to me rather too emphatically. Bearing this in mind, scramble down a broken rock buttress to reach easier ground. The crest remains sharply pronounced for a while, with a soft-option path soon available on the southern flank if you're that way inclined. Beyond a shallow rise is a small col, marking the end of the good stuff.

The shapely but somewhat neglected pyramid of Catstye Cam can be bagged from here in about 10 minutes. Back at the col, a well-trodden path drops quickly into the cove, crossing the Red Tarn outflow and contouring beneath the eastern arm of Striding Edge to regain the approach route at the stile.

Looking back along Striding Edge from the snow slope leading to the plateau

Route 3 – East Ridges of Nethermost Pike and Dollywagon Pike

Grade Easy	I (½ would be more appropriate, if such a grade existed)
Distance	11km
Ascent	800m
Time	5 hours
Start/finish	See route 2
Maps	OS Landranger (1:50000) 90; OS Explorer (1:25000) OL5; Harvey British Mountain Map (1:40000) Lake District
Accommodation	See route 2
Sleeping out	Nethermost Cove and Ruthwaite Cove are both isolated and dramatic settings for a wild camp. On a harsh winter night there's not much chance of company.
Public transport	See route 2
Seasonal notes	A pleasant, little-trodden and only very mildly scrambly hillwalk in summer. NB Under full winter conditions the corries slung between these ridges become a rather wilder version of Helvellyn's Red Tarn face, with a variety of traditional mountaineering gullies and more modern mixed lines; one of the ridges would make a nice way to descend after a climb. The corries tend to hold snow better than the ridges that divide them.

The view south from Helvellyn.

Left to right: Fairfield, Dollywagon Pike and Nethermost Pike; the twin ridges are seen in profile

Dollywagon Pike (left) and Nethermost Pike seen from the lower reaches of Grisedale

On a sunny Sunday Striding Edge from afar can resemble an ant highway, a teeming throng of comings and goings. Not so its relatively under-appreciated southern neighbours. The east ridges of Nethermost Pike and Dollywagon Pike are an antidote to the Red Tarn horseshoe (route 2), a wander through lonely country that's at its best in winter. Seen along the length of Grisedale, the rugged eastern flank of the massif presents a snowbound

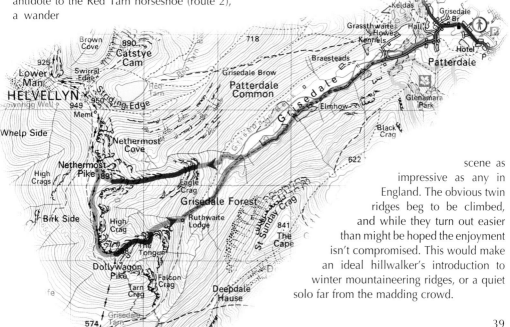

scene as impressive as any in England. The obvious twin ridges beg to be climbed, and while they turn out easier than might be hoped the enjoyment isn't compromised. This would make an ideal hillwalker's introduction to winter mountaineering ridges, or a quiet solo far from the madding crowd.

APPROACH

Walk up Grisedale as for route 2, but instead of turning off the road stay with it as it becomes a farm track along the valley floor. Continue past Elmhow farm and two small plantations. Beyond the second wood, where the path begins to climb out of the flat lower valley, branch right to cross a footbridge over Grisedale Beck. The squat mass of Eagle Crag marks the foot of Nethermost Pike's long East Ridge; pass through a stone walled enclosure and follow a sketchy path up scree towards the crag, which can be skirted by looping wide either to left or right. Alternatively:

Optional scramble: Eagle Crag, grade 2

While the upper ridge may be white these low level rocks are often snow free; if so they provide an interesting approach scramble, technically harder than anything above. To start, head for the broken grassy ground between the two main crags and directly above some old mine workings. Take a shallow groove to the right of an obvious deep gully to reach a scree covered ledge, then follow slabby tiers just right of the upper groove. A steeper outcrop is dispatched via a slabby scoop on its left side, bringing you to more mine workings. Plod up the spoil heap, then continue between outcrops just to the left of a deep mine cutting, to reach the broad grassy shoulder at the start of the East Ridge.

CLIMB

Nethermost Pike East Ridge, I

Head W on a faint path over tussocky grass (or, with luck, thick snow), the ridge with its steep right flank gradually taking shape as you go. At about the 750m contour the ridge abruptly steepens into a ragged pyramid, stony ground leading on up the front of the prow. If it isn't buried under snow a path can be followed, threading up through grass and rock ribs. It is more fun to climb the rocks direct with some very modest scrambling or winter climbing. Ideally the turf will be hard frozen and the snow plentiful. Whatever the conditions underfoot you can be sure that modern contrivances such as ropes and technical axes will not be needed – forget the grade, and just enjoy the gentle airiness and tranquillity of your situation. A brief narrow arete marks the end of the 'difficulties', beyond which a short walk rightwards tracking the rim of the plateau at a safe distance (possibly quite heavily corniced) leads to Nethermost Pike's summit cairn.

From here a round trip to busy Helvellyn takes about 20mins – time well spent on a clear day. Back at Nethermost Pike head S to the edge of Ruthwaite Cove. Follow the corrie rim in preference to a flanking path (and walkers' motorway) on the right, passing over High Crag to a little col, from where a short climb gains the summit cairn of the endearingly named Dollywagon Pike.

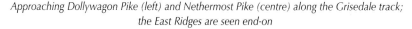

Approaching Dollywagon Pike (left) and Nethermost Pike (centre) along the Grisedale track; the East Ridges are seen end-on

On the East Ridge of Nethermost Pike, with the snowcapped North Pennines in the distance

Nethermost Cove from the East Ridge of Nethermost Pike

DESCENT

Dollywagon Pike East Ridge

Marked as The Tongue on OS maps this pleasant ridge is even easier than Nethermost's, and doesn't warrant a climbing grade. The ridge starts directly below the summit cairn; rocky and reasonably exposed at first, it soon eases, a grassy path leading down the broadening crest. The upper ridge fades into crags, forcing a rightwards descent to reach the wide lower spur. While it's possible to continue down the crest of this, the route leads into complex craggy ground that's best avoided in darkness or mist. A sensible poor-visibility alternative quits The Tongue at about the 650m contour, dropping N into the lower reaches of Ruthwaite Cove. Rough slopes below The Tongue now lead to the magnificently located private hut of Ruthwaite Lodge. Pick up the main Grisedale path back to Patterdale here.

41

Route 4 – Pinnacle Ridge, St Sunday Crag

Grade	3
Distance	12km as described (can do much less)
Ascent	700m
Time	4½ – 5 hours
Start/finish	See route 2
Maps	OS Landranger (1:50000) 90; OS Explorer (1:25000) OL5; Harvey British Mountain Map (1:40000) Lake District
Accommodation	See route 2
Sleeping out	There's nowhere particularly suitable in the lower reaches of Grisedale, except perhaps hidden in a plantation.
Public transport	See route 2
Seasonal notes	An absorbing winter mixed grade II with few unavoidable difficulties. Although a decent build up of snow is said to be comparatively rare on this crag, the route ought to be OK in any condition. It might be a good choice in unconsolidated snow, as there's little turf to damage.

The impressive Grisedale face of St Sunday Crag; Pinnacle Ridge is just one of several buttresses

PINNACLE RIDGE may be prosaically self-explanatory, but the route by any other name would climb as sweet. Lakeland's finest ridge scramble is a grand Alpine-style outing up a complex rambling face, never difficult but certainly atmospheric. For a 'mere' scramble the exposure is exhilarating, hanging high over the deep trench of Grisedale; yet quality rock and a short lived crux make this an ideal ridge for people looking to push their grade. From below the line is unclear, but like all the best routes it unfolds logically as you climb, the lower blocky section building to a sudden and photogenic crescendo on the shark's fin pinnacles. If only it were a bit longer; always leave them wanting more, as they say.

APPROACH

Start as for route 2, walking up the steep hill on the minor Grisedale road. Just before reaching a small pine plantation on the left, the main path for St Sunday Crag branches off left; it looks logical on the map, but takes too high a line as it nears the NW face, necessitating a loss of hard-won height. A cannier approach is to continue on the Grisedale road, which soon becomes an unsurfaced track. After about 1.5km, pass Elmhow farm and the adjacent pine plantation of the same name. At the far side of the trees turn left immediately on a minor path, then left again around the back of the wood, to reach a grassy path that zigzags cunningly up the steep flank of St Sunday Crag. On about the 440m contour the hillside eases off into the shallow scoop of Blind Cove (not named on the 1:50000 map). Head roughly SW to reach a grassy terrace at about 500m; traverse along this, following signs of passing boots beneath the screes that skirt the base of the craggy NW face. A higher traverse on sheep paths is also possible, but leads through steep broken ground. Unless you already know what you're looking for (and even if you do, frankly) it's hard to discern the correct line of Pinnacle Ridge among the jumble of buttresses and gullies overhead. A scree-filled gully bounds its right side, and a scrappy scree slope runs directly from its base. Other identifying features include a small tree about 40m up on the right side of the ridge, a horizontal left-pointing spike a little higher, and a horizontal left-leaning tree higher up still. From the terrace a faint path climbs grass and scree to reach a cairn at the foot of the ridge.

By the left-pointing spike

CLIMB

Pinnacle Ridge, 180m grade 3

Climb a heap of flakes and blocks – easy clambering on rough sound rock. A broad ridge soon develops. The best (and airiest) line is on the right edge, while to the left it's possible to slink onto easier and less pleasant ground in a little vegetated gully that bounds the N side of the route all the way to the pinnacles. This would be a wasted effort. Follow polish and crampon scratches to reach the prominent left-pointing spike; climb its exposed right side, with an interesting step right along an obvious fault. Easier scrambling then leads to the base of a big steep tooth. Flank this on the left to gain a niche behind. If a rope is going to seem necessary anywhere, this is the place to belay.

Leaving the niche is the short sharp crux of the route, and might take an effort of will if you're not used to such things. Enter the obvious vertical corner, bridging up on polished rock for a couple of metres. Transfer to the left wall, where unexpected jugs are a welcome reward. Continue direct up the wall to reach the spiky ridge crest, and an optional belay.

Dispatching the crux was the key to success; you've now burst out onto the eponymous pinnacles, a jagged rank of spines with a vertical drop to either side. Though thrilling, the scrambling is rather easier henceforth. Linger over the pinnacles, as they are sadly short lived. A careful slabby downclimb from the final point leads to a narrow neck. Continue out the far side on easy vegetated slopes, from where there's a grandstand view back over the pinnacles. Up on the left a heap of spiky blocks provides a last burst of scrambling, soon leading to easy ground above the face. Head S over the plateau to reach the summit cairn.

DESCENT

The simplest option is to follow the main path NE back down to Patterdale, an easy descent of around 40mins.

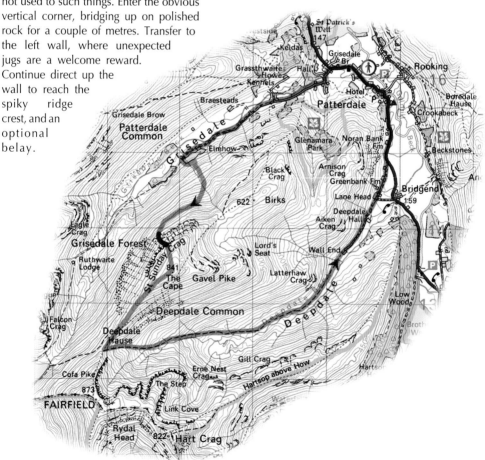

Murky conditions on the pinnacles

CONTINUATION

However if you don't mind a bit of a leg stretch (and if not, what are you doing here anyway?) then this is a good chance to climb Fairfield via the very mildly scrambly Cofa Pike. Alternatively, how's about taking a closer look at the lonely bowl of Sleet Cove at the head of Deepdale? A clear path descends St Sunday's well-defined southwest ridge, reaching the low col of Deepdale Hause in a little under 1.5km. From the Hause ascend about 20m (height gain, not distance) towards Fairfeld to pick up a rough path that cuts down E to reach the grassy floor of Sleet Cove beneath an impressive array of crags, the hanging gardens of Hutaple. This might be the time to try Portcullis Ridge (a good VDiff, if quite short). Continue beside waterfalls into the lower level of the dale. Now clearer, the path passes through glacial moraines, following the N bank of Deepdale Beck through the wide lower valley. Meet a track just before Wall End farm; this leads past several houses to reach the A592 about 1km S of Patterdale.

Route 5 – Westmorland's Route, Dove Crag

Grade	108m Severe
Distance	8km
Ascent	720m
Time	6 hours
Start/finish	Car park off the A592 just N of Brothers Water (NY403133); get there early on peak weekends.
Maps OS	Landranger (1:50000) 90; OS Explorer (1:25000) OL5; Harvey British Mountain Map (1:40000) Lake District
Accommodation	See route 2
Sleeping out	The middle reaches of Dovedale are well suited to a wild camp. Another obvious option is the famous Priest's Hole, a sheltered bivvy cave that can be seen as a long low slot in the broken face above Dove Crag's overhanging right wing. As it's hard to locate it safely from above, the cave is best accessed from below, a short scramble from the main Dovedale path described in this chapter. Don't bank on getting it to yourself at weekends.
Public transport	See route 2
Seasonal notes	While it's too low lying to come into regular nick Dove Crag occasionally offers superb winter climbing. Westmorland's Route is said to be a challenging mixed IV,5 but it doesn't tend to hold snow well. Do not contemplate climbing here in the wet unless you've got several grades in hand.

Dove Crag seen from Dovedale

CONNOISSEURS OF THE QUAINT AND QUIRKY will find it in spades (or trowelfuls) here. Westmorland's Route may be the only wholesome offering at a venue thick with E-numbers, but it's no sheep among wolves for all that. Not for this venerable excursion the indignities of the clean-picked, chalked-up, smooth-polished Cumbrian crowdpleaser. Half obscured beneath its cloak of vegetation the line still preserves a faint whiff of the tweedy pioneers. It is a grand mountaineering adventure in imposing surroundings, with sufficient lichen and looseness to guarantee that elusive traditional feel; expect greenery, but no walk in the park. Strictly speaking only about a third of it is ridge-like, but for an experience this eccentric who cares? The old fashioned Mild Severe grade has been given a modest increase in this book to reflect the relative seriousness of the undertaking.

APPROACH

Take the obvious track along the beautiful wooded W shore of Brothers Water. Just beyond a big old farmhouse fork right, and then right again, on a good path that steadily ascends across the N flank of Dovedale, one of the most idyllic little valleys in the Lake District. As you approach the head of the dale Dove Crag begins to look mightily imposing. Beyond a small ruin the path steepens, climbing a scree trough between lines of out-crops. Luckily what looked from a distance as if it'd be purgatory turns out to be a helpful flight of stone steps. At a more level area just N of Dove Crag leave the main path, descending slightly beneath the crag's forbiddingly overhung right wing. Westmorland's Route is the vegetated ridge buttressing the far end of the crag, starting from a lower base than the main walls. From the rub-bly gully at the S side of Dove Crag a short green scramble gains a ledge at the foot of the climb.

CLIMB

Westmorland's Route, 108m Severe
This is the Arthur Daly of Lakeland ridges – a lit-tle dodgy maybe, but underneath it's alright; see past the lichen and moss and you'll find generous

Pitch 2 of Westmorland's Route

5 Westmorland's Route
A South Gully
B Priest's Hole

Pitch 2, 12m

Climb the exceedingly exposed ridge, with a hard final mantelshelf onto a sloping belay ledge.

Pitch 3, 15m

Take a step left, then heave up a short juggy crack to regain the jagged arete, which terminates at a grassy ledge under the steep wall of the upper crag.

Pitch 4, 20m

Move gingerly right over some mucky vegetated ground to reach a little rib. This leads to the base of a long slender left-leaning slab, the only obvious line of weakness through intimidating ground. At the time of writing the slab was pretty mossy, though it should clean up nicely with more traffic. Good belay ledge at the top.

holds and sufficient gear placements. Watch out for the odd wobbly bit.

Pitch 1, 21m

From blocky rocks at the base of the ridge move right, climbing a mucky slabby wall on good holds. Bear slightly right, but not so far as to stray onto the hanging gardens that festoon the right flank. A hard step-up gains a left-leaning line of weakness, leading to a well positioned spike belay on the crest of the ridge.

Pitch 5, 20m

A short step-up gains a left-leaning gangway. Inch along this with much exposure and little meaningful protection (more might be unearthed if you're carrying a trowel). Tenuous final moves lead out onto the blocky edge overlooking the gully at the S side of the crag. From here step carefully right, heart in mouth, and then swarm up steep grass to a broad jungly ledge. Walk a

Pitch 3 of Westmorland's Route – the ridgey bit

few metres right along this to belay below the final juggy wall.

Pitch 6, 20m

Pick a line to suit – fairly easy, though airier and dirtier than you might think, and not over-protected. The crag soon fades into grassy scrambling. If the ground is wet a seventh pitch to total safety is a good idea.

CONTINUATION

From the drystone wall at the top of the crag those lost souls not wishing to indulge in a post-climb hillwalk can descend carefully N to regain the approach path. However to abide by the traditional spirit of the climb a summit really ought to be conquered. Continue up the grassy spur, soon bearing right to reach the col between Dove Crag (the hill, not the cliff) and Hart Crag. Turn right here for the short climb onto Hart Crag's stony summit, to be rewarded with grand views over the central fells. Energetic parties could conceivably go on over Fairfield, then traverse the Grisedale face of St Sunday Crag to round off a fine day's mountaineering with an ascent of Pinnacle Ridge (route 4).

DESCENT

If that sounds like too much of a good thing a less ambitious route back to the car is at hand, and a satisfying way to round off the trip it is too. Descend Hart Crag's rough northeast spur, then follow the clear path, in parts boggy, along the elongated grassy crest of Hartsop-above-How. Beyond a knobbly minor summit the path meets a drystone wall, which is followed until reaching a ladder stile. Cross the wall here to pick up a narrower path. After the odd wiggle this descends steeply E through the woods, returning directly to the car park.

Pitch 4 of Westmorland's Route

Grade	East Ridge, Harrison Stickle 1; West Ridge, Pike of Stickle 2/3
Distance	5km
Ascent	750m
Time	3½ hours
Start/finish	National Trust pay and display car park near the Stickle Barn Tavern (NY294063) or the nearby national park pay and display car park (NY295063)
Maps	OS Landranger (1:50000) 90, OS Explorer (1:25000) OL6; Harvey British Mountain Map (1:40000) Lake District
Accommodation	Great Langdale campsite (National Trust) 015394 37668; Elterwater Youth Hostel 0845 371 9017; Langdale Youth Hostel 0845 371 9748
Sleeping out	The only wild thing about camping rough down in Langdale would be the farmer when she finds you. Up on the Pikes Stickle Tarn is the age-old favourite, often busy. The pool-dappled expanses around Martcrag Moor and Thunacar Knott are more original options.
Public transport	Langdale is linked to the West Coast Mainline by bus services via Ambleside and Windermere.
Seasonal notes	Lowly position and southerly aspect make for slim winter pickings, but given a miracle the West Ridge of Pike of Stickle might make an entertaining II/III; the East Ridge of Harrison Stickle would be I/II. There's turf on both, so, to ensure that that remains the case, wait for a prolonged freeze.

The Langdale Pikes from Esk Hause – Pike of Stickle is the middle peak

THE BOLD ROCK PEAKS and rambling crags of the well-named Pikes form an attractive frieze above Langdale, a familiar Lakeland skyline that has kept postcard publishers in pennies for centuries. A sunny outlook and acres of quality rock mean that whatever grade you operate at, there's something superb here. The scrambles tend to be fairly short, but several can generally be linked together to give an extended trip. The combination of Harrison Stickle's easy East Ridge and the rather more testing West Ridge of Pike of Stickle is just one of many possibilities. Sound rock, steady scrambling and a soupcon of exposure give the latter a mountaineering ambience. The one hard step is over almost as soon as it's begun; cynics might say the same about the whole route. On the plus side, if it were longer then you'd be much less likely to have it all to yourself.

Pike of Stickle from Martcrag Moor

APPROACH

Only S'n M enthusiasts (that's *Suffering on Mountains*) should consider a direct approach to Pike of Stickle up breakneck scree out of the depths of Mickleden. From either of the car parks close to the Stickle Barn and the New Dungeon Ghyll follow a stone-paved path NW along the W bank of Mill Gill (marked as Stickle Ghyll on OS maps). Cross a footbridge to the opposite bank, where a better path climbs steeply past some waterfalls (the rock beside the falls can be scrambled at about grade 1). The path passes below the slabby outcrop of Tarn Crag (more optional scrambling detours at grade 2 or 3), where it's best to re-cross the stream for the

final ascent to the little dam of Stickle Tarn. Above on the left are the rambling rocks and heather of Harrison Stickle's East Ridge, a ridge only in name but worthwhile nonetheless. Head W on a path along the lake shore, which soon branches left for a steep pull towards the saddle between Harrison Stickle and Pavey Ark. Leave the path on reaching the bottom rock tier of the East Ridge.

CLIMB

Harrison Stickle East Ridge, 1

Skirt left of this dank tier, heading back right above the crag on grass and scrappy rock. A vague rocky groove leads to a grassy patch; keep heading right (care in the wet) to reach a slope of stunted heather; this trends up and left onto the indistinct crest. Follow the crest up ledges and little outcrops of knobbly rock, soon reaching the base of a well-defined wall. A blocky gangway crosses this face from right to left, with one brief off-balance move that could give pause for thought. Above, the ground quickly eases off, a short walk bringing you to Harrison Stickle's crowning knobble. Scramble a broken groove on the right to reach the summit.

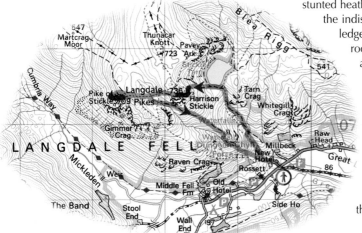

Above the crux corner on the West Ridge

Now descend W onto a path across the plateau backing the peaks. Skirt behind Pike of Stickle to reach a little saddle just to its west. From here the West Ridge is obvious, a stepped buttress running down the flank of the peak towards Mickleden. The scramble begins about 100m down the slope; descend steep grass beside a scree ribbon to reach a grassy promontory at the base of the ridge.

CLIMB

Pike of Stickle West Ridge, 2/3

From the grass, ascend a series of walls and ledges to reach a steepening. This is best skirted on the right, climbing a slabby groove before moving back left onto the shelving crest. Continue into a pronounced corner, formed by a jutting nose. Tackle a short crack in the back of the corner with difficulty – this is the crux and needs a confident approach. Easier-angled (though quite exposed) ground then leads on to a vegetated ledge. Direct access to the slab above is made problematic by a steep little wall; step right as if to acquaint yourself with the grotty gully that defines the right side of the ridge, but instead of doing so climb an obvious line of weakness on good rock to reach the slab, and thus an airy 'tower' that has been prominent above for a while. A head-on assault of the top block might be possible for the brave, but the canny will favour a fault just to its right. Easy rocks now lead up and right onto the summit of Langdale's pointiest Pike.

DESCENT

A short clamber regains the plateau between the Pikes as mentioned in the approach. Now follow the clear path E towards Harrison Stickle, then drop SE where a path – steep and eroded in parts – descends between crags to reach the dale. Or for something a little different, head NE to Pavey Ark and fight your way through the ascending hordes to make a descent of the justly popular grade 1 scramble Jack's Rake.

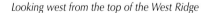

Looking west from the top of the West Ridge

Route 7 – Crenation Ridge, Pikes Crag

Grade	110m Difficult
Distance	7km
Ascent	920m
Time	5 hours
Start/finish	Brackenclose car park (NY182075) or Wasdale Head car park (NY187085)
Maps	OS Landranger (1:50000) 90; OS Explorer (1:25000) OL6; Harvey British Mountain Map (1:40000) Lake District
Accommodation	Campsite at Wasdale Head adjacent to the Barn Door Shop (great for outdoor gear and advice on local routes) 019467 26384; Wasdale Head Inn 019467 26229; National Trust campsite at Brackenclose, Wasdale 019467 26220 www.nationaltrust.org.uk; Wastwater Youth Hostel 0845 371 9350
Sleeping out	Hollow Stones would be an impressive place to pitch a tent; a few sunny days up here climbing on Pikes Crag and Scafell Crag would be time well spent. Several small sites can be found among the boulders but during weekends and holidays it's worth being discrete as the main path through the cirque sees a lot of Scafell Pike-bound traffic.
Public transport	The closest bus stop is several km down the valley at Gosforth, on the Whitehaven–Ravenglass bus route; walking to Wasdale Head from here would take a whole morning. Seascale on the Barrow–Carlisle railway line is the closest train station, but that's not saying much. ▶

Pikes Crag (left) and Scafell from Hollow Stones

Seasonal notes   Crenation Ridge is grade II in winter, with some enjoyable snow-and-rock climbing. It can be quite hard with thin cover, so consider waiting for a decent consolidated build-up. As it's west-facing an early start on a cloudy day might yield best results. In dry summer conditions this climb would suit a party of mixed abilities as the difficulties are short-lived and belay ledges numerous; when wet, however, it's best left to those with several grades in reserve, as the soap-like friction makes for an 'interesting' alternative to rock climbing.

WITH THEIR WEEKEND QUEUES and cacophony of climbers' calls, Lakeland's more predictable crags can sometimes be jading. On Shepherd's or Gimmer the track isn't so much beaten as thrashed within an inch of its life. But cast the net wider and peaceful solitude can still be yours. Although it's a magnificent chunk of rock it is rare to have to share even the best-known routes on Pikes Crag – and Crenation Ridge isn't one of those. If you don't baulk at a bit of moss and the odd loose block then the untrodden atmosphere of this little mountaineering jaunt is very rewarding. Those who make the effort are repaid with a series of interesting short pitches and grandstand views over the amphitheatre of Hollow Stones. The fact that it tops out on a mini-summit from which the only escape is by abseil or downclimb certainly adds something to the day.

APPROACH

The two most logical ways to Pikes Crag are the short sharp sprint from Wasdale and the long scenic bimble from Borrowdale via Sty Head and the Scafell Pike Corridor Route. The first is described here. From the car park by Brackenclose National Trust campsite head ESE on the busy Scafell Pike walkers' path to reach Lingmell Gill. (From Wasdale Head there's a shortcut across the hillside which meets Lingmell Gill higher up.) Beyond a footbridge the path follows the pretty N bank of the stream, passing through a couple of gates on the way. Cross a ford over the beck and ascend the steep stone-paved path up the spit known as Brown Tongue to enter the dramatic boulder-strewn cove of Hollow Stones. On the right is the Shamrock and the peerless Scafell Crag; straight ahead stands Pikes Crag, a row of buttresses and gullies culminating in the pyramidal Pulpit Rock. The path now splits into several strands, but all roads eventually lead to Rome (well, Scafell Pike). The various left-hand routes aim for Lingmell Col and a junction with the Corridor Route; the straight-ahead option climbs steepening scree in the trough between Sca Fell and Pikes Crag, heading towards Mickledore, the famous col slung

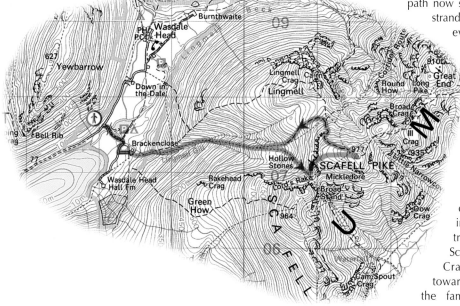

Pikes Crag from Mickledore – Crenation Ridge is seen end-on here

between England's two highest peaks. Stay with this, ignoring a faint path (easily missed) that traverses the screes below Pikes Crag. When you can, peel off left across rough ground to reach the rubble-filled gully bounding the right side of Pulpit Rock. Crenation Ridge is the right-hand skyline of the Rock, and will have been prominent for much of the approach.

CLIMB

Crenation Ridge, 110m Difficult

Much of the route is suited to moving together, although a couple of steeper steps might be better pitched; belay ledges can be found everywhere. Take care that the rope doesn't dislodge loose stones onto your buddies.

Start in the very bottom of the gully, where it forms a narrow slot between rock walls. A mucky 'path' up left gains mixed vegetation and rock steps at the base of the ridge. Climb this by a choice of lines (care in the wet), to reach the scree-strewn ridge crest. Continue until the route is barred by a steep wall, climbed by a right-to-left line to reach more rubbly ledges. Soon comes the next notable obstacle, another step, split by a pair of little chimney/grooves. The left one is the easier of the two, but a forceful attitude and a big-ish hex might both be required.

Continue over more precarious debris, slanting left of a steepening and then cutting through a gap to the right of another steep rock mass to

On the first steep wall

Ⓐ	D-Gully
Ⓑ	The tower
Ⓒ	Summit of Pulpit Rock
❼	Crenation Ridge
❽	Pikes Crag Ridge

enter a little scree-filled bay. Take an easy line up the back of this, then traverse leftwards along a ledge to return to the crest. A short pull on sloping holds and a final easy scramble bring you to the summit of Pulpit Rock.

Descent of Pulpit Rock

Pulpit Rock is a distinct mini-summit standing proud of the mountainside, and separated from it by a short vertical step. This can be descended either by abseiling from a block set slightly back from the edge, or by downclimbing a line a little to the right (facing downhill). In slimy conditions the former is recommended.

CONTINUATION

The mucky gully S of Pulpit Rock could be descended with care, but given that the monarch of England is now just a stroll away it'd be a shame not to pay your respects. Ascend the rough slope, the angle soon relenting as you head E across the stony summit plateau to the cairned crown of Scafell Pike.

DESCENT

As the summit area is ringed by steep broken slopes a bit of attention is called for if descending in the mist. Hollow Stones can be reached either via Mickledore or the Lingmell Col; the main paths are so well trodden that it's almost impossible to lose them once found, except for at the point where the Corridor Route and the Lingmell Col path merge (a large boulder close to the junction is a useful marker in mist).

Abseil off Pulpit Rock – Scafell Crag in the background

Route 8 – Pikes Crag Ridge

Grade	141m Severe
Distance	7km
Ascent	920m
Time	5 hours
Start/finish	Brackenclose car park (NY182075) or Wasdale Head car park (NY187085)
Maps	OS Landranger (1:50000) 90; OS Explorer (1:25000) OL6; Harvey British Mountain Map (1:40000) Lake District
Accommodation	See route 7
Sleeping out	See route 7
Public transport	See route 7
Seasonal notes	Although it seems unlikely for such a well-climbed place as the Lakes the summer line of Pikes Crag Ridge has no guidebook-documented winter ascent. Done via the optional easier pitches it would be at least grade III. The harder choices described below would naturally bump up the grade somewhat – IV,5 perhaps. Without snow, an ascent is best saved for dry conditions, unless your tastes are unconventional.

Pikes Crag (left) and Scafell

◄ **FOR TOPO SEE ROUTE 7**

THOUGH RIDGE CLIMBS are often described as 'alpine' this one deserves the honour more than most. Pikes Crag's other ridge is a rather more committing affair than its easygoing neighbour (route 7) – longer than average for this neck of the woods, and unjustly ignored. A daunting prelude in the opening groove leads to an airy block-strewn crest and some exciting moments on a great square-cut tower; still some way above is the isolated summit of Pulpit Rock, one of the few true rock peaks in England. With its diverse collection of pitches – some pretty stiff for the grade – and a couple of abseils, Pikes Crag Ridge isn't an outing to take lightly. Lichen, greenery and the occasional hollow-sounding hold only add to the mountain ambience and attest to a relative neglect that makes an ascent all the more worthwhile. Bring spare abseil tat.

APPROACH

Approach as for route 7 initially. Pikes Crag Ridge is hard to recognise as a defined arete from directly below, but the line is obvious when seen from the floor of Hollow Stones. Briefly climb towards Mickledore to reach a turnoff onto a traverse path that contours across the scree below Pikes Crag (only marked on the 1:25000 OS map). Follow this faint path until below deep, dank D Gully, which cuts up behind the left side of Pulpit Rock.

Climb steep grass and scree to reach the base of the stepped rock rib just right of the entrance to D Gully.

CLIMB

Pikes Crag Ridge, 141m Severe

The original first pitch is a scrappy green VDiff which frankly looks a waste of time. It's better (and longer, and harder) to start the climb via the first two pitches of an adjacent route called Isis, so that is what is described here, but beware that the second pitch of this is top-end Severe.

Pitch 1, 12m

Scramble up the stepped rib to belay on a narrow ledge just below and left of a little square-cut overhang.

Pitch 2, 30m

This is the crux of the route, exciting but well protected. Climb a juggy crack up a steep open groove which soon deepens into a pronounced slabby corner. Bridge spectacularly up this, unearthing small wire placements when the need arises, to reach a markedly steeper 'thin' bit. This can be climbed direct with a long reach and smears; alternatively wibble left onto an airy rib which is ascended on flat holds until it's possible to step back right into the corner at an obvious flake hold. The corner continues past a jammed block – easier, if quite green – to finish at a grassy ledge and spike belay (a stance shared with the original pitch 1 of Pikes Crag Ridge).

Pitch 3, 16m

Go up grass to the back of a deep right-angled corner. A thuggy pull up slightly overhanging jugs leads to a ledge on the broad ridge crest. From here it's possible to climb an obvious layback crack, but quicker to avoid it by scrambling right and then back left

Exiting the corner on pitch 2

onto another big ledge on the crest. Belay off a huge spike.

Pitch 4, 25m
Climb the pleasant groove behind the spike, then scramble easily up the blocky ridge crest in a fine position to reach the lip of a defined cleft beneath a chunky tower; downclimb boulders to belay in the gap.

Pitch 5, 10m
The vertical wall beyond the gap is climbed on its left side following a line of juggy flakes for a few metres. Then instead of entering a niche behind a big block traverse airily right above the wall, passing a delicately balanced rock with care to reach the flat top of the block. Stride over the intervening gap to scramble onto the grassy summit of the main tower.

Pitch 6, 8m
The far side of the tower drops vertically into another tight gap. It'd be possible, but inadvisable, to downclimb. A quick abseil is more sensible. The best anchor is a little blunt spike on the right – care is needed when lowering over the lip so that the sling doesn't accidentally ride up.

Pitch 7, 25m
Exit the gap up a vague left-leaning ramp, following good holds and gear (if you spend time digging moss out of the placements). Then continue more easily up the broad vegetated crest, with the odd wobbly rock for added interest. Belay in a big niche.

Pitch 8, 15m
Climb clean solid cracks on the right flank of the ridge to gain a ledge. The short final wall goes direct via some unexpected flake holds. Surrounded by steep ground, the top of Pulpit Rock has a satisfying summit feel.

DESCENT

See route 7.

Scafell from the summit of Pulpit Rock

Route 9 – Yewbarrow Traverse

Grade	2
Distance	5km
Ascent	620m
Time	3 hours
Start/finish	Overbeck car park (NY168068)
Maps	OS Landranger (1:50000) 89; OS Explorer (1:25000) OL6; Harvey British Mountain Map (1:40000) Lake District
Accommodation	See route 7
Sleeping out	Not really a route for wild camps, but Dore Head is a possibility
Public transport	See route 7
Seasonal notes	Bell Rib might be worth avoiding in Lakeland's typical unconsolidated snow; the rest of the route would make an attractive winter ridge walk.

ASCENIC RIDGE WALK over a wedge-shaped mini-mountain, the traverse of Yewbarrow is a satisfying little leg stretch, perhaps best saved for a lazy half day when the high crags are dank. The hands-on stuff is optional and very short-lived, but the position high over Wastwater more than compensates. For a bigger day out this route could be incorporated into a peak-bagging horseshoe around Mosedale or the Nether Beck valley.

APPROACH

From the car park climb NW on the path roughly parallel to Over Beck to meet a drystone wall at a path junction at the foot of Yewbarrow's S spur. A path now follows the left side of the wall up the spur, a long slog up a bracken-cloaked slope rising towards the bold pyramid peak-let of Bell Rib. Branch right at a path junction just under a steep little crag. Now quite rough underfoot, the standard

The Scafells and Wastwater from Bell Rib

non-scramblers' path climbs just right of this buttress, and then stays on the left flank of Bell Rib to reach the summit ridge beyond what limited scrambling there is. It's much more interesting to climb Bell Rib direct. To do so, leave the path as the ground steepens, bearing right over grass and scrappy outcrops to reach the foot of the unmistakeable rock prow on the crest of the ridge.

CLIMB

Bell Rib, grade 2

There's only about 30m of sustained scrambling on this route but the exposure is disproportionate to the scale and the mossy rock needs careful footwork in the wet. A short corner crack up the right side of the front face of Bell Rib is perhaps the most intuitive start, but it's rather more than grade 2. For an easier alternative, walk a short distance right to the Wastwater flank of the crag, then climb an obvious line of weakness that leads up for a few metres to reach the foot of a pronounced steepening. Skirt this by stepping left along a narrow mossy ledge in an exposed position to gain a broader sloping ledge which cuts up rightwards to less airy ground. A final easy rock step leads to the top of the buttress. Continue up Yewbarrow's grassy spine, where the onward route is rudely interrupted by a square-cut gap slicing through the crest. Clamber across this, with a couple of scrambly moves, and then carry on along the ridge to reach a second similar cleft. Beyond this the standard walker's path is re-met, and followed over an extended row of little grassy summits. Yewbarrow's north peak (point 616m) marks the drop-off point from the main ridge.

DESCENT

The path now descends Yewbarrow's short sharp north spur. A brief burst of grade 1 scrambling leads down a flight of polished little rock steps beside Stirrup Crag, the best route being well-worn and obvious. Soon reach grassy ground at Dore Head. From here a very steep and eroded path drops NE to the floor of Mosedale – a good option if pints of beer are beckoning from Wasdale Head. The quickest way home is SSW down the little Over Beck valley to the car park at its mouth – there's a path on either side of the stream.

(Above) Starting up Bell Rib, the hard way; (Right) *The Scafells from the first gap above Bell Rib*

Route 10 – Sphinx Ridge via the Climber's Traverse, Great Gable

'Threading the Needle'

Grade	2
Distance	8km
Ascent	830m
Time	4 hours
Start/finish	Of several possible bases the obvious two are Wasdale and Borrowdale. The Wasdale approach is more direct, but as Borrowdale is easier to get to for most people it is described below. There is verge parking along the minor road to Seathwaite (approx NY235122).
Maps	OS Landranger (1:50000) 90; OS Explorer (1:25000) OL4; Harvey British Mountain Map (1:40000) Lake District
Accommodation	Campsites at Seathwaite, Seatoller and Stonethwaite; Thorneythwaite Farm B&B near Seatoller 017687 77237; Borrowdale Youth Hostel 0845 371 9624; see route 7 for options in Wasdale
Sleeping out	A wild camp at the ideally situated Styhead Tarn is almost as much a Lake District rite of passage as an ascent of Napes Needle (route 14) or a traverse of Striding Edge (route 2); overnighting here could give you two long days of climbing on The Napes. Just don't expect to be alone at weekends.
Public transport	Regular buses from Keswick to Seatoller. Wasdale is less well served; see route 7.
Seasonal notes	The Climber's Traverse needs care under snow. Since it's turfier and easier-angled than the more technical Napes ridges, Sphinx Ridge is likely to hold snow more readily. Given the southerly aspect, night might be the best time for frozen conditions. Grade I/II seems a fair guess. The glassy polish would make 'threading the Needle' a bit of a struggle in ice or wet.

THE MASSIVE SQUAT LUMP of Great Gable might seem an unlikely contender for Lakeland's ridge-climbing Mecca, but of any single hill in this book its selection of awesome aretes is unmatched. Most are true rock climbs with the exception of Sphinx Ridge, the westernmost and easiest of the unique brace of ridges that make up The Napes. Combined with the famous Climber's Traverse and the rather less well-trodden ridge route up Westmorland's Crag this makes one of the longest and most spectacular of Lakeland scrambles. The terrain is complex and a little daunting, and despite being discontinuous the scrambling is both excellent and diverse. The harder sections may all be readily avoidable, but this still isn't a route best suited to children or the large parties of beginners that are often seen here. The traverse beneath The Napes is exposed to any falling material sent down by climbing teams, while the scree gully at the base of Sphinx Ridge is a serious health hazard when busy. A helmet would be a sensible precaution, but other safety gear is unlikely to be needed.

APPROACH

From Seathwaite farm in Borrowdale take the main path S, reaching the E bank of Grains Gill. Follow this for about 1km, then cross the stone arch of Stockley Bridge and climb W on a good path, passing above the Taylorgill Force gorge to reach Styhead Tarn. Sty Head itself is a short stroll SW; this point is also easily accessible from Wasdale Head.

From the mountain rescue stretcher box on the pass briefly take the heavily used path climbing towards the summit of Great Gable. Almost immediately branch left to pick up the less well-trodden Climber's Traverse. This does what it says on the tin, crossing the huge scree-covered south slopes of Great Gable aiming for the grand old traditional mountaineering ground of The Napes. The path first crosses tumbled boulders below

10 Sphinx Ridge
11 Arrowhead Ridge
12 Eagle's Nest Ridge
13 Napes Needle and
     Needle Ridge
A The Sphinx
B Napes Needle
C Westmorland's Crag
D Great Hell Gate
E Little Hell Gate

Under The Sphinx

the steep compact buttress of Kern Knotts, then makes a rising traverse over scree slopes to reach craggy ground beneath The Napes. This complex sprawling cliff is hard to navigate on first acquaintance. Starting on the right, the first major feature is the clean sweep of Tophet Wall; continuing below the crag Napes Needle soon hoves into view, and to its right the steep lower buttress of Needle Ridge (route 13). Leave the main traverse path and climb steep broken ground leading to the base of the gap between Napes Needle and the main crag.

CLIMB

Climber's Traverse, grade 2

The scramble starts with a bang, with the hardest of the day's pitches. Climb the extremely polished chimney/groove on the right side of Napes Needle with some difficulty, then descend the shorter but equally steep and shiny W side of the gap to complete the manoeuvre known as 'threading the Needle'. Cross a broken gully and climb leftwards onto an exposed ledge called the Dress Circle, from where the classic post-card photos of Napes Needle are taken. Directly above is the precipitous lower section of Eagle's Nest Ridge (route 12); continue scrambling W with care, passing through a tight gap between a flake and the main crag, then descending steep polished rock to enter a gully bounding the left side of Eagle's Nest Ridge. Arrowhead Ridge (route 11) can now be seen above. The Climber's

On the slabby rib of Sphinx Ridge

Sphinx Ridge, grade 2

The unroped alternative leaves the traverse path just before reaching the buttress that backs The Sphinx and picks its way up a short grotty gully full of precariously poised scree – an accident waiting to happen if more than one party climbs at once. As soon as possible move left out of the gully to reach the crest of Sphinx Ridge at a level, toothed section. Clamber over a couple of exposed pinnacles to reach a slabby rib, which is climbed excitingly until thinner more technical ground forces a rethink. Foot traverse a narrow heathery ledge across the rib's right flank to briefly re-enter the gully. Now continue up the broken crest, where the difficulty can be varied to suit – either a simple scrambly path weaving around the outcrops or a more direct hands-on line. A steep wall with some suspect blocks and a final polished groove lead to a distinctive grassy neck at the junction of the various Napes ridges.

Westmorland's Crag, grade 1/2

Above the grassy neck is the sprawling confusion of Westmorland's Crag. A non-scrambling path cuts left below the crag before plodding up

Traverse continues across scrappy (though non-trivial) ground, heading straight towards the pinnacle dubbed The Sphinx for obvious reasons. This Pharaonic monolith and the compact buttress behind it can be climbed at about Moderate/Difficult.

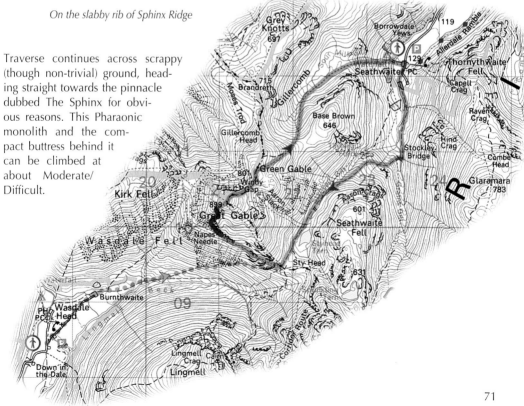

Great Gable's rubbly SW shoulder to the summit plateau; this is an inferior choice. To maintain the scrambling interest walk a short way up the grass crest to pick up a sketchy little path on its right side, traversing across scree to the base of Westmorland's Crag. Finding the correct ridge among the various tottering options is notoriously difficult. Pass the first rib, and then a second set slightly higher, to reach a third rib with a block at its base, a big gully to its right and a sharp pronged tower high on the skyline. Look carefully and you'll spot signs of wear leading up a short corner. This gives access to the broad crest, where follow-your-nose ground leads up a series of entertaining short walls, blocks and ledges. The little rock pinnacles can all be scrambled direct or bypassed on the right. It's great stuff, and the top comes too soon. Turn right to stroll onto Gable's summit.

DESCENT

The quickest way off is the paved path down Gable's SE shoulder back to Sty Head, but it is fairly brutal. On a nice day it's worth staying high; continue NE over the plateau, where a rough path makes a careful descent behind Gable Crag (route 14) into the well-named notch of Windy Gap. A quick hop over Green Gable and a long easy descent (at first ENE, then N) into the hanging valley of Gillercombe brings you to a point overlooking Seathwaite. The flagstone-paved path now drops steeply down the rugged slope beside foaming Sourmilk Gill to reach the valley floor.

Wasdale from the pinnacles on Sphinx Ridge

Grade	80m VDiff
Distance	7.5km (taking the long route home over Great Gable)
Ascent	830m (ditto)
Time	6 hours
Start/finish	See route 10
Maps	OS Landranger (1:50000) 90; OS Explorer (1:25000) OL4; Harvey British Mountain Map (1:40000) Lake District
Accommodation	See route 10
Sleeping out	See route 10
Public transport	See route 10
Seasonal notes	Although it has been done as a snowy rock climb the aspect, altitude and general nature of Arrowhead Ridge doesn't tend to permit good winter climbing conditions – in common with the other Napes ridges.

The steep first pitch

◄ **FOR TOPO SEE ROUTE 10.**

A N INSPIRING LINE on unimpeachable rock, Arrowhead Ridge is in many ways the best of The Napes' big three, and certainly the most arete-like. Its comparative unpopularity is hard to account for, but lacking the queues and polish of Needle Ridge is just one of its selling points; the climbing is also harder, airier and more interesting – assuming, that is, that you don't bother with the disappointing indirect route (Diff). The ridge crest architecture equals anything else described in this book.

APPROACH

The quickest approach is from Wasdale via an unsubtle slog up Gavel Neese. But the famous Climber's Traverse from the pass of Sty Head is more satisfying, and a logical route for people starting from either Wasdale or Borrowdale. This is described fully in route 10; follow the Climber's Traverse past Napes Needle and the Dress Circle, squeezing through the gap between a flake and the main crag and then descending steep polished rock to enter a gully bounding the left side of Eagle's Nest Ridge (route 12).

Arrowhead Ridge is now visible up on the left, its slabby lower reaches rearing up to the distinctive spire that earns it its name.

CLIMB

Arrowhead Ridge Direct, 80m VDiff

Pitch 1, 25m
Climb the lowest rocks on the left, or alternatively a grassy rake and corner system further right (better than it looks). Belay in a blocky niche on the arete, just below the slabby wall that runs up to The Arrowhead.

Pitch 2, 15m
The crux; a spectacular bit of climbing at the grade. Gain the exposed slabby wall with a stiff pull, then follow obvious holds and plentiful gear placements up to the base of the Arrowhead block. The brave will surmount it direct, but it doesn't make a spacious belay. It might seem preferable to step right across the face just below the block instead, before pulling onto a ledge to belay comfortably in the gap behind The Arrowhead.

Looking down on The Sphinx (Route 10) from the upper crest

Below The Arrowhead

DESCENT

Don't attempt the gullies between the ridges at any cost; broader, relatively safer scree fans bound either side of The Napes, Little Hell Gate on the W and Great Hell Gate on the E. The names are a subtle clue. From the grassy neck the way to go is painfully obvious – both gullies have plenty of steep loose ground demanding care in descent. Sphinx Ridge (route 10) provides a better alternative descent on the W side of the crag, but this too involves some precarious scree. The savvy will have carried suitable footwear on the climb, and will keep their helmets on.

CONTINUATION

Old school mountaineers, with rucksacks, can enjoy the last laugh as they can cheerfully continue over Great Gable without descending the crag. Either continue uphill via the scramble on Westmorland's Crag (route 10) or take the path that skirts left below the rocks, then plods up the rubble of Gable's SW shoulder to reach the summit cairn; descend as for route 10.

Pitch 3, 40m

Bridge up the gap between the pinnacle and the ridge to gain the short sharp knife edge above. Cross this (à cheval if you must), and follow the airy crest above, a rising series of rock steps and narrow level aretes – the epitome of a classic ridge. A precarious stride over a gap behind a pinnacle leads to a belay ledge. It might be worth staying roped up on the final scrappy scramble.

Climb the jumble of broken rocks and grass where the various Napes ridges converge, continuing up to the distinctive grassy neck that connects the crag with the main mountainside, as for route 10.

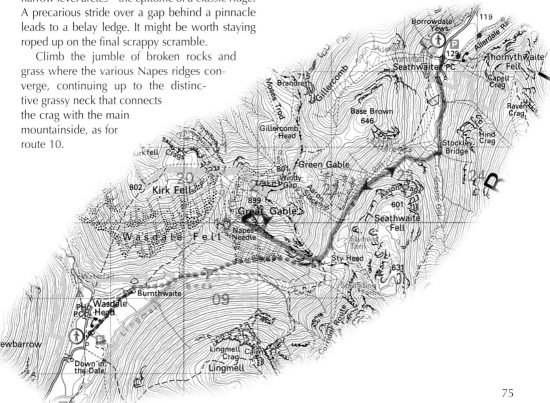

Route 12 – Eagle's Nest Ridge, Great Gable

Grade	97m Mild VS via the Direct Start (or 114m Diff via Ordinary Route)
Distance	8km (see route 11)
Ascent	830m (see route 11)
Time	6 hours
Start/finish	See route 10
Maps	OS Landranger (1:50000) 90; OS Explorer (1:25000) OL4; Harvey British Mountain Map (1:40000) Lake District
Accommodation	See route 10
Sleeping out	See route 10
Public transport	See route 10
Seasonal notes	The initial Direct pitch wouldn't lend itself to winter climbing. Even the Ordinary Route is only likely to be in nick once in a blue moon.

An eagle's eye view of Eagle's Nest Ridge

◄ FOR TOPO SEE ROUTE 10.

Along, lonely lead high above the screes, the Direct start to Eagle's Nest Ridge has a superbly spacious feel. With delicate climbing on flawless rock it's one of the best single pitches described in this book. The blocky traditional Diff continuation up Eagle's Nest Ordinary gives a slightly unbalanced route grade-wise, but the two combine very well. The Ordinary Route is a classic in its own right, offering varied climbing with an airy Alpine feel; it starts up a chimney system just left of the Direct route. Starting with the Direct makes this the hardest of the Napes' three main rock ridges, while by the Ordinary Route it is the easiest. Both routes are described here and either way Eagle's Nest Ridge has that unbeatable combination of quality climbing and bird's eye perspectives.

APPROACH

Follow route 10 to the base of The Napes. By either variation the climb starts directly above the Dress Circle. Accessing this from below is unpleasant, so it's probably best to thread the needle as described in route 10. Gear up on the little rock slab at the Dress Circle.

CLIMB

Eagle's Nest Ridge Direct, MVS 4b

Pitch 1, 37m

The route was first climbed with 19th-century protection, and as such renowned for its boldness. Carry plenty of smallish modern nuts and there's nothing to fear; the gear is spaced just wide enough to hone the climb's exciting edge.

Climb the obvious rib, gaining and following a deep crack just right of the arete, to reach a tiny ledge on the crest known – unsurprisingly – as the Eagle's Nest. Continue straight up for a few metres in a spectacular position until you can pause to gather your thoughts on a second little ledge, the Crow's Nest. A small wire in a slot here protects the subsequent arete, where balancey moves on slopers await. It's stimulating stuff but the angle soon eases, bringing you to a deep belay ledge in a corner. You're now at the top of pitch 3 of Eagle's Nest Ordinary Route.

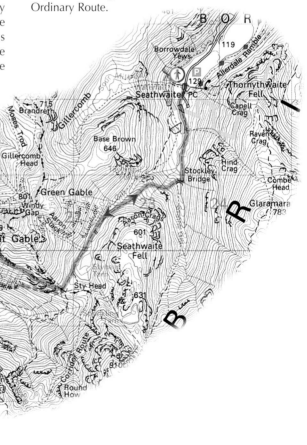

Eagle's Nest Ridge from Needle Ridge (Route 13)

Alternative start:
Eagle's Nest Ordinary Route, Difficult

This softer option begins 15m left of the rib of the Direct. Pitch 1 follows a chimney (30m); pitch 2 moves right through a little gap and up a slab to belay in a corner (12m); pitch 3 takes another little chimney and then a smooth slab to belay as for the top of the Direct (12m).

Pitch 2, 20m

(This will be pitch 4 if you've taken the Ordinary Route.) Take the short steep chimney/crack on the right with a couple of interesting moves, then bear left up a scrambly line of weakness until you're overlooking Eagle's Nest Gully; now follow the blocky crest to a stance on a square-topped ledge in front of a sort of crevasse (spike belay).

Pitch 3, 40m

Step over the gap and bear right of a steep prow. More ridge-crest fun follows, with nice positions but no nasty surprises. The ground soon merges into the confusing grass-and-rock jumble at the top of the Napes ridges. Keep scrambling up to the pronounced neck joining the crag to Great Gable.

Needle Ridge (Route 13) seen from the excellent Eagle's Nest Ridge Direct

CONTINUATION

See route 10.

DESCENT

See route 11.

(Right) Wasdale from the top of Eagle's Nest Ridge

Route 13 – Napes Needle and Needle Ridge, Great Gable

Napes Needle and Needle Ridge from Eagle's Nest Ridge (Route 12)

Grade	Napes Needle 18m HS; Needle Ridge 100m VDiff
Distance	8km (see route 11)
Ascent	830m (see route 11)
Time	7 hours
Start/finish	See route 10
Maps	OS Landranger (1:50000) 90; OS Explorer (1:25000) OL4; Harvey British Mountain Map (1:40000) Lake District
Accommodation	See route 10
Sleeping out	See route 10
Public transport	See route 10
Seasonal notes	See route 11

On the Wasdale Crack, Napes Needle

◄ **FOR TOPO SEE ROUTE 10.**

THE SPECTACULAR PINNACLE of Napes Needle is Lakeland rock's ultimate must-do. Arguably the most iconic symbol in the history of the sport, this short sharp exercise in rope management needs little introduction. But for the benefit of those who aren't yet bored to stone by the fossilised old adage, the first ascent by Walter Parry Haskett-Smith in 1886 is (rather too) often said to mark the moment that rock climbing gained its independence from mountaineering. The historical significance may have been lost on the man himself, but he must have been pleased with his audacious on-sight solo. 'Hanging by the hands and feeling with the toes...provided an anxious moment... It was an undoubted satisfaction to stand once more on solid ground below' he later confided, and today's visitors tend to share that sentiment. Although not particularly technical it's a polished climb of high excitement. Effecting a safe reverse is arguably the real hard part, not suitable for beginners. The pinnacle guards the foot of Needle Ridge, an exposed and compelling route in its own right; combining the two makes perfect sense.

APPROACH

Follow route 10 to The Napes. There's now a choice between 'threading the Needle' as for route 10 to reach a ledge on the W side of the pinnacle, or continuing below Napes Needle until a scree gully or the scrambly rib to its right permit access to the same point. The first option is less unpleasant.

CLIMB

Napes Needle, 18m HS

There's a choice of traditional first pitches, all of which meet at the belay below the final block. The HS grade for the harder second pitch takes into account the descent as much as the climb. For the second pitch twin ropes are a good idea; clip one into protection on the way up and leave one free; the reason will soon be clear.

Pitch 1, 13m

From the ledge on the W side of Napes Needle climb either of two slanting cracks that meet up to form a vertical offwidth – the Wasdale Crack. It's better than it looks (if shiny). Easy ground on the left then leads to a belay on the narrow shoulder just below (right) of the summit block.

Pitch 2, 5m

'Feeling as small as a mouse on a milestone' in the words of the plucky first ascensionist, step out onto the exposed flank facing Needle Ridge. Make a big mantel (crux) to gain a standing position on the obvious horizontal break. Sidle left along this. Arrange protection in a higher

break; grope for insufficient holds and curse the polish; then step around the corner onto the undercut Wasdale face, where small holds lead to the smooth top out. How many climbers can dance on the head of a needle? Three is possible, although given the detached nature of the summit block it would seem rash. Belay anchors are conspicuously lacking. The one vaguely unsafe option is to drop a loop of rope under the overhanging beak of the pinnacle, and another for your second to secure on the shoulder. The wise won't bother trying.

DESCENT

Given the anchor situation, an abseil can't be recommended (and has led to accidents in the past). Ignore the butterflies in your belly and carefully reverse the route of ascent. By running the spare line over the Needle's top it's possible to contrive a canny top rope, so that your belayer

simultaneously pays out one rope and takes in the other. Unclip from the gear as you go, leaving it in situ for your second's summit bid. It's all a far cry from the solo heroics of Haskett-Smith and probably just as well. Your second now replaces

Looking down on Napes Needle from high on Needle Ridge

you at the sharp end. Once they've also basked in their moment of glory and made it back in one piece, downclimb from the shoulder to reach an obvious spike at the top of the offwidth of pitch 1; abseil from here.

CLIMB

Needle Ridge, 100m VDiff
A satisfying – if rather easier – continuation.

Pitch 1, 30m
From the notch behind Napes Needle step onto a short polished wall, soon leading into a niche/chimney. Climb this, then move leftwards over a possible stance to take a steep cracked wall direct (crux). Easier ground leads up the crest to a good belay ledge.

Pitch 2, 35m
Now less steep, the ridge rises in an airy rock staircase. The best line is obvious, and the ground is quite easy until you reach a big right-facing corner formed between a rib on the left and a slabby cracked wall. Climb the corner until near the top, when a step left gains better holds on the rib. Above is a spacious belay ledge.

Pitch 3, 35m
From here the crest levels into a pinnacled arete, a grade 2 scramble in a magnificent position. You might opt to move together, or even dispense with the rope. After a short distance the ridge kinks left to join the jumble of rock and grass where the various Napes ridges meet.

CONTINUATION

See route 10.

DESCENT

See route 11.

Route 14 – Pinnacle Ridge, Gable Crag

Grade	III
Distance	9km (Honister approach)
Ascent	730m (Honister approach)
Time	7 hours
Start/finish	Of the three possible bases – Ennerdale, Wasdale and Honister, the approach described most fully here is from Honister Hause. Start at the National Trust car park by the quarry and youth hostel (NY226135)
Maps	OS Landranger (1:50000) 90; OS Explorer (1:25000) OL4; Harvey British Mountain Map (1:40000) Lake District
Accommodation	See route 10; also consider staying in Ennerdale. Various options include: Ennerdale Youth Hostel 0845 371 9116; Ennerdale Camping Barn (YHA-run) 01629 592700; or the unique bothy-style Black Sail Hut Youth Hostel 07711 108450.
Sleeping out	The perennially popular 'wild camp' at Styhead Tarn is one overnight option, although the long exodus from here up rubbly Aaron Slack is an uninspiring way to start the morning (perhaps it's best to Levite for another day?). For more substantial shelter in the wilderness there are two small quarry workers' bothies in the hanging valley between Haystacks and Fleetwith Pike, one of which is maintained by the Mountain Bothies Association. The precise locations are an open secret; some time spent with a large scale map is instructive. Moses Trod would be the easiest access route from here to Gable Crag (see Descent section below).

Ennerdale from the top of pitch 2

Public transport   The 77 and 77A bus from Keswick serves Honister and Buttermere on a circular route

Seasonal notes   In summer this makes a fairly unpleasant scramble by all accounts, with copious vegetation and grubby loose rock. In winter well-frozen turf is crucial – don't climb it soft.

Nominally a ridge but actually more of a buttress, this is an atmospheric winter trip up a big remote crag. Pinnacle Ridge saves the best for last, building from a rather indeterminate start into a sudden grand climax high above the screes. The excitement and quality of its upper reaches have earned it a degree of popularity, but on a quiet midweek the chances are it'll be all yours. As it is by some considerable margin the hardest of the few winter routes described in this book some axe-wielding aptitude is called for. Relying on frozen turf, and with ample rock protection, the line is climbable as often as anything north facing and high hereabouts. Sod's Law dictates a weekend thaw, so if you've a hunch it's in nick then get out midweek while the going's good. You can get your work done when the route has dribbled into the Irish Sea.

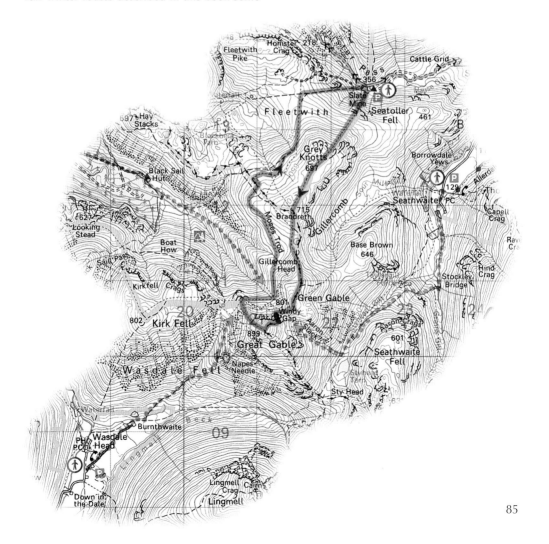

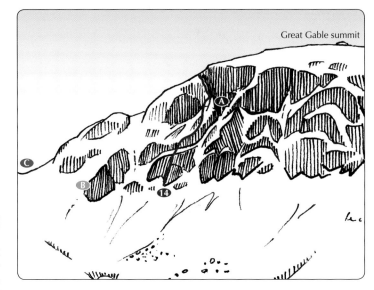

14	Pinnacle Ridge
A	The Pinnacle
B	Windy Ridge
C	Windy Gap

APPROACH

With its pivotal position at the terminus of three major valleys Great Gable can be approached in a number of ways. From Wasdale Gable Crag is best reached via the col of Beck Head; from just above the pass a bouldery traverse path leads directly under the mountain's N face – clearly marked on the OS 1:25000 map. For lovers of remote country a long hike (or a nifty cycle) along the forest track in the depths of Ennerdale might be the favoured option, particularly if combined with a stay at the enviably-located Black Sail Hut. The Borrowdale alternative is brief but butch; park at the end of the minor road to Seathwaite and follow the oft-trodden motorway to Styhead Tarn, then grunt up the scree trough of Aaron Slack to Windy Gap, from where a short bouldery descent gains the traverse path below Gable Crag. Last but not least is the approach from Honister Hause, attractive for its high start, its tally of summits and the good view of Gable Crag from the adjacent peak of Green Gable. The route is described below.

Beyond the stark quarry works a path climbs steeply SSW along a fence line, passing rock bands to reach the boggy hollows and outcrops on top of Grey Knotts. Stay with the fence onto the wide summit of Brandreth, with an unfolding panorama down Ennerdale, and over Glaramara to the Helvellyn range. An easy descent to Gillercomb Head is followed by a rough ascent to the small stone wind break on the summit of Green Gable. This is a good vantage point from which to familiarise yourself with the layout of Gable Crag, just opposite. Make the short steep descent into Windy Gap, which may sometimes

carry a modest cornice. Now head due W below Gable Crag, passing under the obvious low point of Windy Ridge (40m III) until you are below a wide inset area of broken ground, bounded on each side by fairly defined gullies. High up, the little pinnacle that distinguishes the top section of the climb provides a useful focal point in the confusion of rock, snow and vegetation. It has been called 'bottle shaped' but looks more like a rock to me.

CLIMB

Pinnacle Ridge, 200m III

Pitches 1–3, 145m
Pitch 1 enters a shallow bay with a big slab on its left side and a chockstone-blocked chimney at its back; it then climbs steep turfy steps immediately right of the chimney to reach easier terrain. For the next two pitches there is hardly an identifiable ridge at all; simply follow a line of least – or most – resistance (as the urge takes you) on the ground between the two gullies, weaving up a succession of steep little rock bands and vegetated ledges, and belaying at will. By feinting left at opportune moments the grade can generally be kept fairly low. The Pinnacle is visible for much of the time to keep you broadly on track; at the top of pitch 3 is a ledge with the deep corner of Bottleneck Blues (IV) above on your left, and The Pinnacle just up on the right.

Belay by the 'bottle-shaped' pinnacle (it looks more like a rock to me)

Pitch 4, 25m

Easy blocky ground leads into a steep corner directly below The Pinnacle; this provides a short high-quality mixed pitch with interesting moves and decent rock protection. Belay at a superb atmospheric stance by the narrow neck between The Pinnacle and the main crag. With big drops falling away on both sides this is the only true section of ridge on the whole route.

Pitch 5, 30m

Gingerly step onto the exposed neck, then mantel a short steep rock wall on the left to end up standing on a narrow ledge – perhaps the crux of the route. Sidle briefly left, where the interest continues up a series of abrupt steps and turfy grooves, with plenty of exposure and sufficient small wire protection. Difficulties soon ease as you reach the snowy promontory at the top of the buttress. Gable's summit is a short walk away.

DESCENT

For the sake of variety it's more interesting to make a circuit. Descend the steep NW shoulder of the mountain, taking care in mist to follow the cairn-marked line a safe distance from the lip of Gable Crag. This scrambly boulder slope can be awkward in deep snow. Not far short of Beck Head turn right onto a path that descends due E through more boulders some way below Gable Crag, into Stone Cove. An unusual mid-height traverse path known as Moses Trod now girdles the flanks of Green Gable and Brandreth, heading N. Once on the wide west shoulder of the latter cross a fence and bear roughly NE on any of several paths heading over open slopes above the hanging valley of Dubs Bottom to reach a dismantled tramway and the adjacent quarry access track, either of which lead quickly back to Honister.

Turfy steps on pitch 1

Grade	Cam Crag Ridge 2, Intake Ridge 3
Distance	9km
Ascent	650m
Time	4½ hours
Start/finish	If you haven't got the bus from Keswick, there's verge parking on the minor road to Stonethwaite (approx NY258141), and a National Trust car park in the nearby village of Seatoller.
Maps	OS Landranger (1:50000) 90; OS Explorer (1:25000) OL4; Harvey British Mountain Map (1:40000) Lake District
Accommodation	Campsites at Seathwaite, Seatoller and Stonethwaite; Thorneythwaite Farm B&B near Seatoller 017687 77237; Borrowdale Youth Hostel 0845 371 9624
Sleeping out	Langstrath and The Combe both have wild camping potential, as do the many sheltered hollows on Rosthwaite Fell. There is also a 'secret' howff under some boulders hereabouts. (If I told you where I'd have to kill you.)
Public transport	Regular buses from Keswick to Seatoller
Seasonal notes	Winter climbing? Not likely. The altitude is too low in anything but an exceptional deep freeze, and neither route seems best suited to the build up of decent conditions in any case.

Cam Crag Ridge above Langstrath – the route follows the skyline from left to right

Although their most ridge-like aspect is their names this brace of fine features offers superb scrambling in an unspoilt but accessible low mountain setting. You could do them separately, but incorporating both into a logical circuit makes for a more substantial day out. These routes were pioneered back in the age of tweed breeches and hobnails by the prolific Borrowdale enthusiast and Alpine mountaineer Bentley Beetham (they don't name 'em like they used to). Both are rather easier than the climbing grades they were originally given.

APPROACH

From the hamlet of Stonethwaite head SE along a farm track, passing through a rustic campsite beside the wide bouldery course of Stonethwaite Beck. On nearing the buttress of Heron Crag turn right to enter

Approaching the crux of Cam Crag Ridge, high above lovely Langstrath

The slabby corner near the start of Intake Ridge, Skiddaw in the distance

Langstrath. Stay W of the beck on a stony track through this idyllic valley, to reach the gin-clear pool of Blackmoss Pot, the area's premier deep water bouldering venue. Above the nearby floodplain Cam Crag rises in a row of rocky tiers scattered up the hillside to make what can, with some poetic license, be described as a ridge. Quit the main path for a fainter one, unmarked on OS maps, that climbs the steep bracken-cloaked slope, passing just right of the lowest pyramidal buttress (optional scramble) to reach a grassy levelling beside a jumble of huge blocks at the foot of the ridge.

CLIMB

Cam Crag Ridge, 200m grade 2

Ascend leftwards through the boulders to a short slabby wall, which gives access to a mini-arete. Climb this on good solid holds, then an easier-angled section above leading to the base of a steep little right angled corner. Exposed and strenuous for the grade, the corner is the route's crux; it may be sensible to offer beginners the security of a rope. Above, the angle quickly relents. Short solid scrambling steps and spells of simple walking alternate up the broad crest. At the next major steepening follow blocky holds up a right-slanting fault. The ground then gradually eases, though a last steep wall climbed on slightly questionable angular chunks provides an optional sting in the tail for the confident.

CONTINUATION

You're now up among the boggy hollows and craggy knobbles of Rosthwaite Fell, a rugged wee hill with an uncrowded feel. Head N through the maze of hummocks, perhaps detouring to pocket peaklet Rosthwaite Cam en route to the secluded pool of Tarn at Leaves. Pick up one of several paths at the left side of the tarn, all of which descend NW towards the hanging valley of The Combe. At a height of about 400m leave your path to contour N along the fellside towards the rounded hump of Glaciated Slab, a popular beginner's crag that forms part of Intake Ridge. Descend scree around the base of the slab, and continue down until nearly level with a drystone wall beneath the route.

CLIMB

Intake Ridge, 120m grade 3

A disjointed line (sc)rambling up a series of buttresses – the interest here is in the detail, with some very enjoyable sections. Start just left of the lowest buttress, climbing a short blocky cleft before moving rightwards over broken ground. A prominent sloping corner then provides some fun; from its top head up and right to reach a well-trodden ledge overlooking Glaciated Slab. As the next section is a tricky scramble above an unforgiving drop, now might be a good time to rope up. Gain a bulging slab leading out right to the edge of the buttress. Make a balancey high step onto a second slab, and step airily rightwards along a line of weakness leading out spectacularly above Glaciated Slab. A small nut here would protect the second. Pad over the top of the slab before following the hog's back ridge to a big grass ledge.

A scrappy spur brings you to the foot of the next steep tier. Climb a grubby depression just right of a clean nose, on steep and slightly iffy rock with plenty of heather. Pull carefully left over blocks to reach grassy ground, then move up and right to a level ledge immediately below the final steep rocks of the ridge. Although easier than the lower crux, this is another spot to consider the merits of a rope. Near the right end of the ledge is a bulging nose; pull up steeply to pass left of this. Now traverse carefully right along a slabby break, quite suddenly popping out onto safer ground. Rocks lead easily to the top.

DESCENT

It's possible to follow the fellside just S of the ridge, but it's steep and loose. Easier is to contour S from the top of the scramble to regain the main descent path into The Combe. Stay E of the gill, passing through a series of enclosures. Go right at a fork in the path, dropping into Borrowdale and soon reaching Stonethwaite.

On the gorgeous Glaciated Slab

Grade	159m up to Mild Severe by the route combination described; harder and easier variations are possible
Distance	6km
Ascent	760m
Time	7 hours
Start/finish	Gatesgarth farm pay and display car park (NY195150)
Maps	OS Landranger (1:50000) 89 or 90; OS Explorer (1:25000) OL4; Harvey British Mountain Map (1:40000) Lake District
Accommodation	Buttermere Youth Hostel 0845 371 9508 or various options in Borrowdale (see route 15)
Sleeping out	Although it's a strenuous enough walk-in even without overnight gear a wild camp high in Birkness (Burtness on OS maps) Combe would give access to a fantastic full weekend of climbing. There are a few small pleasant plots beside the stream.
Public transport	See route 14
Seasonal notes	Clean, south-facing Grey Crag isn't an ideal winter cliff; Harrow Buttress can (very) occasionally provide a grade III climb on snowed-up rock; Chockstone Ridge would be a similar grade. The crag is quick-drying in summer.

CONTENDER FOR THE MOST IDYLLIC of Cumbria's mountain venues, Grey Crag is the perfect place to while away a leisurely sunny day. Routes here tend to be straightforward rather than stretching; the rock has a rough honesty and the position is unmatched, high over the green and blue of Buttermere. The crag forms a collection of discrete buttresses rambling up the hillside, each furnishing old fashioned low-to-mid-grade sport. The most fruitful approach is to string together a route on each successive buttress to create a long and satisfying linkup from the lowest rocks to the lofty summit of the crag. The combination described here is just one of many possibilities; beginning with the classic Harrow Buttress (Difficult), it continues via the airy and unjustly neglected Chockstone Ridge (Moderate) to reach a final thrilling climax on the near-perfect arete of Oxford and Cambridge Direct (Mild Severe). Back on *terra firma*, a gorgeous ridge walk rounds things off in High Stile.

APPROACH

The approach is short (on paper), but sharp; two hours wouldn't be an excessive time to allow. From the car park cross the B5289 and follow the signed path past the farmyard. A track heads across the flat valley-bottom meadow, crossing a wooden footbridge to reach the hillside of Buttermere Fell (not named on the 1:50000 OS map). Climb past a small pine plantation for a minute or two on the popular paved Scarth Gap trail to reach a junction where the main path veers off hard left. Leave the Scarth Gap path here, going more or less straight on on a less well used path that contours the hillside below a line of dank crags, passing a memorial plaque to reach Combe Beck. Cross the stream, following its W bank quite steeply to a stile over a drystone wall. Now stay with the beck to ascend into the upper reaches of Birkness Combe (named Burtness on OS maps), a rugged cirque of exceptional character. Ahead is the great flat-topped bulk of Eagle Crag; Grey Crag is the more broken collection of rocks high up on the right. When opportunity affords turn right, trudging up nasty scree to reach the base of Harrow Buttress, the lowest of Grey Crag's four sections. Start climbing just left of the very bottom rocks.

CLIMB

Harrow Buttress, 45m Difficult

Pitch 1, 10m
Climb the obvious short steep corner on glassy polish, to a ledge on the right.

Pitch 2, 13m
Step back left to enter the smooth chimney; this is a struggle if wearing a rucksack, particularly when slimy. Pull left out of the chimney to belay on a ledge.

Pitch 3, 22m
Climb a vague groove, above which fairly easy rocks lead into a little roofed niche. Swing left out of this (crux) to reach the top of the buttress.
From the top of Harrow Buttress scramble down easily into a gap. From here

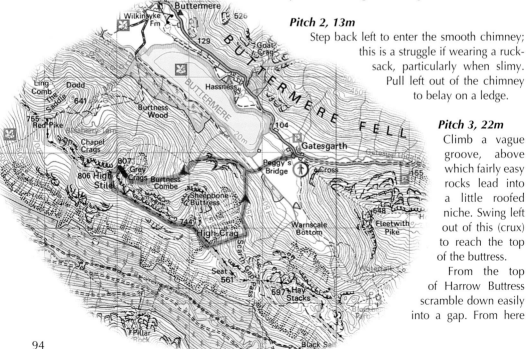

A Harrow Buttress
B Chockstone Ridge
C Oxford and Cambridge Direct Route
D Mitre Buttress

a loose heathery path leads up a fault between crags to reach a point overlooking the scree gully that runs along the foot of Chockstone Buttress. Chockstone Ridge is well seen from here, a slender pillar bounded by shallow gullies, with extensive slabs to its left and a steeper rock mass to its right. Cross the gully to reach the rock.

Chockstone Ridge, 72m Moderate

Pitch 1, 25m
Starting from a blocky ledge just above the lowest steep wall swing up easily onto the crest, which is followed to a block belay.

On pitch 3 of the underrated Chockstone Ridge

Pitch 2, 10m

Make a steep pull to reach a little square-cut pinnacle on the crest; belay here.

Pitch 3, 15m

Step up right in an airy position, then follow the line of least resistance back left onto the blunt arete, which is followed to a generous ledge.

Pitch 4, 22m

Move right to enter a narrow and fairly exciting chimney on the right side of the ridge, to finish the route in fine style.

Now scramble onto the grassy terrace that separates Chockstone Buttress from the upper tier, Oxford and Cambridge Buttress; this is Grey Crag's crowning glory. Walk briefly left, descending a little to reach the foot of Oxford and Cambridge Direct, the pristine right-angled arete running the full height of the crag to divide the slabby frontal face from the steeper delights of the crack-seamed right wall.

Oxford and Cambridge Direct Route, 42m Mild Severe

Pitch 1, 15m

Ascend a short crack just right of the edge, then pull out onto the prow. Delectable climbing leads straight up this to reach a comfortable ledge.

Pitch 2, 27m

Appropriately, the day's final pitch is also its finest. Step left to climb a prominent steep little crack (jamming useful). Above this, slabbier ground leads up rightwards to the breezy crest

The wonderful second pitch of Oxford and Cambridge Direct – bound to bring a smile to your 'boat race'

(Left) Oxford and Cambridge Direct

of the buttress. Staying just left of the edge, pad ecstatically past a second little steepening leading, too soon, to blocky ground at the top. A wonderful pitch, bound to bring a smile to your face.

DESCENT

Descents back into Birkness Combe can be made down steep grass and scree ribbons flanking the various buttresses. Alternatively the quickest route to Buttermere is the walker's path down the NNE spur of High Stile.

CONTINUATION

But having come this far climbers with any soul will eschew an early descent for the longer more scenic route home over tops. A short walk SW gains the summit of High Stile. From here stroll easily S to reach the narrow grassy ridge running along the back of Birkness Combe. The 1km stride over to High Crag is a soothing wind down from the excitements of climbing, as shadows gather in the depths of Buttermere and Ennerdale and the high fells rust in the evening glow. Payback comes soon after, with a knee jarring descent from High Crag towards the low saddle of Scarth Gap. Look out for a path on the left as you go, since this cuts quite a corner. Once down on the path N of Scarth Gap, Gatesgarth is quickly reached

Buttermere from the top of Chockstone Ridge

THE REST
OF ENGLAND

Although the Lake District is England's only real mountain area and the natural centre of ridge climbing activity, it isn't the last word. The various ridges scattered widely and randomly around the rest of the country are an eclectic collection, each very attractive and adventurous in its own way.

With the exception of the landlocked Peak District the locations are all sea cliffs, those wild ragged edges where our island splinters into the ocean. None offers an entirely typical sea cliff experience (if there is such a thing), and could perhaps best be described as mountaineering-on-sea. Waves and tides are all part of the fun with these coastal shenanigans, and can often provide challenges to equal the weather and remoteness of mountain climbs.

Waiting for the tide at the bottom of Skeleton Ridge (Route 18)

Route 17 – Ridges of Winnats Pass, Peak District

Grade	Elbow Ridge 80m Moderate, Matterhorn Ridge 60m Difficult
Distance	1.5km
Ascent	150m
Time	2 hours max
Start/finish	Pay and display car park opposite Speedwell Cavern, very busy at weekends (SK139827)
Maps	OS Landranger (1:50000) 110 isn't detailed enough; OS Explorer (1:25000) OL1 is a lot more useful; Harvey British Mountain Map (1:40000) Dark Peak is a good alternative
Accommodation	Castleton Youth Hostel 0845 371 9628
Sleeping out	Nowhere particularly suitable for a wild camp nearby
Public transport	The nearest train station is Hope on the Sheffield–Manchester line, several kms down the valley. The 272/4 bus from Sheffield to Castleton runs hourly; from here it's a short walk uphill.
Seasonal notes	Slimy in the wet, and not recommended. Although the ridges are south facing and low lying, there are reputedly rare occasions when a true winter ascent is possible. It'd only be worth doing if the turf was frozen. Grade III seems a fair estimate.

At the top of Matterhorn Ridge

Marching up the flanks of the rugged little gorge of Winnats Pass, these compelling twin features are the only significant ridge climbs in the Peak, and the only routes on limestone described in this book. Run together they give about 140m of superb mountaineering-style excitement in an incongruously non-mountainous setting. The climbing is technically easy, but these knife-sharp crests have a sense of exposure out of proportion with their modest scale, and should be treated with respect. Sprouting from the ground just metres from the tarmac, and sandwiched between Sheffield and Manchester, this is the most roadside of convenience clambering. You could virtually belay out of your sunroof. And therein lies the problem. Although you have a right to climb on this access land, landowners the National Trust have expressed legitimate safety concerns and the BMC officially advise against climbing here. The hillside hangs over a popular public road and footpath. Although the rock is less unsound than it looks, loose blocks do exist. The potential for passers-by to be hit by falling material (or climbers) is obvious. To add insult to possible

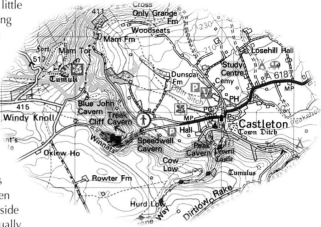

injury, the grassy strip beside the road hides a shallow high-pressure oil pipeline. Overkill, you might say. Considering all this, if you're still keen to climb then it would be sensible and sensitive only to visit early or late in the day, midweek. Take out public liability insurance, climb only in small groups, and do so with extreme caution – it's not just your own welfare in your hands.

Starting up the bottom section of a greasy Elbow Ridge

A Elbow Ridge
B Matterhorn Ridge
C Winnats Pass Road

APPROACH

Walk up the verge from the car park to enter Winnats Pass. Elbow Ridge is the lower of the two, starting at road level. Matterhorn Ridge is the two-tiered 'peak' higher up the hillside on the left.

CLIMB

Elbow Ridge, 80m Moderate
If you're going to rope up for any of Elbow Ridge, do it here. Starting easy-angled, the rocky base of the ridge soon steepens, before levelling and tapering into a pronounced crest. Follow this

On the lower arete of Elbow Ridge

High on Elbow Ridge

Meeting the locals on Matterhorn Ridge

with due care. This is some vegetation and much exposure; in the damp you might be reduced to an undignified à cheval. It's possible to arrange infrequent runners. The sharpest section terminates at a little grassy col, from where it's probably safe to proceed unroped. Less narrow but still quite airy, the ridge continues up a rising series of scrambly rock steps and level grass crests to reach a final steep nose. Taking this direct would be brave – an obvious line breaches the easier rock tier on the left.

Now descend diagonally across the steep grass slope to reach either the base or the half-height break of Matterhorn Ridge.

Matterhorn Ridge, 60m Difficult

The name might overstate the case somewhat – for one thing there are fewer sheep in Zermatt – but this remains a respectable climb, and probably not best suited to unaccompanied beginners.

The lower tier is the technical crux. Start with blocky scrambling, which becomes steadily steeper and more exposed before some final tricky moves bring you with relief to the half-height break. Soloists and wet weather stoics might consider slinking right to avoid the top couple of metres of this lower tier. It's now worth belaying before the upper tower. This might be a little easier, but it is more vegetated, and if anything more exciting; reliable runners are quite spaced. Again, the sting is in the tail, and by now the passing traffic seems a long way below.

DESCENT

Traverse left on a rough path that passes some old mine workings, then crosses the slope to meet the road a little way W of the ridges.

Route 18 – Skeleton Ridge, Isle of Wight

Written and researched with the help of Joe Williams

Grade	125m HVS/MildXS 4c
Distance	3km
Ascent	150m
Time	6 hours
Start/finish	Private car park at The Needles pleasure park (SZ307853); you may have to pay in high season. On busy days there can be queues of traffic waiting to get a space – worth bearing in mind if the schedule is tight. Note: there is no public parking at the Old Battery itself.
Maps	OS Landranger (1:50000) 196
Tides	Consult the Totland Bay tide table. The climb can be accessed without wading for only an hour or so either side of low water, preferably on a spring tide. Even then it may be impossible to reach the rock dry shod if there's a swell running. The beach between the abseil and the ridge is covered at high water, so once committed there's no way back.

The Needles from a crumbly pitch 5

Gear

On the approach at least 90m of abseil rope is necessary, static line being highly advisable; a further length of c40m is needed if planning to leave an in situ rope as a belay anchor at the top of pitch 6 (also highly advisable). On the descent dedicated abseil devices are safer and more comfortable than a belay plate. For the climb itself carry: a generous selection of pegs of all shapes and sizes; piton hammers; a range of medium to large cams; one set of nuts; several short tape loops for tying off rusty in situ pegs; some long slings for equalising dodgy belays and throwing over wobbly chalk piles; a couple of shock absorbing quickdraws for reassurance; double ropes, the stretchier the better. Chalk bags are redundant. Rope climbing gizmos (Ropeman, jumar and the like) are a sensible insurance; it's an awfully long way to climb back up the abseil line using chalk-clogged prussiks.

Accommodation

Stoats Farm campsite 01983 755258 just S of Totland (and not far from The Needles) is friendly, good value and next door to an excellent pub or Totland Bay Youth Hostel 0845 371 9348

Sleeping out

Discounting benightment on the ridge there's not a lot of scope for this on the Isle of Wight.

Public transport

Wightlink ferry from Lymington to Yarmouth (www.wightlink.co.uk); while convenient to take a car across it is also possible – and a lot cheaper – to travel as a foot passenger, then use public transport on the island. Regular bus services connect Yarmouth, Totland and The Needles pleasure park; the difficulty is meshing bus timetables with tide times.

Seasonal notes

The ridge should probably be avoided in the rain, since water and chalk don't mix well. High wind can also be a show stopper if it raises a dangerous swell. If the wind is strong enough to buffet you at the Battery then you're unlikely to feel safe teetering along the razor edges of the ridge.

DEATHLY WHITE AND DEADLY SERIOUS, Skeleton Ridge has a sinister sepulchral resonance that seems fitting for something formed over unfathomable aeons from countless compressed corpses. It is the island's fossilised spine jutting free, its lower vertebrae fragmenting into the waves as a line of detached sea stacks, the famous Needles. The route follows the landward rib from shore to clifftop, unique both as a landmark and a climb. Skeleton Ridge is a Mick Fowler creation, and while comparatively gentle by his standards it remains by far the gravest climb in this book, the one on which the unwary are most likely to come to grief. It also ranks among the most characterful adventure routes in the British Isles, with melodramatic climbing in a serious sea cliff setting. In places the ridge is a collapse-prone pile, in others it narrows to perhaps the

keenest blade in the country, a soaring white fin on the edge of all things.

Unlike most chalk climbs Skeleton Ridge is best tackled conventionally, not with ice tools, yet the rock still needs a delicate touch and holds may detach at random. The medium is inherently suspect and the climb uncommonly airy, yet it's neither sustained nor particularly technical. Then

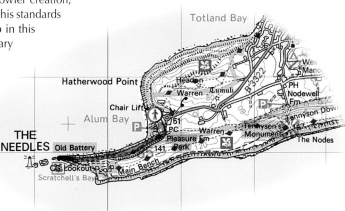

Leaving the groove on pitch 1

again, with belays this questionable, falling would not be healthy. Cool mountaineering judgement, canny rope work and a comfortable grade margin are demanded equally of both leader and second. Climb if you must, but look well to each step (and handhold).

NB Given a long enough timeframe any guidebook will eventually be rendered obsolete by subsequent erosion. On Skeleton Ridge, however, significant rockfall may happen sooner rather than later, and descriptions from about 20 years ago are already unusable. Before climbing seek the latest information possible – ask on internet forums perhaps, or call Solent Coastguard. And remember what they say – geological time is now.

ACCESS ARRANGEMENTS AND TIMING

Access must be pre-arranged with the friendly National Trust staff at the Old Battery (01983 754772), with whom good relations have to be preserved if climbing is to continue here unhindered; phone in advance and then make yourselves known to staff on arrival. To prevent an

unnecessary emergency callout it is also essential to inform Solent Coastguard (02392 552100) before abseiling to the beach, not forgetting to call in again when back safe at the top of the route.

Given the complications of access and rigging, and the dusty faff of a long loose abseil, it's wise to leave plenty of time to reach the foot of the climb. Arriving at the Old Battery three hours before scheduled low water would not be excessive; better to await low water down on the beach than miss your moment and have to jug back up the abseil rope in defeat.

APPROACH

From the pleasure park follow the busy clifftop track to the Old Battery, a commandingly sited historic naval fortification owned by the National Trust. Although the climb itself is invisible from the fort abseilers will attract the attention of the general public; meeting the Battery staff is first priority as they may want to be in attendance. To pre-rig a belay anchor for the top of pitch 6 (there's not much else to tie onto), climb the fort's perimeter fence, heading W onto the promontory at the top of Skeleton Ridge. Rig a rope from a WW2 observation post, running it down the headland to be left in situ.

Back at the fort, hop over the SE corner of the fence. Rig an abseil from the fence; it is almost exactly 90m to the beach. A wide ditch separates the fort from the main headland; abseil the short drop into this. The official climber's descent anchor is a metal post in a little niche on the cliff edge overlooking Scratchell's Bay. Equalise the rope to the post and the fence above.

The main drop starts in a chossy gully before curving a little to take the fall line down insecure grass patches, powdery soil and crumbling rock steps. It is a big and serious descent. Teams lacking a single very long rope will have to pass a knot; the average angle of the cliff is not vertical, so you shouldn't be free hanging when carrying out this manoeuvre. Knocking debris down is practically unavoidable; take care that the rope does not dislodge rocks onto your head from above. Once safe on the beach **stand well back** while your partner descends.

Head W along the shore, clambering over a mound of boulders. Until some years ago this was a tower on the ridge, a fact that should emphasise the fragility of rocks and people. Skeleton Ridge is

An unwelcome breeze on pitch 3

the pinnacle-topped wall at the end of the beach – you can't miss it. Walk (or wade) along the base of the wall until roughly halfway between the two prominent pinnacles. Belay on a ledge just above the sea, at the bottom of a shallow left-facing groove.

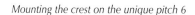

CLIMB

Skeleton Ridge, 126m HVS/MildXS 4c

Pitch 1, 12m, 4b
Climb the groove – good runners – then traverse boldly left along a line of flints embedded in soft pale chalk, ascending to the ridge-top niche between the pinnacles. The in situ peg belay needs backing up.

Pitch 2, 12m
Traverse along a sloping ledge on the left flank of the ridge, passing left of the big tower (good gear) to a block belay on the next col.

Pitch 3, 12m, 4c
Crux. A narrow fin looms menacingly overhead. Clip (and preferably back up) a couple of rusty old pegs, then climb the left flank of the arete in a tremendous position to belay on a spacious ledge. Don't fall off.

Pitch 4, 15m
Climb to the knife-edged arete and follow it until a traverse ledge can be seen on the left flank. Belay here.

Pitch 5, 50m
Sidle along the obvious foot traverse line. This leads to a distinctly loose but thankfully easy bouldery ridge crest, which is followed to an uninspiring block belay at the base of the final steep fin.

Pitch 6, 25m, 4b
If there is a more sensational pitch anywhere then you don't want to climb it. Ascend the left side of the fin past old in situ pegs to pull carefully onto the inches-thick crest. Straddle the chalk very carefully, proceeding à cheval onto the Battery headland. Clip the line you left earlier... and breathe.

Mounting the crest on the unique pitch 6

Traversing the coast east of Heddon's Mouth

Grade	236m+ Difficult (or HVS, in this case for 'Huge Vertical Shrubbery')
Distance	4km
Ascent	200m
Time	5 hours
Start/finish	National Trust car park by the Hunter's Inn (SS655481)
Maps	OS Landranger (1:50000) 180; OS Explorer (1:25000) OL9 – recommended
Tides	Consult the Ilfracombe tide table. A low spring tide and very calm sea state are needed to access this route (NB for non-sailors, spring tides occur around full and new moon, and have nothing to do with the season). Approach along Bloody Beach while the sea is still falling to leave a sensible time window in case you need to retreat back along the beach – this can only be recommended during the first hour or so after the tide turns. To be climbable the entry pitch requires a tidal height of at most 0.9m. The forecast height will only obtain when incoming swell isn't keeping the water level up. High pressure and easterly winds help suppress the water level, but if conditions are rough then waves will break over the entry pitch at any state of the tide. The Pembroke weather buoy (ID 62303) is a useful indicator of potential swell here – 1m+ will be fun; 2m+ means don't bother. For buoy data visit http://www.ndbc.noaa.gov.
Gear	Add a few pegs to your standard rock rack. This necessitates carrying a hammer or an ice axe apiece; the latter may be welcome if forced to climb steep grass slopes above Bloody Beach, but on The Claw itself it's needed only for pegs. Leather work gloves prove handy.
Accommodation	Several campsites in the vicinity, but none in convenient walking distance. Since the unfortunate closure of Lynton Youth Hostel the nearest budget accommodation is Ocean Backpackers Hostel, Ilfracombe 01271 867 835 www.oceanbackpackers.com.
Sleeping out	To avoid upsetting National Trust wardens it's best not to.
Public transport	Barstaple to Lynmouth buses stop at Parracombe, from where it's 5km on foot to Heddon's Mouth.
Seasonal notes	Summer's luxuriant overgrowth can conceal vital belay stakes, and make the upper heather slopes even more purgatorial than normal. At any time of year sub-optimal weather will increase the difficulty of the beach approach and add extra excitement to the ascent – as if that were needed.

HAD HE SET HIS DECKCHAIR on the Exmoor coast King Canute would have enjoyed a short, soggy reign. At up to 15m, the Bristol Channel's tidal range – the vertical difference between low and high water – is famously the second largest in the world. Here on the frayed edge of Exmoor these huge tides suck at the base of England's biggest cliffs, hogsback precipices crumbling onto inhospitable boulder beaches, drenched by leviathan swells that roll off the open ocean. Tricky to access and escape, the complete sea level traverse of this wild littoral is a unique multi-day climbing expedition, subject to the full force of nature. The Claw offers just a brief dip into this world of surf and stone; even still, it's a big day out. Technically easy it may be, yet with its adventurous approach, copious vegetation and questionable protection it requires a commitment and competence normally associated with harder routes. Indeed few climbs show as profound a gulf between on-paper grade and on-route experience. Beginners beware.

Looking east from The Claw

A sea level scramble through mighty surroundings, the access is as memorable as the climb itself. There's a rarity value too, since it is possible for just a few hours a day, on a few days in every fortnight – if the sea permits. That the inexorable Atlantic will soon swamp the beach under several storeys of water is a certainty, and slow parties face being cut off or worse. If progress stalls then timely retreat is a better option than attempting to scale the friable vegetated cliffs that menace Bloody Beach, where cunning safe routes are likely to be found only by Exmoor old hands. The Claw is the sole obvious way out; once committed however, the only way is up. Timing being key is a truism of Alpine climbing; it is novel to have to apply the same sense of urgency to a Devonshire Diff. Time and tide wait for no one it seems.

APPROACH

Start the walk-in two or three hours before scheduled low water at Ilfracombe. From the car park take the track just right of the Hunter's Inn, leading N down the beautiful wooded combe (or cleave, as they say hereabouts). A few hundred metres short of the beach at Heddon's Mouth cross the River Heddon on a wooden footbridge and follow the W bank past an old limekiln to the seashore. Once on the shingle beach wade back E over the River Heddon; this can be tricky when the river's in spate.

When wet the rocks are extremely slippery, making the access traverse painfully slow. Consider donning a harness before proceeding to the crags bounding the E side of the beach. Ascend gently sloping slabs beneath the crumbly main cliff to overlook a channel at the bottom of a two-tiered drop. If you've left a suitable time margin this will still be flooded, in which case scramble up and right to the neck of the slabs overlooking the next rubble-floored inlet. If dry it is possible to downclimb ledges on the landward side of the obvious chimney, but the bottom couple of metres are smooth and overhanging. If in doubt abseil from a thread under a chockstone.

Continue E over the boulders to the base of Highveer Point, a cathedral-sized chunk detached from the main cliff. Skirt right of the buttress to

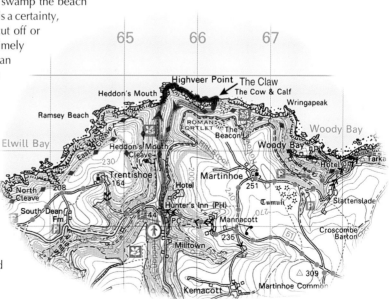

scramble over a neck on the landward side. In calm conditions it's also possible to scramble along its seaward foot via a watery channel. As a rough guide, if waves are still breaking strongly here one hour before scheduled low water then the bottom pitch of The Claw may prove unclimbable.

Now clamber along the 650m stretch of Bloody Beach, all slimy weed and barnacled boulders. Despite appearances the chossy cliffs overhead are breached by two cunning escape paths, established in the 19th century by James Hannington, the first to systematically explore here. They are steep, vegetated, unobvious and best left to Exmoor experts.

Seen from a distance The Claw blends into the general mass of rock and greenery, but up close it is unmistakeable, a steep serrated ridge bounding the E end of the walkable beach, with a sloping platform at its base. Pass a series of monolithic cave mouths (Hannington's Cave) to reach the boulder-floored inlet under the short steep wall that guards the bottom of the sloping platform. The impressive height of the water stain on the crags above is a warning not to tarry. Either commit straight away or return directly along Bloody Beach.

CLIMB

The Claw, 236m+ Difficult
There are two ways onto the platform.

Pitch 1(a), 10m
The customary Diff start; inadvisable (perhaps impossible) if wet. From a big boulder step onto smooth sloping holds and traverse insecurely left (cams protect) to the seaward end of the wall. Ascend rightwards onto the platform.

Pitch 2 of The Claw on a wild day

Pitch 1(b), 10m, 5a

Possible in slightly higher seas, and might be aided if you're quick. Further right is a prominent vertical crack, the Curate's Corner. Climb this strenuously to a little niche. Now hand traverse left (sketchy footholds) to gain the platform.

Pitch 2, 45m

The most atmospheric section of the route. From the seaward end of the sloping platform go up steeply to gain the jagged arete, which is climbed direct via steps and ledges (some questionable rock). Peg/nut belay on a generous ledge at the top of the arete.

Pitch 3, 25m

Climb precipitous pampas and friable lichenous rock steps to belay excitingly on a narrow grassy ledge under a small rock wall. The old metal stake nestled near the lip of the ledge ought to be backed up.

Pitch 4, 10m

Move a little left to gain a sloping grass shelf which leads up and right to a sapling belay in a grubby corner (a backup nut placement may need to be excavated).

Pitch 5, 45m

Step right onto the exposed blunt ridge, then weave up vegetated ledges and wobbly outcrops. A hard-to-spot in situ stake provides security; natural placements can also be unearthed. About 25m up bear right into a shallow plant-choked gully, a hanging garden of exceptional botanical diversity. Swim up brambles to a welcome tree belay.

Pitch 6, 8m

Enter the little corner above the tree, where a metal stake is hiding, then move up and right to belay from an outcrop at the head of the gully (medium/large cams helpful).

Pitch 7, 48m

Sidle right onto the vague crest (with luck uncovering a stake in passing). Now climb the ridge, wading steeply uphill through tenacious armpit-deep heather. There is a path of sorts, but you'd be forgiven for missing it; part the forest canopy and all may be revealed. Four metres above a boulder hunt closely at ground level to find a wobbly stake.

The infernal ferns and house-high heather of the upper canopy

Pitch 8, 45m

Continue straight up through the infernal heather jungle, perhaps placing an optimistic sling around a spindly sapling in passing. Make for a large square-cut block, the Coffee Table, where a surprisingly secure belay awaits.

Although this could be considered the end of the climb proper, safe ground is still far above, while the slopes below barrel off into the distant swell. Especially in damp conditions it might seem prudent to remain tied in, perhaps moving together. A couple of trees en route provide runners. Two more full rope lengths of strenuous heather-bashing will be required; plenty of time to curse your humble author. Once triumphantly united with the South West Coast Path drag your mate up hand over hand to the bemusement of passing walkers.

DESCENT

The path heads W in a tremendous cliffside position before curving leftwards and descending towards the Hunter's Inn. Retire to the bar for the remainder of your holiday.

Route 20 – Commando Ridge, Bosigran, Cornwall

Grade	200m VDiff
Distance	1km
Ascent	140m
Time	3–5 hours
Start/finish	National Trust car park on the B3306, by some old mine ruins (SW422364)
Maps	OS Landranger (1:50000) 203
Tides	Consult the tide table for Cape Cornwall. Pitches 1 and 2 may be inaccessible at high tide or when there's a big swell; save your visit for a relatively calm day a couple of hours either side of low tide.
Accommodation	Climber's Club hut at Bosigran – not always available to non-members www.climbers-club.co.uk; Whitesands Lodge backpackers, Sennen 01736 871776; there are also many campsites and B&Bs throughout West Penwith
Sleeping out	It would be hard to wild camp inconspicuously, but doubtless it has been done.
Public transport	Penzance is the nearest train station; local buses run from here to Pendeen, the nearest sizeable village.
Seasonal notes	Given a calm dry day climbing here should be quite pleasant throughout the year, but a winter storm might be too exciting. The rock is quick drying, but that's because it's exposed to the Atlantic breeze (a mixed blessing).

The jagged upper section of Commando Ridge

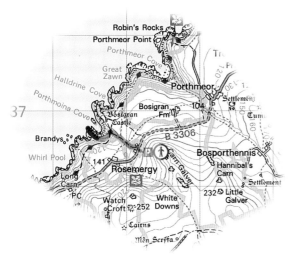

37

is varied and the situations as exciting as any you're likely to find on a mountain arete. Because of its exposed traversing this isn't the best route to drag a total beginner up, especially as a big swell can make the approach gripping.

APPROACH

A short path descends northwest from the car park, at first through a stunted thicket and then open slopes leading down towards the dramatic inlet of Porthmoina Cove. The squat promontory of Bosigran main cliff can be seen ahead, enclosing the east side of the cove; it is one of the best crags in southern England, and has something exciting at virtually every grade. Save it for later.

There's no mistaking the sawtoothed crest of Commando Ridge, rising from the waves on the other side of the cove. Turn left onto the coast path, cross a little stone bridge and then branch off over soggy ground leading, with a short scrappy scramble, to a pile of boulders beside the top section of the ridge. A memorial plaque bolted to the crag here commemorates the antics of the WW2 Cliff Assault Wing of the Marine Commandos who trained here; no prizes for guessing where the ridge got its name.

S TAR OF THE SMALL SCREEN and a contender for the longest and best VDiff in England, Commando Ridge is a perennial favourite. The climb has an interesting character as it's essentially an Alpine-style ridge with a wave-washed tidal base. Instead of a view over ranges and valleys, its backdrop is the peaks and troughs of the mountainous North Atlantic, just as inspiring in its own way. The rock is Cornish granite at its chunky best, the climbing

Thankful for the jugs on pitch 2

Cross to the west flank of the ridge via either of two obvious notches, one on each side of the memorial plaque. The right hand notch is accessed by a short groove behind a detached flake. There's a short steep Moderate downclimb on the far side of both gaps; if you prefer to abseil it's easy to rig at the right hand notch. Once on the west side of the ridge follow a vegetated path towards the sea to reach a rock corner running to a slab. Although it's easy enough to downclimb, the handy in situ abseil tat may be too much to resist. Now walk down the slab to a terrace at the foot of the ridge, (with luck) just above the breaking waves and spray. These blocks and slabs can be submerged at high tide and occasionally deluged by 'freak' waves even on ostensibly calm days, so it's probably worth roping up here and treating the rest of the approach as the first pitch, as described below. With the swell sucking at the rock just below your feet you might be glad of the lifeline. If a big sea is running it's possible to access the ridge at a higher point and miss out the first couple of pitches.

CLIMB

Commando Ridge, 200m VDiff

Pitch 1, 20m
Walk right along the terrace, stepping down to pass around the foot of the ridge with a slightly awkward move to gain a ledge on the east flank, just above a deep surging zawn. Belay when rope drag gives you no choice. Communication with your partner is limited to sharp tugs.

Pitch 2, 15m
The atmospheric crux pitch, often moistened with spray. Continue to the end of the terrace, move up on steep blocks and then gain the jug-riddled black wall. Swing up this to gain a deep crack, where curvy flake holds lead out of the booming zawn to a bouldery stance on the sunny ridge crest.

Pitch 3, 20m
Cross a neck of boulders to gain a conspicuous chimney in the arete. An old fashioned squirm up

The knife edge on pitch 4

On the blocks of pitch 6

this leads to a spike belay on the next ledge, some way below a prominent 'beaked' pinnacle.

Pitch 4, 20m
Sidle up and left along a break to gain a short knife edge. Hand traverse its left side to reach the 'beak', then ease leftwards into a gap between pinnacles on the crest. Downclimb a slabby corner for about 8m to a little grass patch on the west flank.

Pitch 5, 20m
Climb blocks in a gap in the ridge to regain the crest at a broad cracked slab. Climb this to the base of a sharp fin. Now traverse a line of ripples along the sheer east face, without much exposure (there's a grass ledge just below) but with minimal protection. Belay at a notch in the ridge just beyond.

Pitch 6, 45m
Easy slabby ground is followed by pleasantly exposed ridge-top scrambling over little blocks.

Beyond this climb a slabby, grassy wall to belay at a good stance where the ridge levels out.

Pitch 7, 30m
Teeter along the square-topped crest to reach a huge detached block (good thread runner beneath it). Foot traverse a break on the right side in a magnificently airy position, then do a tricky downclimb over a spike (remember to protect the second) and stay on the right flank to descend into the gap just beside the memorial plaque. The ground is now just a few metres away on the E side, so many people call it a day here.

Pitch 8, 30m
It is possible to continue in the same line for this final pitch, mostly scrambling with one avoidable 4b mantelshelf.

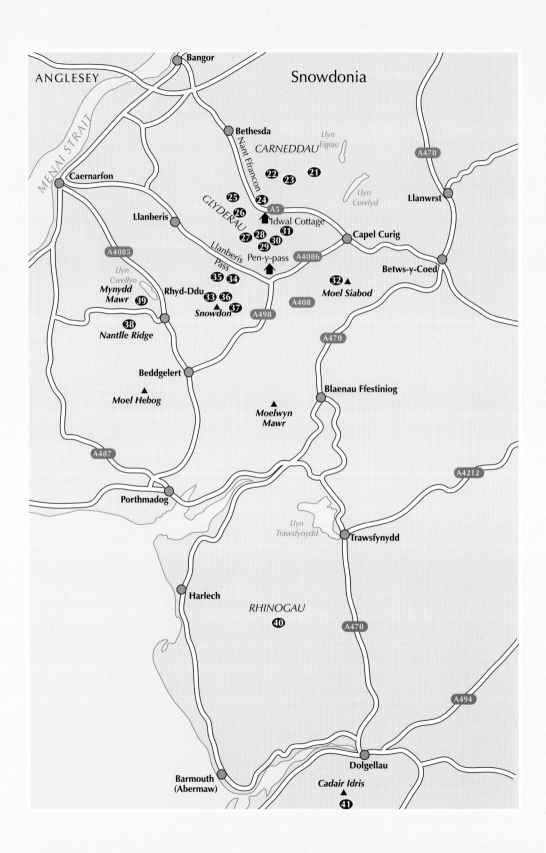

SNOWDONIA

Its rocks nibbled by industry and its turf by sheep, Snowdonia is not so much immaculate and wild as lived-in and well-worn; like an old familiar pair of slippers. From the cavernous quarry pits to the chalked-up holds of the Cromlech the hills bear the marks of generations of human toil. Yet there is real natural grandeur here too. The clustered peaks of the north squeeze a lot into their close-packed folds, and although they jostle cheek-by-jowl the three major mountain groups each have a distinct character: the grassy sweeping Carneddau, the bristling boulder graveyard of the Glyderau and the high graceful crests of Snowdon all contain ridge routes of stature and quality. The big names inevitably pull in most punters, but beyond the centres of climbing gravity orbit satellite ranges with attractions of their own. The Nantlle hills are all the better for being a relative backwater, while those who really want to avoid the crowds can lose themselves in the heather-choked outcrops of the Rhinogau (aka Rhinogs). Further south still, and a world away from the bustle of Ogwen and Llanberis, the majestic mini-range of Cadair Idris holds plenty of mountaineering promise too.

Snowdon from Llynnau Mymbyr

Route 21 – Amphitheatre Buttress, Craig yr Ysfa

Grade	VDiff
Distance	8km
Ascent	650m
Time	6½ hours
Start/finish	Car park at Gwern Gof Isaf (SH685603) for the more popular southern approach, or road head at SH732663 if coming in from the north
Maps	OS Landranger (1:50000) 115; OS Explorer (1:25000) OL17; Harvey British Mountain Map (1:40000) Snowdonia
Accommodation	Idwal Cottage Youth Hostel 0845 371 9744; Capel Curig Youth Hostel 0845 371 9110; Caban Cysgu bunkhouse in Gerlan, Bethesda 01248 605 573; Gwern Gof Uchaf campsite and bunkhouse 01690 720294, Gwern Gof Isaf campsite and bunkhouse 01690 720276 – both in Ogwen. If coming from the north: Rowen Youth Hostel 0845 371 9038
Sleeping out	A pleasant wild camp is possible near the S end of Ffynnon Llugwy. There is also a small rough bothy in Cwm Tal-y-Braich (named on 1:25000 map) between the southern arms of Pen yr Helgi Du and Pen Llithrig y Wrach, although its precise location is best left to the motivated to work out. For those making the northern approach to Craig yr Ysfa a camp in the wild upper reaches of Cwm Eigiau would really add atmosphere to the trip.
Public transport	The A5 start is well served by Capel Curig to Bethesda buses; coming in via Cwm Eigiau, Dolgarrog would be the closest bus stop.
Seasonal notes	Amphitheatre Buttress tends not to be done as a winter route. It dries quickly after rain, but if wet the polished crux pitches are tricky.

Tryfan (centre) and Y Garn (right) from the Ffynnon Llugwy track

'CLASSIC' is a tag too-often applied in climbing circles, but in this case it is entirely fitting. How better in one word to sum up a venerable and venerated excursion that's more than a century old and nearly a thousand old-fashioned Imperial feet in length, with a spacious Scottish-scale setting, a grand compelling line and a medley of interesting airy pitches on good honest rock? So worthwhile is it that even the unfortunate mid-height hands-in-pockets heathery ramble barely dents one's enjoyment. With generally short-lived difficulties and generous stances Amphitheatre Buttress is low in the grade, and does not demand newfangled contrivances such as rubbers and camming devices. However the approach stroll and the climb itself are of a length sufficient to guarantee most parties a big day out. Add imperfect weather and you might have good reason to deploy that other over-used climbing term – 'the epic'.

High above the amphitheatre on the short-but-stimulating pitch 4

APPROACH

Two approaches are customary for Craig yr Ysfa. Coming from the N, a minor road leaves Tal-y-Bont in Dyffryn Conwy, climbing to a large layby in the wide mouth of Cwm Eigiau;

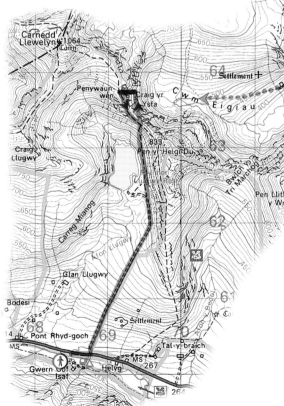

from here the 1½ hour walk-in up-valley needs no description. As well as being gentler on the legs this is the more characterful route. However the rather more strenuous 1½ hour approach from Ogwen in the S is more popular thanks to the convenience of its starting point, and this is the route described here.

The first half of the walk is on the private access road that connects Ffynnon Llugwy reservoir to the A5. Parking is possible at the entrance to this but space is very limited and the gate must not be obstructed; it's probably more responsible to pay the modest parking fee at nearby Gwern Gof Isaf campsite, and stroll back E along the pavement. Turn NNE to follow the tarmac track, which climbs steadily for roughly 2km in a straight line over the grassy slopes, with

21 Amphitheatre Buttress
A The Amphitheatre
B Amphitheatre Right Wall

superb views of Tryfan. As the track bends left towards Ffynnon Llugwy take a path on the right, marked by a small cairn. This makes a rising traverse above the lake's E shore, then zigzags up the steep headwall onto the narrow saddle of Bwlch Eryl Farchog. Craig yr Ysfa is now visible in profile.

From the pass a narrow path descends N, cutting across the steep vegetated slope towards the bottom of the huge rambling crag. After a couple of hundred metres it makes quite a steep and eroded descent past a tree, then bears left and zigzags down a patch of grass. The route now climbs slightly along the base of the crag, a short sharp ascent soon leading to the start of the route, a two-tiered slabby rib. Amphitheatre Buttress is hard to miss – its right side is bounded by the deep scree gully of the Amphitheatre (also home to other grand mountain routes).

CLIMB

Amphitheatre Buttress, c300m VDiff

Pitch 1, 30m
The pitch starts easily, but it's probably worth roping up straight away for what comes a little higher. Climb the two slabby tiers to reach a little niche. Exit this by exposed delicate moves, sidling left onto a higher slab which leads to a vague groove running up to a large ledge.

Pitch 2, 30m
Simple scrambly ground leads up the ridge to a ledge below a big detached block that leans against the mountain.

Pitch 3, 40m
Take polished holds just right of the block, then pull awkwardly onto its top. The long slab above is superbly exposed but well protected. Follow a series of rounded cracks just left of the arete, with reachy moves between the best holds. A blocky break leads to a continuation of the slab, and more gear-hungry cracks. Eventually reach a ledge; move left along this, then continue up easy blocks to a belay stance below a distinct steep wall.

Pitch 4, 12m
Said by some to be the crux – it's certainly stimulating. Climb a vague polished groove on the right end of the wall, then tremble right onto the airy face overlooking The Amphitheatre to gain the top of a pronounced block. A little crack in the wall above leads to a reassuring ledge.

Pitch 5, 15m
Walk a couple of metres left, then swing up a steep blocky wall, bearing left onto a ledge. A delicate move right then gains another (sloping) ledge. Belay at will.

Pitch 6 and 7, 75m
A scrambly walk leads up the heathery crest. A rope will only be needed if either you or the route

are wet. Belay on a generous flat stance on top of a little tower, at the point where the ridge pinches tight to form a sharp edge.

Pitch 8, 30m

This pitch needs considerate rope work to protect your second. Downclimb carefully from the far right corner of the platform to reach a little neck in the arete. Now follow the blocky ridge direct to the foot of a proud upright pinnacle. This gendarme can be sneakily outfoxed on the left, but that would be a crime. Climb the right side of the pinnacle with trepidation, moving left to top out (and dance a little jig?). You may need to talk yourself into it, but descending the far side is easier. Beyond is a short pinnacled crest which fizzles all too soon into scrappy slopes.

Pitch 9, 30m

There are two scruffy 'ridges' above. Walk up to regain rock on the right hand one. Blocks now lead up and right to an unexpected impasse, an exposed and very stretchy step rightwards onto a little spike. A thin crack in a slab at head height protects the move; climb this slab to a ledge.

Pitch 10, 30m

Fairly thuggy moves up steep blocks lead to the base of the final wall. Climb an awkward polished groove on the left of this to reach a line of rounded flake holds overlooking the green gully on the left. The top comes quite suddenly.

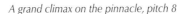

DESCENT

While it might be fitting to extend the outing with a walk over Carnedd Llewelyn most people will find themselves short of motivation and/or daylight by now. From the route top-out the quickest way home is SE over a knobbly minor summit. Continue down the slabby, scrambly ridge crest back to Bwlch Eryl Farchog; in summer this is trivial, though much less so under snow (see route 23). From the bwlch a descent can be made either N or S on the paths described in the Approach section.

A grand climax on the pinnacle, pitch 8

Route 22 – Crib Lem, Carnedd Dafydd

Grade	1
Distance	14km (including the Cwm Llafar circuit, as described)
Ascent	1100m
Time	6½ hours
Start/finish	Parking is very limited on the dead-end road from Bethesda, so drivers may be best off parking in Gerlan (part of the town), close to the Post Office and chapel in the vicinity of (SH632664).
Maps	OS Landranger (1:50000) 115; OS Explorer (1:25000) OL17; Harvey British Mountain Map (1:40000) Snowdonia
Accommodation	see route 21
Sleeping out	Wild camping opportunities abound in Cwm Llafar, especially in the rugged seclusion of Cwmglas Bach; you're unlikely to be competing for space here.
Public transport	Regular buses link Capel Curig, Bethesda and Bangor (the latter also served by mainline rail)
Seasonal notes	High, north-facing and adjacent to arguably the most exciting winter climbing venue south of the border, Ysgolion Duon, Crib Lem has the makings of a classic winter mountaineering route. Grade I/II seems fair and aside from the relative seriousness of its remote position it would make a good first experience of this sort of winter ridge climb. And if the wet warmth of a typical Welsh winter has spoiled your grand plans, Crib Lem remains an amenable damp weather option.

Ysgolion Duon and Crib Lem (right) from Cwm Llafar

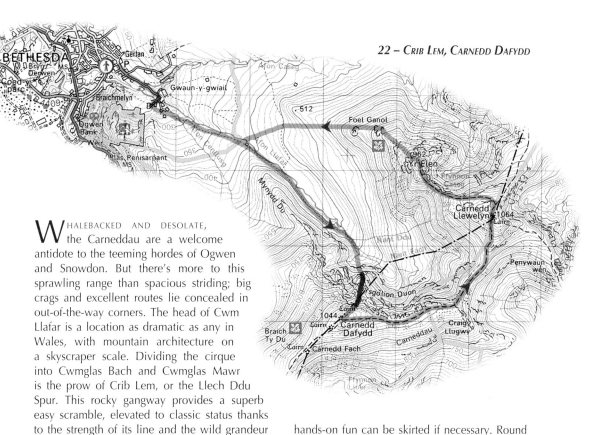

W HALEBACKED AND DESOLATE, the Carneddau are a welcome antidote to the teeming hordes of Ogwen and Snowdon. But there's more to this sprawling range than spacious striding; big crags and excellent routes lie concealed in out-of-the-way corners. The head of Cwm Llafar is a location as dramatic as any in Wales, with mountain architecture on a skyscraper scale. Dividing the cirque into Cwmglas Bach and Cwmglas Mawr is the prow of Crib Lem, or the Llech Ddu Spur. This rocky gangway provides a superb easy scramble, elevated to classic status thanks to the strength of its line and the wild grandeur of its position. It would be an ideal introduction to ridge scrambling, since practically all the hands-on fun can be skirted if necessary. Round off the day with a walking circuit over the three 3000ft-ers that hug the cwm.

In Cwmglas Bach

On the tilted block, Yr Elen behind

APPROACH

The initial approach is quite confusing in the dark. From Gerlan follow the minor road uphill SE. Shortly after leaving the houses the road crosses a bridge over the Afon Caseg. Beyond this, take a right fork, then cross a bridge over the Afon Llafar. Pass the water treatment works, following a footpath sign over a stile into rough boggy pastures. Vague at first, the path becomes more obvious as it climbs through various enclosures parallel with the south bank of the Afon Llafar, crossing several stiles and passing a small ruin on the way. Beyond a final drystone wall you reach the open hillside. Now level and drier underfoot the path continues alongside the river into the open arms of Cwm Llafar. The scale of the cirque at the head of the cwm isn't obvious until you're beneath it, the blocky corners and roofs of Llech Ddu contrasting with the vast rambling gothic facade of Ysgolion Duon.

Feeling suitably ant-like, trend right towards the bottom of Llech Ddu, following a vague path uphill past large boulders (the climber's descent path from the crag). Stay right of the cliff, climbing beside a waterfall and then zigzagging up a scree slope to enter the rugged upper bowl of Cwmglas Bach. Once safely above Llech Ddu the path veers left along a grassy shelf between layers of outcrop, to reach the nose of the ridge.

CLIMB

Crib Lem, grade 1

Crib Lem begins straightforwardly, a worn path weaving up a series of grassy ledges and broken scrambly steps. Beyond an easy section the ridge levels off and pinches into a distinct narrowing, the crest split into little teeth – some of them wobbly. Clamber photogenically over an unusual tilted block, then shortly afterwards thread through a series of small square-cut pinnacles to reach the bottom of a steep step. Climb this direct up cracked blocks to regain easy ground. A second step can be climbed via an obvious blocky groove, or skirted on a well-used path. Above this the ridge soon merges into the scree of Carnedd Dafydd's barrelling upper slopes; plod SW up a scrappy path to reach the summit cairn.

POSSIBLE DESCENT

For the lazy or weather-challenged the quick-est descent from Dafydd's summit is the broad northwest ridge. But as you've come this far it'd be a crime to miss the excellent Cwm Llafar horseshoe.

CONTINUATION

Head E descending gently from Carnedd Dafydd on a clear path that follows the stony ridge along the lip of Ysgolion Duon. After about 1.5km the ridge swings NE and descends to a pass, Bwlch Cyfryw-drum. From here a stony climb gains the rounded summit of Carnedd Llewellyn, marked with a cairn and a stone-walled wind break. Striking the correct line off the third highest summit in Wales can be tricky in mist, as the best-used path loops slightly further N than

might be expected. If you can't locate it head WNW over the plateau, quickly dropping to a col at 900m. The slender satellite peak of Yr Elen sprouts out of Llewellyn's bulky shoulder, linked to its giant neighbour by a narrow arete. Taken direct this provides some very easy (and entirely avoidable) scrambling on sharp flakes; a well-scuffed path stays just left of the crest. The ascent is negligible, but the little table top does still have the character of a separate moun-tain, ringed on all sides with crumbling faces. From here there's an interesting perspective on the Cwm Llafar cliffs.

Steep at first, the descent NW soon reaches gentler slopes, easy grassy striding then leading onto the little outcrop of Foel Ganol. From the next outcrop on about the 660m contour, bear W to descend pathless marshy slopes into the mouth of Cwm Llafar. Cross the river to regain the approach route.

Ysgolion Duon from the steep step on Crib Lem

Route 23 – Circuit of the Southern Carneddau

Grade	I
Distance	15km
Ascent	1030m
Time	8 hours
Start/finish	Layby beside the long straight on the A5 between Gwern Gof Uchaf and Llyn Ogwen (SH670605)
Maps	OS Landranger (1:50000) 115; OS Explorer (1:25000) OL17; Harvey British Mountain Map (1:40000) Snowdonia
Accommodation	See route 21
Sleeping out	Cwm Lloer and Cwm Llugwy are both peaceful secluded locations to pitch a tent, with impressive surroundings in winter. Wild camping wouldn't add convenience to the day, but it'd certainly pile on the atmosphere.
Public transport	Regular buses linking Capel Curig and Bethesda stop at various points along the A5.
Seasonal notes	Minus snow this is simply a long ridge-top stride with a smattering of mild hands-on entertainment – a classic walk, but not mountaineering. To up the ante, wait for a big snowfall. In wild winter weather the narrow ridge sections can be precarious, while the windswept featureless summits pose a different sort of challenge.

Looking up to Cwm Ffynnon Lloer from the Ogwen Valley

In the howl of a winter storm the bald domes of the high Carneddau must be the most committing summits in Wales, a little Snowdonian version of the Cairngorms. Given the massif's generally buxom curvy image the slender crests encountered on this route may come as a surprise. Snaking around the lake-filled cwms of Lloer and Llugwy, treading four fine tops (including the three highest in the range), and offering clifftop perspectives of the monumental Ysgolion Duon (route 22) and Craig Yr Ysfa (route 21) this is a long testing tramp through the best of the Carneddau. During summer these are walkers' ridges, but add a generous snowfall and three sections become modest mountaineering terrain: a step on the East Spur of Pen yr Ole Wen; the tricky descent into Bwlch Eryl Farchog; and the wonderful scrambly ridge from here to Pen yr Helgi Du. Moody weather up here demands careful navigation in a serious setting. Technicalities may be modest, but this grand high country should never be taken for granted.

APPROACH

From just E of Llyn Ogwen turn off the A5 onto a farm track by a stand of pines. Pass a cottage then leave the track near Tal y Llyn Ogwen farm, following a footpath N, at first beside a stone wall and then on a long gentle ascent beside the Afon Lloer. Soon cross from east bank to west, continuing past falls and over a ladder stile across a drystone wall. The path then curves leftwards into the mouth of secretive Cwm Lloer. Before reaching the lake head W to the steep lower tier of Pen yr Ole Wen's East Spur.

CLIMB

A short gully on the left is the easiest breach of this tier, but by bearing right a longer and more entertaining passage of turfy grade I climbing can be found. Continue easily up the rock-strewn spur to the rounded top of Pen yr Ole Wen. Now trace the rim of Cwm Lloer, passing over a mound of

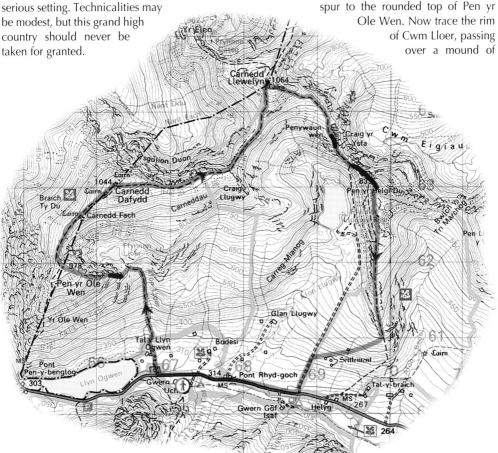

stones at Carnedd Fach, reputedly a prehistoric burial cairn. The ridge then broadens considerably, leading up over stony (or, with luck, snowy) wastes onto Carnedd Dafydd's wide summit.

Descending gently E, an attractive stretch of ridge soon takes shape, defined on its left by the buttressed crags of Ysgolion Duon. To avoid getting too closely acquainted with the biggest cliff in Wales pay heed to any cornices along the edge. Stay with the high ground as the hill widens again, curving gradually left (attention needed in low cloud) to descend briefly NE. Here the crest pinches in once more, a lovely airy ridge undulating over Bwlch Cyfryw-drum. There are no difficulties but cornices may be substantial. The unfolding perspectives over Cwm Llafar, Ysgolion Duon and Crib Lem (route 22) are inspiring. Beyond the pass a dull scree or snow plod gains the day's high point on the cupola of Carnedd Llewellyn, where the summit windbreak might prove welcome.

Wide, featureless, ringed by treacherous ground and exposed to the full ferocity of the weather, diligent navigation can pay dividends here.

On the East Spur of Pen yr Ole Wen, above a stormy Ogwen valley

Approaching Pen yr Ole Wen's East Spur

Climbing the Northeast Ridge of Pen yr Helgi Du in foul conditions

Descend around the scoop of Ffynnon Llyffnant, heading roughly E at first and then trending more SE to meet the edge of Craig Yr Ysfa on the lip of its yawning Amphitheatre. Clamber through boulder heaps above the crag, passing the top of Amphitheatre Buttress (route 21). The ridge leading towards Bwlch Eryl Farchog soon terminates in a steep rocky drop-off that must be descended to reach the pass, as per route 21. Without a cloak of snow a worn path can be followed with only trivial scrambling but it calls for a lot more care in winter conditions, particularly if icy.

This brief burst of grade I downclimbing safely negotiated, follow the crest of the narrow ridge down to the low point of the col, a dramatic wedge slung between Crag yr Ysfa and Pen yr Helgi Du. Steep escape routes are available from here both N and S, although a hefty cornice might pose problems. It's better to stay on top a while longer since the continuation to Pen yr Helgi Du is the most enjoyable part of the day. Taking the rugged ridge out of the pass, an abrupt steepening soon rears up. Stick with the crest for a short ascent on turf and rock steps – easy grade I climbing in an airy position. Too soon the hill's flat grassy top is underfoot.

DESCENT

The gently sloping south ridge is the best way off. Stay with a path along the soft rounded crest for just under 2km. At about the 500m contour bear right to reach a bridge over a concrete leat, from where a rough little path is followed more or less WSW through squishy ground to join the Ffynnon Llugwy access road close to the A5 (as per route 21). A 15min stroll along the main road then brings you back to the layby between Gwern Gof Uchaf and Llyn Ogwen.

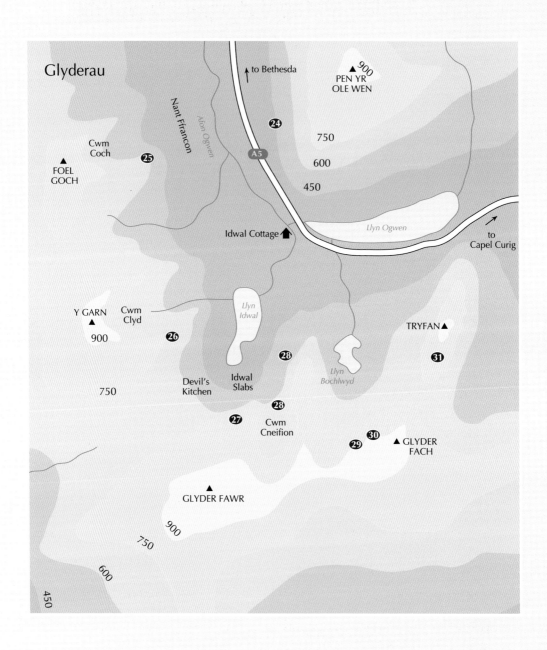

Glyderau

to Bethesda

PEN YR
OLE WEN ▲ 900

Nant Ffrancon

Afon Ogwen

Cwm
Coch

②④

FOEL
GOCH ▲

②⑤

A5

750

600

450

Idwal Cottage 🏠

Llyn Ogwen

to
Capel Curig

Y GARN ▲

900

Cwm
Clyd

Llyn
Idwal

②⑥

TRYFAN ▲

750

Devil's
Kitchen

Idwal
Slabs

②⑧

Llyn
Bochlwyd

③①

②⑧

②⑦

Cwm
Cneifion

②⑨ ③⓪ ▲ GLYDER
FACH

▲
GLYDER FAWR

900

750

600

450

Grade	95m VDiff
Distance	1km
Ascent	150m
Time	1½ hours
Start/finish	Idwal Cottage pay and display car park (SH649603) or a small layby on the W side of the A5 a few hundred metres nearer the route.
Maps	OS Landranger (1:50000) 115; OS Explorer (1:25000) OL17; Harvey British Mountain Map (1:40000) Snowdonia
Accommodation	See route 21
Sleeping out	Unless you want to annoy local farmers and National Trust wardens then camping close to the road in the busy Ogwen area isn't a bright idea.
Public transport	Regular buses linking Capel Curig and Bethesda stop at Ogwen, including the Snowdon Sherpa service.
Seasonal notes	The chances of this low level route ever being in winter condition are slim. But given what would these days be an almost unheard-of cold snap it'd likely be grade II by the scrambler's line – avoiding the first pitch, and taking the pinnacles indirect. Higher on this massive complex face there's a better chance of ice action in frozen streams or snow gullies.

PINNACLE RIDGE is a rather tired moniker, but this one certainly does what it says on the tin. A strenuous start builds to a spectacular photo finish on an airy horned crest, the stuff of climbing daydreams. It doesn't go anywhere near a summit, and passing traffic is audible throughout, but this unusual roadside ridge is attractive all the same. Instant gratification doesn't tend to be a feature of mountaineering-style routes; here, though, you'll be roped up 20 minutes after leaving the car. Low and accessible, this quick hit is a good bet when summits are wreathed in murk.

Despite the nearby tarmac the baffling scale of the Braich Ty Du face lends a mountainous air to the proceedings. The energetic could continue up the scattered outcrops above, to the mountain's distant summit.

APPROACH

They don't get faster or looser than this. Stroll NW along the A5 (pavement) for a few minutes. Pinnacle Ridge is just one of many buttresses on the huge rambling face above the road, but distinctive from below thanks to its obvious twin horns. Just before a fence protecting the road from rockfall cross over and climb the unstable hillside on a sketchy path that makes a rising traverse rightwards below a steep outcrop to reach the gully running down the right side of the ridge. Be careful not to knock stones onto the cars below.

From a good distance below the dilapidated stone wall that crosses the gully, walk 15m left along a heathery ledge at the foot of the ridge to reach a vertical rib, cut by a right-angled left-facing corner. This provides the meat of pitch 1.

Idwal Cottage from pitch 3

CLIMB

Pinnacle Ridge, 95m VDiff

Pitch 1, 35m
Climb to a gorse-covered ledge about 6m up; now gain the steep corner at the right side of this – the crux. Despite good runners (large cam useful), this is a stiff little obstacle demanding a forceful attitude. First surmount a square block, then heave up the corner to exit right. Easy ground above soon leads to a spike belay.

Pitch 2, 20m
Continue up scrappy rock steps and heather ledges, staying just left of the front of the ridge to reach a belay ledge and spikes.

NB This stance can be reached by a vegetated ramp starting from a point about 10m above the stone wall, thus completely avoiding the difficult pitch 1. If this option is followed by the easiest line on the pinnacles the route's technicality reduces to a grade 2 scramble, with an attendant loss of quality.

Afon Ogwen from the pinnacles of pitch 4

24 Pinnacle Ridge

Pitch 3, 10m
Step up, then walk right along a ledge above a steep wall, leading around the crest of the ridge to its right flank. A steep pull up spikes lands you on another ledge at the base of the first horn.

Pitch 4, 30m
Because of the exposed traversey nature of this pitch the leader should protect the second by placing plenty of gear, especially after down-climbing from each of the horns. Scramblers can stay right of the horns on an easier and less exposed line, but for best results step onto to the left side, staying high to use the top of the ridge for holds and runners. Move across the exposed face of the first horn, and make a tenuous long step into a gap beyond. Now swing up spikes to grab the tip of the second horn. Hand traverse along this, cross another gap and make a final belay at the neck of a promontory.

DESCENT

Head away from the edge on a path through heather and bilberry until it's practical to descend right into the gully bounding the S side of the ridge.

Route 25 – Needle's Eye Arete, Foel Goch

Grade	Moderate
Distance	4km
Ascent	620m
Time	4 hours
Start/finish	Drivers should park beside the single track road that connects Idwal Cottage and Ty'n-y-maes, between Pentre and Blaen-y-nant; space is limited and gates and passing places shouldn't be blocked (roughly SH641612).
Maps OS	Landranger (1:50000) 115; OS Explorer (1:25000) OL17; Harvey British Mountain Map (1:40000) Snowdonia
Accommodation	See route 21
Sleeping out	It'd be possible to camp in the middle reaches of Cwm-coch, but as there's nothing practical to gain by it you'd have to be seriously keen.
Public transport	See route 24; from the bus stop at Idwal Cottage it's a 1km stroll along the minor road to the start of the off-road walk.
Seasonal notes	Grade III in winter, but a pleasant ascent requires a firm re-freeze after heavy snowfall; the first section of arete looks like it'd be technical for the grade. In summer the crest is quick drying but lichenous and greasy when wet; with its slime-prone start this route is really best left for fair weather.

Creigiau Gleision from below – the route is just to the right of the obvious gully at the left end of the crag

The sole feature to have bucked the trend and maintain its popularity over the years has been Needle's Eye Arete, a route for adventurous mountaineers rather than convenience-fixated craggers. A scrambler's taste for greens certainly helps. However given the general seriousness and a short stretch of trickier climbing the grade 3 it was previously given seems a modest – though crucial – understatement. In all but perfect conditions Needle's Eye Arete should be left to those with experience of harder things. This superb excursion looks a mess from a distance, but unfolds to give a logical and exciting route up a big face that still retains a whiff of the ancients.

THE RAMBLING ARETES and surreal tottery pinnacles of Creigiau Gleision appealed to our doughty Edwardian forbears, and it is from this era that most of the routes date. As climbing fashion moved on, this complex sprawl fell out of use, returning to heather and goats. (Interest may now be re-kindling as romantics turn away from climbs more trodden in search of lost treasure.)

APPROACH

Random pinnacles pepper the mountain, so the line of Needle's Eye Arete is best identified from a distance. It bounds the right flank of Eastern Gully, a rubbly trough that curves up into Creigiau Gleision near its left side, spilling

On the lower pinnacles

out into an erosion scar on the slope below the crag. From the single track road about 200m S of Pentre farm walk up a gradually steepening grass slope into Cwm-coch, crossing a fence at its top corner. A hellish slog beside an erosion scar now leads in about 40min to the mouth of Eastern Gully.

Ascend the gully (helmets recommended), picking carefully over rubble and slime until barred by a greasy little slab. Follow a vague path rightwards below this step to reach a grassy saddle, with a good view of the forbidding bottom section of the climb. Step back left along a ledge above the slab and continue up the gully briefly until opportunity knocks in the form of a heather ledge that cuts rightwards around the base of the first pinnacle.

CLIMB

Needle's Eye Arete, 150m Moderate

If the unpleasant entry section is greasy a rope is highly recommended. Step right along the airy ledge to belay just around the corner. An awkward move right across steep green rock then leads to heathery ground on the right flank of the ridge. Now go up, and a little left, to gain a vegetated chimney/corner. Slither up this to reach the clean rock of the crest with relief; belay in a little notch overlooking Eastern Gully.

A short slabby wall on the crest – crux – now leads to an indecently exposed knife edge. Straddle this and soon reach a curious hole through the ridge, the Needle's Eye. A direct ascent of the next wobbly-looking tower may not appeal. More sensible is to cross to the left

The Braich Ty Du face of Pen yr Ole Wen (Route 24) from the pinnacles

Pen yr Ole Wen (Route 24) from the top of Creigiau Gleision

flank, following a rising traverse some way below the crest on a mix of heather and decent rock to regain the ridge at the next prominent little gap.

A very airy pinnacled section follows – take it direct, belaying at will (if at all). At one point an escape left into Eastern Gully is available, but by now the hardest climbing is already in the bag. Beyond the possible get-out the ridge leads on over several more enjoyable steps and little gendarmes. Soon a steep prow rears up ahead, more substantial than the rest. Step up off a spike to gain a juggy groove on its right flank, with an exit onto yet another vertiginous pinnacle. Now walk up a short slope to the final rocks, which lead uneventfully to the grassy shoulder at the top of Creigiau Gleision.

CONTINUATION

This being a hearty traditional excursion one really ought to conclude proceedings with a brisk perambulation. Ascend W around the rim of the crags, then curve right up a gentle grassy incline to the summit of Foel Goch, a quiet contrast to the bigger, busier Glyderau. The highest point is at the apex of two grand crumbly faces and an even grander, more crumbly ridge Yr Esgair (see Appendix 1 for reasons to be fearful).

DESCENT

Drop steeply WNW around the edge of Cwm Bual to reach a grassy saddle linking Foel Goch to Mynydd Perfedd. This latter and neighbouring 3000-er Elidir Fawr can be visited on a quick there-and-back dash from here. All descents of the eastern flank of these hills are pretty steep; from the saddle a good option is the spur that divides Cwm Bual and Cwm Perfedd. Cross a stile on the saddle and follow a clear path down the scarp to reach this spur. Easy grassy walking now leads NE down the broad crest. The path soon dwindles and the ground steepens considerably; bear left towards Cwm Perfedd to avoid a crag at the foot of the spur. Cross a fence and continue down spongy ground to regain the single track road near Maes-Caradoc farm; the layby is about 1km from here.

Route 26 – East Ridge, Y Garn

Grade	2/3
Distance	4.5km
Ascent	650m
Time	4 hours
Start/finish	Idwal Cottage pay and display car park (SH649603)
Maps	OS Landranger (1:50000) 115; OS Explorer (1:25000) OL17; Harvey British Mountain Map (1:40000) Snowdonia
Accommodation	See route 21
Sleeping out	Cwm Idwal is unsuitable but the hanging cirque of Cwm Clyd might offer a fun wild camp. Less fun would be carting the kit up there.
Public transport	See route 24
Seasonal notes	The lower spur is unlikely to be high enough for winter climbing; the more interesting upper section is grade III.

Y Garn from Gribin Ridge (Route 31);
the lower crest of East Ridge is centre frame, and the upper buttress is higher on the left

THE MAJESTIC OGWEN FLANK of Y Garn is a symmetrical bowl cradled by encircling ridges. A popular hillwalk traces the skyline; excitement can be injected by starting the southeast ridge direct, a testing scramble on a subsidiary spur that goes by the unimaginatively named East Ridge. Although a well-known outing it seems less mobbed than many, and has a mildly exploratory feel. It's a route of two halves, a scrappy (though fun) introductory rib leading to the much harder upper ridge. The traditional grade is 2, but loose rock and high exposure ought to earn it a modest upgrade. A rope is a sensible precaution, particularly in the wet; so too a helmet.

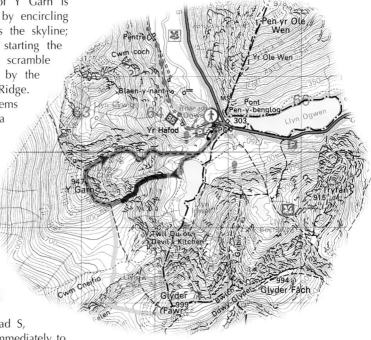

APPROACH

From Idwal Cottage car park head S, leaving the main flagstone path immediately to enter a little slate-walled ravine. Walk along the base of this to the far end, then follow a path SW over open ground to reach a shingly beach at the N end of Llyn Idwal. On a hot day the water may be irresistible but it would be rather a public place to strip off. Skirt W around the lake, then quit the path and head for the foot of Y Garn, aiming at the blunt broken rib that flanks the S side of the Llyn Clyd stream (you can't miss it). This is the beginning of the scramble.

CLIMB

East Ridge, grade 2/3

Turn the first steep rock band on the left. A well-worn trail now weaves up through outcrops and heather ledges on the crest of the rib, skirting some of the harder sections. You needn't do the same. The hands-on interest is discontinuous but there are several pleasant short problems on sound rough rock, some of which is wonderfully featured. A final steep wall can be breached up a groove on its left side, or missed out altogether by looping further left. When the rib fizzles out, walk 200m left over steep vegetation and scree to reach the foot of the compact pyramidal continuation buttress.

A direct assault appears unlikely, so slink around to the left flank. Even this is a relatively serious pitch, and might be worth roping up for – especially if slimy. Climb a little shattered gully on spikes of dubious quality. Towards the top of the gully pull right onto a scree-covered ledge on the ridge crest, taking care not to shower

Llyn Idwal from the wobbly first pitch of the upper buttress

Llyn Idwal and Llyn Ogwen from the level crest below the final crux

debris over those still below. Then tackle a steep little groove that leads to another scree patch – a possible belay. The ridge now levels out briefly, thinning into a blocky square-cut crest. An exposed move up a vertical step brings you to a final steepening, which looks particularly unfriendly in the wet. Again, a rope may prove sensible. Turn this obstacle with trepidation, via a series of flakes and ledges on the airy right flank of the ridge. From a ledge covered in boulders sidle right along a narrow gangway, to make an abrupt and exposed finish up a steep blocky step. Thankfully this move can be easily protected with a thread runner.

A 10min hands-in-pockets stroll up Y Garn's SE ridge now leads to the mountain's surprisingly spacious summit.

DESCENT

Unfortunately, despite its grand sweep, the northeast ridge is a much gentler proposition than what came before. Follow a well-scuffed descent path – quite eroded in parts – at first just right of the true crest, then on the arete itself. It's gravelly underfoot, but by no means a scramble. Lower down the path is paved with firm blocks leading quickly back to Llyn Idwal.

Y Garn from Idwal; the upper buttress of the East Ridge is prominent on the left

Route 27 – Central Arete, Glyder Fawr

Grade	200m VDiff
Distance	5km
Ascent	700m
Time	5½ hours
Start/finish	Idwal Cottage pay and display car park (SH649603)
Maps	OS Landranger (1:50000) 115; OS Explorer (1:25000) OL17; Harvey British Mountain Map (1:40000) Snowdonia
Accommodation	See route 21
Sleeping out	In bustling Cwm Idwal wild campers keen not to advertise their presence to passing school groups and wardens would be well advised to pitch up only for the hours of darkness, and pack everything away next morning. If you're determined to camp out (and you'd have to be, as there's no need to do so in a range as close to roads as the Glyderau) then Llyn y Cwn above the Devil's Kitchen might prove more appropriate.
Public transport	See route 24
Seasonal notes	Fairly high, north-facing and backed by a sizeable snow-gathering plateau – it's hard to believe that this route hasn't seen winter suitors in the century since its first ascent. Yet while the neighbouring gullies are recorded in the guidebook literature, Central Arete is conspicuous by its absence. The initial slabs would be hard and sketchy (perhaps little more than dry tooling), but the upper ridge looks to have the makings of a fine grade III mixed climb. It might be worth a try from the left.

A<small>N OUTSTANDING ROUTE</small> in an inspiring position, Central Arete is Snowdonian ridge-climbing at its best. The arete is a prominent feature of the Upper Cliff, big in its own right yet only a part of a still vaster sprawl of rock. From the shore of Llyn Idwal to the summit of Glyder Fawr it's possible to enchain one route after another to give hundreds of metres of climbing. But while tides of climbers engulf the Idwal Slabs at the bottom of the heap the tiers above filter many out, and only a comparative trickle seem to make it as far as Central Arete. Their reward is a memorable adventure, with a hard start and stirring exposure, and a vague hint of the Alps. Replace the lake with a glacier, sheep with chamois, ignore the distant Menai Straits, and Ogwen could (almost) be the Oberland.

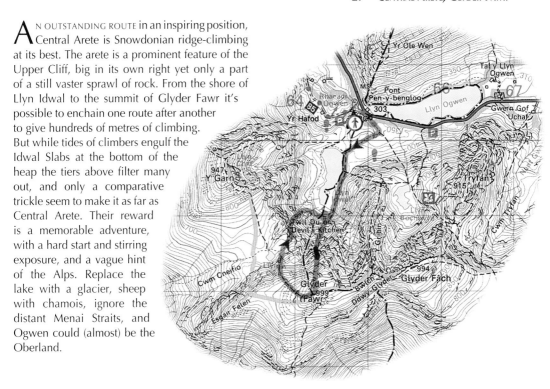

A helicopter buzzes Cwm Cneifion. Glyder Fawr's cliff tiers can be seen, from the Idwal Slabs to the Upper Cliff; Central Arete is high up on the right

- **27** Central Arête
- **28** Sub Cneifion Rib and Cneifion Arête
- **A** Sub Cneifion Rib
- **B** Cneifion Arête
- **C** Gribin Ridge (route 31)
- **D** Idwal Slabs
- **E** Llyn Idwal

APPROACH

From Idwal Cottage head SE on a flagstone path, usually mobbed with dog walkers, school parties and climbers. Just beyond a wooden footbridge the path kinks hard right to reach the N end of Llyn Idwal. Cradling the lake is a monumental cirque, sweeping from the complex Glyder Fawr crags to the sinister black fort of the Devil's Kitchen and the gentle giant Y Garn. If clouds aren't blotting the view then the line of Central Arete should now be discernible high above and to the right of the obvious Idwal Slabs. Stay on

On the slab of pitch 2

the path along the E shore of the lake, going through a gate in a wall and passing beneath Sub Cneifion Rib (route 28) to reach the foot of the Idwal Slabs.

Given a full day in hand the interesting (read: long and winding) approach to Central Arete starts here, with a big route up the slabs plus any combination you fancy on the higher walls, followed by a short walk to the Upper Cliff; no description is given here since none of the lower climbs are remotely ridge-like. For the direct approach continue beneath the pockmarked wall of Idwal Buttress, then immediately quit the decent path with regret. Hack up a steep ribbon of scree on the right of Idwal Buttress, on the sketchiest of paths. Once near the Upper Cliff trend right to reach the base of the broken buttress bounding the right side of the grassy fault of Central Gully. The line of Central Arete doesn't stand out from below – it starts at the lowest rocks.

CLIMB

Central Arete, 200m VDiff

Pitch 1, 45m
Gain and then follow the left side of a long slabby rib that cuts through the messy vegetation; easy climbing, if bold. Reach a heathery terrace and belay at its far side below the start of the arete proper. *NB Further right is an inset slab with a ledge at its base – this is not on line.*

Pitch 2, 35m
The crux – delicate and exposed. Move up and then right to gain the slabby right flank of the arete. Head straight up this, staying slightly right

The spectacular spikes of pitch 4

of the edge. The position is spectacular as you pad carefully up the rippled slab, where incut holds and reliable runners are both equally sparse. Belay at a bijou stance on a thin horizontal ledge on the arete (uncomfortable for more than two people).

Pitch 3, 15m

Continue quite steeply up the slab, again just right of the outside edge, to discover a more comfortable belay ledge.

Pitch 4, 50m

Take plenty of slings on this pitch. The crest now narrows into a spectacular rank of spikes, with a gulf of air below. Make a steep pull up a series of stacked flakes – monster jugs, though some feel slightly hollow – then continue by the line of least resistance over the blockier pinnacles above. Cross the right flank of a particularly sharp spine to a spike belay on a sloping quartz-dappled ledge.

Pitches 5 and 6, 55m

Belay at will. The arete gradually merges with the jumbled chaos of blocks and bushes that scatters the hillside; follow it as directly as possible, watching out for looseness and slimy grass. Bridge up a little gully, then continue up broken ground until there's no further need for a rope.

DESCENT

The summit of Glyder Fawr is some 500m S over rough ground. From here a path curves back N, descending to the soggy level ground at the top of the Devil's Kitchen cliffs. A paved path weaves through a breach in the suitably satanic crags, soon returning to the E shore of Llyn Idwal to rejoin the approach route. Those with a cragging (as opposed to a bagging) mentality can spare themselves the summit trek by turning right at the top of the climb, traversing over a steep block pile and boggy bits to reach the top of the Devil's Kitchen.

Route 28 – Sub Cneifion Rib and Cneifion Arete

Sub Cneifion Rib, pitch 4

Grade	Sub Cneifion Rib 125m VDiff; Cneifion Arete 135m Moderate
Distance	4km (not including the extended circuit)
Ascent	500m (as above)
Time	4 hours (as above)
Start/finish	Idwal Cottage pay and display car park (SH649603)
Maps	OS Landranger (1:50000) 115; OS Explorer (1:25000) OL17; Harvey British Mountain Map (1:40000) Snowdonia
Accommodation	See route 21
Sleeping out	The level floor of secluded Cwm Cneifion looks suitable, but it's a fairly long way to carry a tent when you could be camping closer to a pub.
Public transport	See route 24
Seasonal notes	Sub Cneifion Rib isn't suited to winter climbing, but Cneifion Arete is a high-quality III under decent snow cover (if you can remember what that is!).

◄ FOR TOPO SEE ROUTE 27.

Scything up out of Cwm Cneifion in a great sweep of stone, the Cneifion Arete is a compelling target for aspirant alpinists. It's a worthy objective in its own right, but Sub Cneifion Rib is the customary prelude. Like any compatible couple these two routes complement each other perfectly, joining forces to create something greater than the sum of its parts – a long, satisfying delve into the rugged depths of Idwal. The styles of climbing are distinct – the thinner, slabbier, cragging feel of the Rib contrasting with the Arete's juggy high mountain exposure. Both are popular, so start early to avoid weekend queues. Once these two are in the bag then an ascent of the Gribin and descent of Bristly Ridge can extend play long into the afternoon (see route 31). Altogether this gives one of the best 'Alpine' rounds in Wales, a classic enchainment with few equals south of the border. Are you tough enough to finish with Tryfan?

APPROACH

As for route 27 as far as the wall beside Llyn Idwal. Beyond the gate quit the lake path for a scruffier route that makes a rising traverse across grassy slopes to pass near the base of Sub Cneifion Rib. Gear up at the base of the most continuous rib.

CLIMB

Sub Cneifion Rib, 125m VDiff

Pitch 1, 30m

Follow the crest of the rib on perfect rock up a series of slabby grooves. The crux is a small overlap; move left around the bulge, then straight

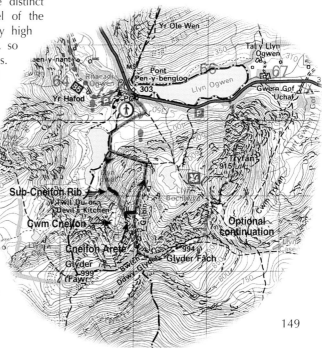

up on small holds (care arranging protection here – small wires). Now follow a crack just left of the crest to a big belay ledge.

Pitch 2, 40m
Climb scrappy bilberry ledges and outcrops, aiming slightly left to a clean rib. Follow this easily to a ledge below a steeper wall. Protection can be placed in a crack on the right before tackling the wall direct to another substantial ledge, flat holds appearing when needed. It's possible to escape the crag from here by scrambling either right or left.

Pitch 3, 20m
An easy walk. Descend a grassy shelf rightwards to regain clean rock on the front of the beautiful upper rib. Climb this for a few metres to a stance a few metres below a prominent square-cut overlap.

Pitch 4, 35m
Sidle right, with a high-stepping off-balance move onto the exposed nose. Continue right into a shallow groove; go up this with a thoughtful move or two to reach a crack running up the front of the rib. Follow this triumphantly to enter a deep corner that provides the most logical finish.

To reach the next route follow a vague path rightwards across the hillside into Cwm Cneifion. The Cneifion Arete is unmistakeable up on the left, a curved stone blade.

CLIMB

Cneifion Arete, 135m Moderate
It's not as scary as it looks, and becomes somewhat easier after a steep start. The first section probably ought to be pitched, but the upper ridge is a good place to move together; some experienced parties treat it as an unroped scramble, but the exposure calls for a cool head.

Pitch 1, 25m
From just right of the toe of the ridge climb a steep shallow groove, with positive – if polished – holds. Make a tricky step right, then continue up to the crest to belay on a little gravelly ledge.

Pitch 2, 10m
The obvious chimney provides a short but inelegant thrutch.

Some easy broken ground follows. Stick to the airy right edge for best results, where the ridge almost seems to overhang the mountainside

Topping out on the Cneifion Arete

The steep bottom section of the Cneifion Arete

OPTIONAL CONTINUATION

If the day is yet young consider making an extended circuit around the Cwm Bochlwyd horseshoe. The route may be several grades easier than those you've already done, but that really doesn't matter on a round this special. Start up the scrambly upper crest of the Gribin Ridge. This soon leads to the plateau, where a clamber through Castell y Gwynt gains the summit tor of Glyder Fach. Continuing E, locating the top of Bristly Ridge is easy in good visibility. Descent of this ridge is slightly harder than the (more usual) ascent; pay particular attention in the scrappy lower reaches, where it's quite possible to miss the top of Sinister Gully and end up drifting too far to the left onto more dangerous ground. From Bwlch Tryfan the ascent of Tryfan's South Ridge is a doddle, but reversing the more complex North Ridge is bound to take time, and isn't recommended in wet or misty weather.

The Cneifion Arete from above

below; to the left it just fizzles into steep vegetation – not a good escape option. A series of sharp flakes lead on up the curving knife edge of the upper crest, providing a profusion of runners and possible belays; the route is obvious. The clambering is easy and juggy, the exposure magnificent. Pop out onto the grassy slopes of the Gribin Ridge.

POSSIBLE DESCENT

If you've had enough fun then head N onto the clear path that quickly descends the bottom reaches of the Gribin Ridge. Lower down, turn left at a T junction to return to Llyn Idwal.

Route 29 – Dolmen Ridge, Glyder Fach

Grade	c170m Moderate
Distance	5.5km
Ascent	700m
Time	5 hours
Start/finish	Idwal Cottage pay and display car park (SH649603)
Maps	OS Landranger (1:50000) 115; OS Explorer (1:25000) OL17; Harvey British Mountain Map (1:40000) Snowdonia
Accommodation	See route 21
Sleeping out	The shores of Llyn Bochlwyd are well suited to a wild camp, but level dry pitches are at a premium; try the W side. There are also a couple of extremely spartan bivvy shelters beneath boulders to the E of the lake but you'd have to be desperate.
Public transport	See route 24
Seasonal notes	The seepy and vegetated lower section might give scrappy mixed climbing after a reasonable freeze; however the ridge itself isn't particularly turfy, so expect a snowed-up rock scramble. Grade III seems a fair bet, but this is merely a guesstimate.

The upper crest of Dolmen Ridge at sunset, seen from the Gribin Ridge (Route 31)

A THRILLING TRIP with a real mountaineering ambience, Dolmen Ridge ticks all the classic ridge-climbing boxes. The route strikes a fine balance between scrambling and climbing proper, with something to amuse (or appal) everyone. From below it's hard to spot, and the prelude is far from auspicious; but then the crux suddenly arrives, and all is forgiven. When the ridge gets into its stride it has a compelling logic, a steep line almost to the mountain's summit, threading through the tumbled chaos of blocks and spikes that give the route its name. Dolmens are prehistoric standing stones, huge and inscrutable – and there's certainly something monumental about this climb.

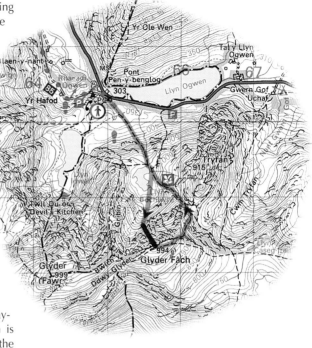

APPROACH

It's possible to reach Llyn Bochlwyd from lay-bys beside Llyn Ogwen, but the initial path is less pleasant. As with many Glyderau routes the convenient starting point is (predictably) Idwal Cottage. Follow the main Llyn Idwal path to its first sharp bend, where a path continues SE, crossing the bogs on flagstones before climbing steeply beside the cascading Nant Bochlwyd to reach the lake. Hop the stream near the outflow (can require care after heavy rain) and pick up a sketchy path along the east shore of the lake, between scattered boulders and boggy hummocks. The path continues beside a stream, climbing a rough slope with the north face of Glyder Fach becoming dominant above. Dolmen Ridge itself begins a considerable distance up the crag, above a vegetated entry scramble. Aim to reach the base of the crag just right of Central Gully, at a point where two quartz stripes are clearly visible.

CLIMB

Dolmen Ridge, c170m Moderate

Although customarily given a scrambling grade of 3, the route's short exposed crux has earned it an upgrade in this book. It can only be recommended to properly equipped parties.

29 Dolmen Ridge
30 East Gully Arête

Accessing the worthwhile bit requires a mucky clamber up uninspiring ground to the right of Central Gully. Start with a bang on a short steep wall of compact rock. Now follow a well-trodden line weaving up a confusion of blocky steps and grassy ledges, with some looseness underfoot, and plenty of slime after rain. On reaching a quartz-dappled terrace step right onto blocks, then go up and back left, climbing a short exposed rib on good holds to reach a wide scrappy bay in Central Gully. The imposing rock mass of Dolmen Buttress rears up to the left of the gully – you can't miss it. Climb greasy vegetation and scree until directly below the buttress. The front face is not a place for Moderates (nor yet, scrambles), but fear not; the idea is to outflank it on the right. Continue up the gully a short way until level with a square cut gangway that slices across the gully flank of Dolmen Buttress.

Creep along this, with a strong suspicion that things are about to get interesting. If you're going to rope up anywhere on this route, then now's the time. Belay in a moderately exciting position at the end of the gangway; a 20m pitch follows. Step into a block-choked groove. Squirm up this, before moving left to reach a steep open-book corner with the full height of the buttress suddenly directly below – that's a great deal of nothing at all. Climb the corner – the crux – with good holds and runners (and a couple of hollow-sounding flakes, incidentally) in the left wall. At the top, swing left onto a welcome belay ledge.

You're now on the ridge crest. Follow it much more easily over a rounded backbone of flakes, and a boulder-strewn section. The next big obstacle is a blunt tower on the skyline, graced with a monumental horizontal block that resembles a megalithic chambered tomb and probably accounts for the route's name. Reach this via an airy step over a jammed boulder (with luck it won't choose this moment to become un-jammed), continuing in a shallow depression in the front of the tower, with one strenuous move up steep flakes. Bear left below the top tier of the tower, walking over the huge reclining block to enter a niche. Regain the ridge crest, either direct (steep) or via a little detour on the left (less so). The arete continues as a series of flakes and tottering pinnacles, exposed scrambling but not hard. It soon curves to the right, before gradually merging into the giant tumbled chunks that litter the mountainside. Scramble thuggishly up

In the crux groove

Approaching the 'megalithic tomb'

The nearby Cantilever stone is worth a diversion if you've not already got a novelty photo in your collection.

DESCENT

To continue the scrambling fun an extended descent via either the Gribin Ridge or Bristly Ridge comes highly recommended (fully-described in route 31). If getting down quickly is the main priority however, then head ENE over the stony moonscape to pick up the rough path that descends below the E flank of Bristly Ridge. The top of the path is marked with a cairn. As far as Bwlch Tryfan it's mostly unpleasant steep scree, but beyond the wall on the pass the path is generally gentler, soon reaching Llyn Bochlwyd and the route back to Idwal Cottage.

these, passing some crevasse-like caves among the leaning blocks, to reach the summit plateau a short walk from the main tor of Glyder Fach.

Nant Ffrancon and Anglesey from the upper crest

Route 30 – East Gully Arete, Glyder Fach

Grade	c200m Difficult
Distance	5.5 km
Ascent	700m
Time	5 hours
Start/finish	Idwal Cottage pay and display car park (SH649603),
Maps	OS Landranger (1:50000) 115; OS Explorer (1:25000) OL17; Harvey British Mountain Map (1:40000) Snowdonia
Accommodation	See route 21
Sleeping out	See route 29
Public transport	See route 24
Seasonal notes	Unlikely to lend itself to the build up of good conditions.

On the steep start of pitch 1

◄ **FOR TOPO SEE ROUTE 29.**

A LENGTHY CLIMB up a big chaotic face, East Gully Arete is a worthwhile excursion with plenty of that distinctive Glyderau atmosphere. It may not be in the same quality league as nearby Dolmen Ridge (route 29), but with sound rough rock, ample protection, generous belay stances and unproblematic route-finding it remains viable in all but the angriest of weather. What's more, there's none of the polish that blights the predictable 'classics'. Since the difficulties are both modest and short-lived it is suitable for relative novices. It's largely a scramble, but there are a still couple of points at which most people will appreciate a rope.

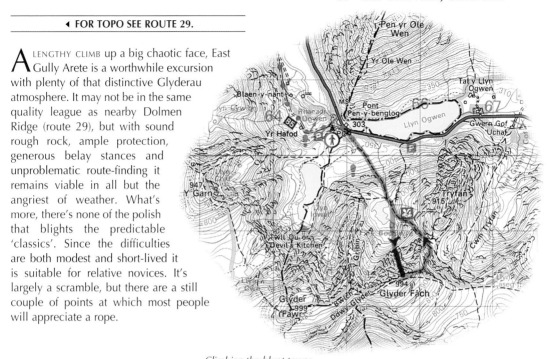

Climbing the blunt tower

157

APPROACH

As for route 29 until beyond Llyn Bochlwyd; now bear slightly left up a rough slope where you'll probably lose what little path there is, a steep scree pile leading to the mouth of the dank gulch of East Gully. As the name suggests, East Gully Arete starts at the steep buttress on the left side of the gully.

CLIMB

East Gully Arete, c200m Difficult

The first 40m-odd is the steepest bit of the route and worth roping up for; it could be avoided by entering the route from the left at a corresponding reduction in grade and quality. Start at the well-scuffed terrace just left of East Gully.

Pitch 1, 15m

Climb onto an obvious rock platform. Now sidle slightly right to gain a line of weakness overlooking East Gully. Go up, then move back left, passing a little ledge and a quartz stripe to reach a good belay ledge.

Pitch 2, 25m

Step onto a spike at the back of the ledge, then move slightly right to follow an exposed slabby section near the right edge of the buttress – good wire runners and holds. Soon, bear left into a pronounced niche. Climb the left wall of this via a tricky slabby groove to reach the first of several broken terraces cutting across the crag. Either belay here or continue easily to a second terrace.

The continuation ridge above the terrace is easier than the entry pitches, and doesn't warrant

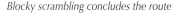

Blocky scrambling concludes the route

Looking down Nant Ffrancon from the Gribin Ridge descent

a full pitch-by-pitch description. A long slabby scramble up the right flank of the ridge leads to a huge poised block – a good belay spot. Above are two broken ribs. Take the better-defined left-hand line up a series of juggy steps; easy ground, though airy. There's a good optional stance in an enclosed grove of spikes about 40m above the huge poised block; it is worth belaying here as the next step is arguably the crux of the route. Climb stacked blocks up the front face of the unmistakeable blunt tower (a sling over the top block protects the next delicate moves). Step up onto an exposed beachball finish, bearing slightly left to reach straightforward ground.

Scrambling is now all that remains. Follow your nose up the broad crest, where an enjoyable (and seemingly endless) series of blocky steps and rounded flakes leads on towards the summit plateau. There is a choice of lines and plenty of scope to keep things entertaining. Eventually the crest merges into the crazy stacks of monumental tombstones that typify these hills. 'Glyder' means 'pile', an apt description of this giant natural slag heap. It sounds ugly, but it's really quite imposing. This is geological decay on an epic scale, with an atmosphere unlike anything else in Britain. The summit tor is a short stroll away, and provides highball bouldering and even a novel underground clamber for cavers suffering subterranean homesick blues.

DESCENT

See route 29.

Route 31 – Cwm Bochlwyd Horseshoe

Grade	1
Distance	6km
Ascent	900m
Time	5 hours
Start/finish	Layby by the A5 just below the climber's venue of the Milestone Buttress (SH663602) – more parking is available along the road towards Idwal Cottage too.
Maps	OS Landranger (1:50000) 115; OS Explorer (1:25000) OL17; Harvey British Mountain Map (1:40000) Snowdonia
Accommodation	See route 21
Sleeping out	See route 29
Public transport	See route 24
Seasonal notes	This is a winter mountaineering expedition of similar quality to the Snowdon Horseshoe, but with rather greater and more sustained difficulties. The climbing doesn't depend on frozen turf and is possible in any sort of snow cover. In full conditions of iced-up rock and firm snow the North Ridge of Tryfan and Bristly Ridge are both testing grade IIs if the most direct lines are taken. The Gribin Ridge is similarly tricky, and tired parties descending at the end of a long hard day might be advised not to follow the crest religiously. However the extreme conditions of yesteryear are nowadays unlikely. Under a frosty dusting or unconsolidated snow the Cwm Bochlwyd Horseshoe may be more a wintry scramble than a full-on winter climb; but always come with respect (and crampons and an axe). Although polished, the route is perfectly feasible in the wet.

Tryfan doesn't have a boring side; the North Ridge seen end-on from Ogwen

WITH ITS GRAND AUSTERITY, atmospheric positions and endlessly varied rocky ground the circuit of Cwm Bochlwyd is unquestionably the finest easy all-day ridge scramble south of Scotland. First comes Tryfan, icon of Snowdonian ruggedness. From some angles it resembles a giant stone dorsal fin dwarfing the ant-like traffic on the A5; from others, the buttressed ramparts and crumbling turrets of a decaying fortress. Tryfan doesn't have a boring side. The North Ridge offers 600m of top quality scrambling that is none the worse for its overwhelming popularity. This outlying peak safely negotiated, an ascent of the fittingly-named Bristly Ridge is the natural next step, exposed but easy clambering over a coxcomb of spectacular pinnacles. A wander over the otherworldly boulder graveyard of the Glyder plateau, a scramble through the shattered spires of Castell y Gwynt and an airy descent of the Gribin Ridge round off an intense trip.

Blustery conditions on Tryfan's North Ridge

CLIMB

Tryfan North Ridge, grade 1

The scale of this scramble is unusual for Wales, the ridge beginning just above the road and leading all the way to Tryfan's summit. A well-worn line (or rather, intertwining collection of lines) weaves up the broad crest via a succession of craggy walls and generous ledges that minimise the sense of exposure.

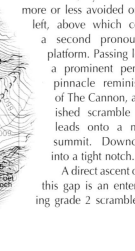

Every tier in turn presents several possible variations, from polished easy options to short challenging pitches that can be a lot harder than grade 1. You're unlikely to find exactly the same route from one visit to the next, and due to the go-anywhere nature of the ground a minute description would confuse rather than illuminate.

From the layby go through a gate and ascend the steep path just left of a drystone wall, bearing left on rough ground beneath the rambling east walls of the Milestone Buttress to reach the lowest heathery shoulder of the North Ridge. Now follow your nose up the blunt crest, making things as hard or as easy as you fancy. The first notable feature is a quartzy terrace; just to the right is the leaning block known as The Cannon, but it's easily missed. The next scrambly section can (if you wish) be more or less avoided on the left, above which comes a second pronounced platform. Passing left of a prominent perched pinnacle reminiscent of The Cannon, a polished scramble then leads onto a minor summit. Downclimb into a tight notch.

A direct ascent out of this gap is an entertaining grade 2 scramble; for

161

an easier option, slant right to find a blocky gully which leads to Tryfan's North Summit. Beyond a bouldery saddle is the crowning Central Summit. Jutting proud of the main massif, this is a magnificent spot. Have a break and perhaps a cheeky apple under the twin monoliths Adam and Eve (which is which seems unclear); tradition dictates taking an airy stride from one to the other, but on a wet or blustery day you'd be risking a precipitate fall from grace down the East Face.

DESCENT

Tryfan South Ridge, grade 1

Beyond another gap is the rocky South Summit. Continue down the rough South Ridge, crossing a slight saddle marked by a drystone wall before climbing briefly onto the little Far South Summit; the most straightforward line is generally right of

the crest, though even the hands-on direct route is easy enough. From this final top of Tryfan the least problematic choice bears slightly right down bouldery slopes to reach a path leading to the major saddle of Bwlch Tryfan. From here obvious paths offer escape routes into the valley.

SCRAMBLE

Bristly Ridge, grade 1

If necessary this scramble can be entirely avoided by taking an unpleasant path below the east flank of the ridge, but that would be missing the point. Parties made of sterner stuff should toil up an eroded trail alongside a drystone wall to reach a scrappy gully – Sinister Gully – that breaches the base of the obvious ridge. Climb this (watching out for loose bits), bearing slightly left where the gully steepens, to gain easier ground on the

Bristly Ridge from Dolmen Ridge (Route 29)

Crib Goch (Route 33) from Castell y Gwynt

crest. The ridge soon narrows, breaking into the short row of lumpy towers that give it its name. Clamber direct over the first rock mass, dropping into a pronounced gap on the far side. Pass just right of the next big tower (the Great Pinnacle), then bear up left through a little niche and back onto the crest. Rapidly easing scrambling now leads up the shattered ridge onto the summit plateau of Glyder Fach.

Bear right and just beyond the highest tor the plateau narrows. The descent to Bwlch y Ddwy-Glyder, the pass between Glyders Fach and Fawr, is barred by the massed stone spears of Castell y Gwynt; there is a rough path to the left of this dramatic minor 'summit', but taking it direct is much more fun. From the bwlch a well-blazed route makes a beeline for Glyder Fawr, which can be quickly bagged if you feel like it. To complete the Bochlwyd Horseshoe however, stick with the rim of the cwm, bearing right onto a level area at the top of the Gribin Ridge.

DESCENT

Gribin Ridge, grade 1

Although it's only a modest and short-lived affair and tends to be underrated the scramble directly down this airy crest is very enjoyable. For best results stay on the lip of Cwm Bochlwyd, where a succession of little rocky problems provides a gradual wind-down from the day's excitements. As usual there's a less pleasant, less hands-on option – a rubbly path just down on the W flank – but why bother?

Below the rocky upper crest the mood of the ridge relents. Cross a broad grassy stretch above the top of the Cneifion Arete (route 28), then follow the obvious path down the lower crest to the T-junction. Turning right here, the outflow of Llyn Bochlwyd is soon reached. Cross the stream and head NE over the hillside to meet another well-trodden path. This descends quite steeply past little Bochlwyd Buttress to reach the A5 a short distance W of the starting point.

Route 32 – Daear Ddu, Moel Siabod

Grade	1
Distance	8km
Ascent	780m
Time	4½ hours
Start/finish	Pont Cyfyng, the road bridge over the Afon Llugwy at (SH734572); if parking on the minor road beyond the bridge be considerate of local residents.
Maps OS	Landranger (1:50000) 115; OS Explorer (1:25000) OL17 and OL18; Harvey British Mountain Map (1:40000) Snowdonia
Accommodation	Capel Curig Youth Hostel 0845 371 9110; Betws y coed Youth Hostel 01690 710796; The Vagabond bunkhouse, Betws y Coed 01690 710850; several other bunkhouses and campsites around Capel Curig
Sleeping out	If you could locate a dry pitch among the bogs, the shores of Llyn y Foel would furnish a secluded and atmospheric wild camp.
Public transport	Regular buses link Capel Curig and Betws y Coed (served by rail)
Seasonal notes	Southerly aspect and relatively modest altitude would suggest that full winter conditions are rare on Daear Ddu, even by Welsh standards. If they did come, it would certainly make an enjoyable winter mountaineering trip; grade I seems a fair guesstimate. The big vegetated crags of Siabod's south face might still hold new route potential for winter optimists.

Moel Siabod from Gyrn Las (Route 35)

M OEL SIABOD stands with its humped back turned sulkily to its neighbours. The dull side dominant in views from Snowdon and the Glyderau belies the mountain's split personality, helping to keep the crowds at bay. From other angles it appears a different beast altogether, a rock-tipped cone with a secretive and impressive eastern cwm. Daear Ddu is the low-angled ridge bounding the south side of this bowl, rising in a flight of knobbly steps from the shores of little Llyn y Foel to the mountain's summit. The scrambling is pretty basic and most of the 'difficulties' readily avoidable, making this an ideal novice's route. Nevertheless it's a rewarding trip with a lonely feel, and worth half a day of anyone's time. To maximise the challenge wait for wet weather, when the rock has all the friction of engine oil.

Starting up Daear Ddu

APPROACH

From the A5 cross the minor road bridge over the Afon Llugwy; the river in full flow is an inspiring sight (and sound), and enough to put you off kayaking for life. Leave the road at the second track on the right, just before reaching some houses. This climbs SW through mossy woods, skirting a farmyard via a signed detour. Beyond a semi-derelict house the track heads straight towards the mountain, rising across moorland with open views over the Llugwy valley to the Carneddau.

Where the track becomes a path stay left to traverse up below the craggy flanks of Siabod's long Northeast Ridge (more on that later), passing a small lake before climbing more steeply to reach a sinister deep dark quarry pool. OS maps show the path terminating here, but it continues in the same line, skirting left of the pool and climbing up and over a broad

shoulder into the mouth of the rugged east cwm. Daear Ddu is the crest dead ahead; pick across bogs beside Llyn y Foel to reach its foot.

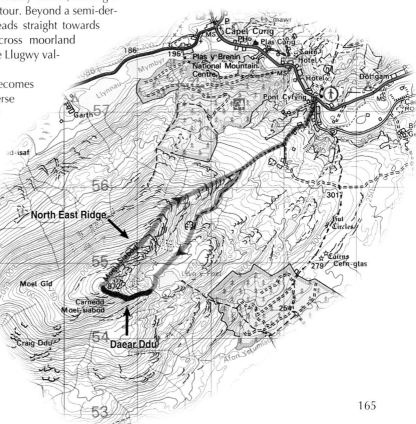

165

On the final summit of the Northeast Ridge

CLIMB

Daear Ddu, grade 1

A clear path now leads all the way to the summit, weaving around boulders and outcrops to contrive a route with little excitement. You don't have to do the same. Far better is to pick your own line, taking the rocks as they come and staying close to the right edge for maximum

Descending the Northeast Ridge

enjoyment. A series of little steps lead to a blocky mass with a slabby right wall – it's quite tricky if taken direct, but it can be readily avoided. The top of this buttress turns out to be a mini-summit; clamber into the gap beyond, then continue more easily. Gradually the crest becomes less sharply defined and more broken, but there's still fun to be had by keeping to the right, where a craggy mass provides a final short scramble. The spacious summit dome is marked by a trig point, with a round-walled wind shelter a little way E.

DESCENT

Head NE. Moel Siabod's broad pate soon narrows into the airy and well-defined Northeast Ridge, an unexpected bonus. Scrambly in places, a series of rock prows descends towards the valley. A short climb onto the final minor peak provides a few brief moments of entertainment, especially if you stay as close as possible to its precipitous SE edge. After this the ridge soon becomes grassy, leading after about 1km to a final steep slope. The path here is quite loose and eroded. Back on level ground, cross bogs and an A-frame stile to regain the approach track.

Grade	I
Distance	11km
Ascent	1060m
Time	6 hours
Start/finish	Pen-y-Pass pay and display car park (SH647556); this is expensive and rapidly fills up at weekends.
Maps OS	Landranger (1:50000) 115, OS Explorer (1:25000) OL17, Harvey British Mountain Map (1:40000) Snowdonia
Accommodation	Pen-y-Pass Youth Hostel 0845 371 9534 is the best placed option, although it's getting a bit shabby; Bryn Gwynant Youth Hostel 0845 371 9108; Pen y Gwryd Hotel for that old school atmosphere 01286 870211; Craflwyn bunkhouse, Nantgwynant (National Trust) 01766 510120; several more options in Llanberis
Sleeping out	Camping out in Cwm Dyli isn't a bad idea in summer, but at the chilly end of the year you could be forgiven for thinking otherwise. Pitch the tent out of sight of the paths.
Public transport	Linking all the major local towns and rail hubs with key mountain access points such as Ogwen and Rhyd Ddu, the Snowdon Sherpa bus is an invaluable service in this neck of the woods. Pen-y-Pass is an interchange between various routes. It's possible to park and ride from several points including Nant Peris, Capel Curig, Betws y Coed and Beddgelert. See www.snowdoniagreenkey.co.uk ▶

Crib Goch broods above Pen y Pass; the East Ridge follows the left-hand sunlit edge, while the North Ridge rises from the right

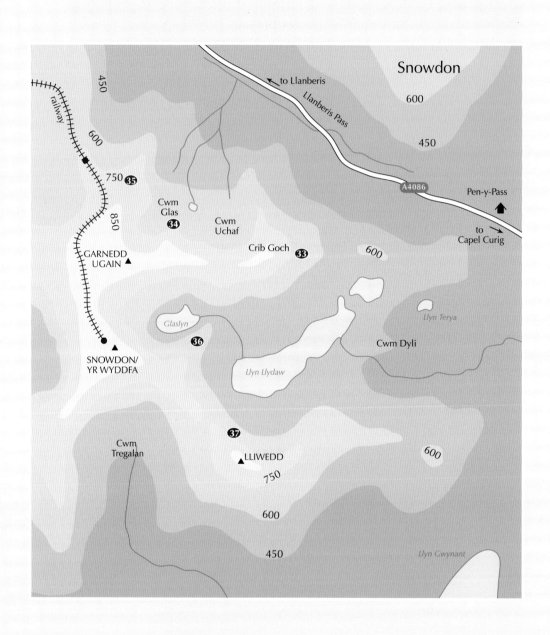

Seasonal notes	In full winter nick the Horseshoe is a top end grade I – indeed, *Welsh Winter Climbs* (Cicerone) goes so far as to suggest I/II, presumably because of its length and seriousness rather than technicality. Solid névé and rimed rocks give you the full experience, but soft wet snow is more likely, and can feel quite hazardous on the shelving crest of Crib Goch. Summer conditions are far less challenging; in its normal state the route is an excellent – if over-popular – grade 1 scramble. High wind and rain can be scary on the long exposed sections at any time, particularly along Crib Goch.

TWO WORLDS COLLIDE on the highest mountain in Wales. Snowdon is a democratic place where trainer-shod families and expensively-equipped Alpine aspirants mingle in égalité – if not always perfect fraternité. All of humanity is here, tiptoeing along the aretes, and the reason that more of them don't plummet to their doom is probably thanks to the drastic reduction in snow cover in recent decades. When the white stuff does make an appearance, the famous Snowdon Horseshoe is by some margin the greatest winter mountaineering ridge traverse in England and Wales. With its spacious scale and airy positions the circuit of the narrow crests linking Snowdon's four fine peaks wouldn't be out of place in the Scottish Highlands. Catch it in sunshine and this really is a magnificent route.

APPROACH

An early start beats the crowds and offers the best chance of finding hard snow, while doing the route anti-clockwise means the harder sections are tackled in ascent. Follow the flagstone-paved Pyg Track W from Pen-y-pass, climbing gradually across the outcrop-studded slopes above Llanberis Pass to reach Bwlch y Moch ('pass of the pigs'). A post here marks the right-hand turnoff for Crib Goch, the gaunt pyramid that dominates the col. Follow this up a broad rocky spur, the ground gradually steepening into the scree and broken crags that form a barrier at the base of Crib Goch's East Ridge.

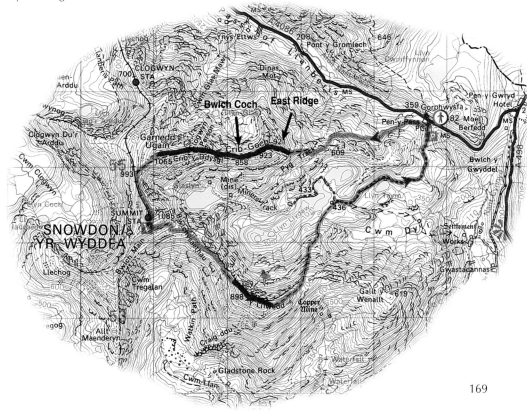

CLIMB

Crib Goch East Ridge, grade I

Given solid frozen conditions the sprawling crumbly face to your right offers an alternative Alpine-style route to the summit, also grade I though considerably more committing. It's worth avoiding like the plague in soft snow. The conventional and more advisable ascent follows the line of the summer scramble up the broad East Ridge. The ground is scrappy and can be climbed pretty much anywhere with care, but do watch for stonefall. Signs of wear show the best way up a steep 'wall' of flakes and then a series of shallow grooves and ledges. The angle soon eases on the upper crest, where the rock has a funny angular structure that makes life awkward in wet or ice. The mountain's East summit is a compact perch at the junction of the East and North Ridges (a third ascent choice; see route 34).

Crib Goch – Garnedd Ugain, grade I

Next comes the photogenic bit where timid souls suddenly discover that they prefer crawling to walking as a means of locomotion. A level rock crest runs W to the slightly higher West summit, narrow on top, shelving steeply away to the left and dropping off more or less vertically on the right. It is an impressive situation, like the top of a giant slate roof. On a dry day some might pirouette the topmost tiles while more cautious others edge along the less intimidating flank using the crest as a handrail; snow, ice, wet or wind tend to discourage show-offs.

Beyond the main summit a slight descent leads to three pronounced jagged Pinnacles. A path of sorts tries to outflank them down on the left-hand slope, but it'll either be rotten scree or steep snow and in either case a higher line is preferable. If you're equipped with a rope or well within your comfort zone then take everything as direct as possible, with some nice brief bits of grade II clambering. A third way finds the middle ground between complete avoidance and head-on confrontation: skirt left of the first pinnacle, then follow a ledge across the left flank of the second to reach a gap in the ridge between it and the third pinnacle, at the head of a steep snow gully. Climb

Yr Wyddfa and Garnedd Ugain from Crib Goch

The Crib Goch pinnacles from Bwlch Coch

an obvious slanting weakness up the right side of the third pinnacle. A brief rough descent then leads to a col, Bwlch Coch, marked by some old fenceposts. Escape could be contrived from here, either S towards the Pyg Track or N into lonely Cwm Uchaf – either requires care.

The continuation ridge Crib y Ddysgl is obvious ahead, an ascending series of blocky rock steps and easier walking sections. There is still some scrambling to come, and if you've been lucky with conditions then the next kilometre or so of sinuous snow crest is one of the highlights of the day. The first and only appreciable step is easiest tackled by staying just left of the steepest rock before regaining the arete, which is then followed in a superb position over a series of false summits to the trig point on the second highest peak in Wales. From here there's an inspiring view over the cirque to the sharp fin of Lliwedd and the gully-seamed winter climbing ground of the Trinity Face. The nearby Pen y Gwryd Hotel famously served as a training base for early Everest expeditions; ignore the railway and summit café, and the tent-shaped bulk of Yr Wyddfa might bear a fleeting resemblance to the big hill.

Yr Wyddfa and Lliwedd

A simple walk around the rim of the cwm brings you to Bwlch Glas, a Spaghetti Junction-like interchange where the railway, the Llanberis Path, the Snowdon Ranger Path and the Pyg Track all converge. This last route climbs steeply out of the cwm on the left at a point marked with an upright stone; in winter its final slope can be sheathed in icy snow and crowned with a cornice, yet people still tackle it in their droves in jeans and golf shoes. Resist the urge to feel superior; it's you who's the odd one out with your daft spiky metalwork. (Where do you think you are? The north face of the Eiger?) Follow the path just left of the railway, passing above the Trinity Face to the roof of Wales. Unless the railway is drifted over then don't expect solitude. Upwards of 350,000 people a year are expected to enjoy the new summit café, where you'll be able to buy the highest cuppa and use the loftiest toilet south of Scotland.

171

The Trinity face of Yr Wyddfa from Crib y Ddysgl

Once you've got over the excitement bid a hasty retreat and leave the hordes behind.

A direct descent towards Bwlch y Saethau runs into crumbly ground, so it's wise instead to follow the SW ridge from Yr Wyddfa's summit for just over 100m, to pick up the Watkin Path as marked by another upright stone. This makes a descending traverse across the ragged south face, and although it's easier than the direct line it is still quite eroded in summer, and may be covered in treacherously icy snow in winter. From Bwlch y Saethau follow the broad ridge crest, or the path just below on its right, to reach Bwlch Ciliau, where a cairn marks the point that you and the Watkin Path part company. From a distance the crest of Lliwedd promises great things, but unfortunately at close quarters it seems to lose the courage of its convictions. Lliwedd is the least likely of the four peaks to hold significant snow. There is some modest scrambling in a dramatic

position if you stick with the left edge overlooking the vast N face (the biggest cliff in Wales; see route 37), but it's not half as exciting as the northern arm of the Horseshoe. First comes the higher West Peak, then the East, and then a while later the little hump of Lliwedd Bach.

DESCENT

From here it's downhill all the way, the ridge soon leading to a cairn on the edge of the slope overlooking Llyn Llydaw. The path now makes directly for the lake, steep and a little rough at first (it might even be icy) but soon easing off. Down in Cwm Dyli cross a stream and follow the lake shore to reach the Miners Track, which leads quickly back to Pen-y-Pass.

Crib Goch (Route 33) and the Clogwyn y Person Arete from Gyrn Lâs (Route 35)   173

Grade	75m Difficult followed by c150m grade 3
Distance	8km
Ascent	850m
Time	6 hours
Start/finish	Pen-y-Pass pay and display car park (SH647556)
Maps	OS Landranger (1:50000) 115, OS Explorer (1:25000) OL17, Harvey British Mountain Map (1:40000) Snowdonia
Accommodation	See route 33
Sleeping out	Although only a mile from the road, few Welsh wild camp sites come as ruggedly atmospheric as Cwm Uchaf and Cwm Glas.
Public transport	See route 33
Seasonal notes	The Parson's Nose is unlikely to offer true winter sport, so access the Clogwyn y Person Arete via Western Gully. From the gap at the top of the gully follow the summer scramble, an excellent mixed II/III by the line of least resistance. It is high and north-facing, and ought to go in most conditions.

SNOWDON'S WILD NORTHERN SIDE is a complex of rock-walled cwms and ice-scoured slabs, pitted with pools and backed by the high pinnacled crests of Crib y Ddysgl and Crib Goch. The busy Llanberis Pass snakes along the foot of the mountain and tourist trains chug beyond the brow of the hill; yet here one can almost forget they exist. In this silent fastness paths are scarce and company scarcer still. A massive spur dividing the hanging cirques of Cwm Glas and Cwm Uchaf, the Clogwyn y Person Arete is a compelling scramble, with options to make

Clogwyn Y Person Arete (left) and the stepped ridge of Gyrn Las (route 35)
high above Llyn Padarn and Llyn Peris

things a little more exciting. Combined with the atmospheric Difficult climb of the Parson's Nose and the Garnedd Ugain–Crib Goch traverse you've got arguably the grandest extended mid-grade ridge circuit in Snowdonia.

APPROACH

Follow the Pyg Track to Bwlch y Moch. Turn off here on the path to Crib Goch (as for route 33) which is taken to the shoulder just below the start of the East Ridge scramble. Now cut right, traversing above a line of broken crags and along the bottom of a scree slope to reach a grassy spur under Crib Goch's sweeping northeast face. Pick up a superbly sneaky contouring path that cuts across the middle reaches of the face, providing the only walkable route through this steep mass of scree, grass and rotting rock – with an eagle's eye perspective on the pass far below. Take care in the wet. The path soon swings W around the base of the North Ridge of Crib Goch, your line of descent later in the day. Enter the high bowl of Cwm Uchaf, cradled beneath the snarling Crib Goch pinnacles.

Contour across the cwm between slabby outcrops and boggy hollows, descending slightly to cross a stream near tiny Llyn Glas. The blocky Clogwyn y Person Arete and the curvy Parson's Nose at its foot are obvious above; ascend steeply SW past another stream and little craggy bits to reach the base of the Parson's Nose slabs. A detached buttress at the bottom of a major mountain ridge, this is has something in common with the Douglas Boulder of Ben Nevis.

CLIMB

Parson's Nose, 75m Difficult
This route has an exciting feel for the grade, and some slightly questionable rock.

Pitch 1, 30m
From the very lowest point of the Nose scramble up through the gently rippled slab sea, sticking more or less to the rounded crest. Bear right to a belay stance below a marked steepening – a point that could also be reached by walking in from the scree slope on the right.

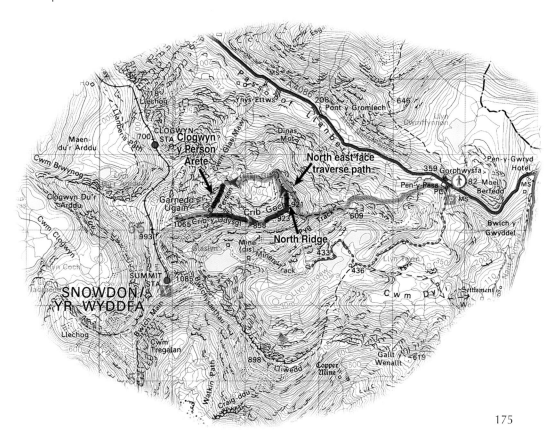

Descending into the gap behind the Parson's Nose

Pitch 2, 20m

The crux – climb about 10m up the steep rock above the belay via the obvious vertical crack or the wall just to its right, to reach a right-leading line of weakness. Follow this to a flat ledge near the right arete of the Nose. A steep pull now gains another exposed ledge overlooking Western Gully.

Pitch 3, 25m

Step up and left airily, then follow the blunt arete more easily to reach the summit.

DESCENT

5m Moderate

A polished downclimb gains the tight gap separating the Parson's nose from the main ridge.

CLIMB

Clogwyn y Person Arete, c150m grade 3

The scrambling line weaves about judiciously, and needs a bit of route finding nous; more direct options involve short exciting bursts of Moderate or Difficult climbing on superb rough-textured rock. Climb out of the gap via a mucky groove

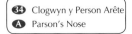

34 Clogwyn y Person Arête
A Parson's Nose

just on the left, leading to a little ledge. A short steep wall then reaches a higher ledge on the broad crest. The next steep rock mass is perhaps best climbed with a rope; alternatively skirt rightwards around it along a ledge, then take a scrappy depression that leads back to the crest. Continue up the ridge, with a mix of short scrambling steps and generous ledges, to meet a second pronounced rock step. A direct assault of this wall requires a few tricky moves on rounded holds; a blocky groove just to the left is rather easier, but it is still worth considering a rope. Both options soon meet at an exposed ledge; bear right along this, then move up on easier ground. A final steep section offers a choice of lines and some appreciable exposure – particularly on the right. Above this the scrambling soon fizzles into the scree and crumbly outcrops of the upper ridge. Plod up this, staying just left of the snaggly crest, to reach the summit ridge of Garnedd Ugain. A short detour W bags Wales' second summit.

CLIMB

Garnedd Ugain to Crib Goch, grade 1

Reversing route 33 along the narrowest bit of ridge on the Snowdon Horseshoe makes a superb continuation to the day. The steep descent leading off Crib y Ddysgl is easiest taken on the right. From Bwlch Coch the famous Pinnacles are most enjoyable climbed direct. From the mountain's true summit stride along the knife-edged rock crest to the 921m peak overlooking Pen-y-Pass.

DESCENT

Crib Goch North Ridge, grade 1

The most direct way off would be via the busy East Ridge, but in descent this can be pretty treacherous for the grade, with plenty of loose material and less than obvious route-finding. It's rather more satisfying to follow the North Ridge, an airy walkway that gets far less attention than it deserves. Narrow at first, and requiring the occasional steadying hand, the rock crest is best tackled direct since the flanks are crumbly. This modest scramble soon peters out into scree, which quickly leads down to the shoulder at the end of the traverse path described in the approach section. Reverse this, then return to Bwlch y Moch and follow the Pyg Track back to Pen-y-Pass.

A steep wall on the Clogwyn y Person Arete

Route 35 – Gyrn Lâs Ridge, Garnedd Ugain

Grade	150m II
Distance	7km
Ascent	900m
Time	4½ hours
Start	One of several laybys in the Pass of Llanberis between Pont y Gromlech and Blaen y Nant (SH626568)
Finish	Beside the A4086 in Llanberis (SH583596)
Maps	OS Landranger (1:50000) 115, OS Explorer (1:25000) OL17, Harvey British Mountain Map (1:40000) Snowdonia
Accommodation	See route 33
Sleeping out	See route 34
Public transport	See route 33; Snowdon Ranger buses pick up and drop off at various points along the Pass of Llanberis
Seasonal notes	Named Cwm Glas Ridge in Steve Ashton's *Scrambles in Snowdonia* this is a snowless grade 1 with only very brief and limited interest. But even in summer it remains worth doing because it's a quiet route through impressive surroundings, on otherwise busy hills. In winter its relatively low position makes Gyrn Lâs Ridge less likely to carry snow than higher reaches of the Horseshoe; it is best climbed with generous cover and frozen turf.

Gyrn Lâs Ridge from Llanberis Pass

Seen from Nant Peris the sheer step high on the Gyrn Lâs Ridge presents an air of impregnability, a forbidding rock prow slicing the wind. Although it is a compelling sight, few people seem to take up the challenge, and the route has a measure of seclusion surprising for a low-grade high-quality mountaineering ridge in Snowdonia's busiest massif. It benefits from this relative obscurity. The technical interest is squeezed into a 150m section below the 800m contour, while the rest of the ridge is just a lot of steep, rough leg work. Even the prominent prow is less of a barrier than it appears from below. But Gyrn Lâs remains notable for the rugged inaccessibility of its location, while the climbing itself is absorbing and airy. With modest difficulties for the grade this would be a suitable step-up for those progressing from the easier winter ridges.

APPROACH

From one of several laybys downhill of the Cromlech Boulders walk down the A4086. Ignore the first track turning off left for Ynys Ettws hut, and take the second left. Cross the Afon Nant Peris on a bridge, and then cross another bridge over the stream draining Cwm Glas Mawr. Now follow a little-used path up steep grass to meet a drystone wall after a few minutes; go through a gap beside a redundant ladder stile. Stay with the path briefly before splitting right up rough grass and rock slopes leading to the broad back of the lower ridge. A faint trail now weaves through little outcrops up the ridge, staying mostly just left of the crest. The view of tiny traffic toiling up the pass below the famous climbers' crags is worth the odd breather. Follow the path to a narrow grassy neck on the crest at about the 650m contour; immediately above, Gyrn Lâs Ridge rears up into the dramatic steep prow as seen from Nant Peris. This is the start of the climb.

On the steep exit from the pinnacles

CLIMB

Gyrn Lâs Ridge, 150m II

The initial prow can be taken direct on broken rock and turfy steps, leading to a steepening finish on slightly suspect rock. The more usual (and amenable) line is further right, following a shallow turfy corner system. After about a rope length (if you're using one) the angle eases considerably. Snow plodding up the ridge leads to the next notable feature, a short pinnacled arete with an exposed feel. Weave easily over the pinnacles to a harder final step. This could be turned up a groove on the right, but it's more entertaining taken direct; step up to gain a little foot ledge just on the right flank, scratch along this and then pull up to safer ground.

A less stimulating section now leads to the base of the ridge's second marked steepening. As with the lower prow this could be climbed direct up a series of turf-and-rock steps, but again a friendlier alternative on the right is available (and more consistent with the grade); another easy-angled chimney/groove provides the key. If it's not totally banked out then there will be a few turf-dependent moves in the obvious narrowing. About 25m of climbing leads onto easier-angled ground. Bear up and left over a more open snow slope, the climbing rapidly fading into the broad shallow-angled spread of the upper ridge. A short walking ascent around the rim of Cwm Glas leads to the summit of Garnedd Ugain.

DESCENT

Various options now present themselves: an easy climb along the Crib y Ddysgl–Crib Goch ridge (route 33), perhaps with a descent of Crib Goch's North Ridge as described in route 34 and a steep walk back down Cwm Glas Mawr to the road; a walker's descent of the Pyg Track followed by a short bus ride from Pen-y-pass to the parking layby; the longer, gentler descent of the Llanberis Path. This latter offers a gentle post-climb wind-down with inspiring views over the magnificent Clogwyn Du'r Arddu to the pinnacled profile of Mynydd Mawr (route 39). Although the path debouches in Llanberis a fair distance down the pass from your car, Snowdon Sherpa buses for Pen-y-Pass run regularly and fairly late.

In the chimney groove of the second step

Route 36 – Lliwedd via Y Gribin

Grade	1
Distance	8km
Ascent	650m
Time	3½ hours
Start/finish	Pen-y-Pass pay and display car park (SH647556)
Maps	OS Landranger (1:50000) 115, OS Explorer (1:25000) OL17, Harvey British Mountain Map (1:40000) Snowdonia
Accommodation	See route 33
Sleeping out	See route 33
Public transport	See route 33
Seasonal notes	The ground doesn't often lend itself to a decent winter build-up – in any case, it's pretty low on the mountain. Grade I/II when in winter condition.

Y Gribin is the sunlit edge running up from the shore of Glaslyn

As a light-hearted half day this cheerful little scramble in the heart of Snowdon's grand amphitheatre is hard to beat. A line of rounded slabs that give enjoyable clambering in a superb setting, Y Gribin is short in length but not on quality, being both better and considerably quieter than the nearby East Ridge of Crib Goch. It's a preferable alternative to the rather boring walkers' paths up Yr Wyddfa too, and might be shoehorned into a clockwise Snowdon Horseshoe (route 33). For a shorter trip the most aesthetic option is a return to Pen-y-Pass via the summit of Lliwedd. The sound and fairly grippy rock makes this an amenable damp weather route; it's also easy in descent.

NB Don't confuse this ridge with the Glyderau Gribin (route 31).

Llyn Llydaw, Y Gribin and Yr Wyddfa

APPROACH

Follow the Miners Track S from Pen-y-Pass, an easy gravel roadway that gradually curves rightwards, passing little Llyn Teryn to reach Llyn Llydaw in the embrace of the magnificent Snowdon Horseshoe (route 33). Crossing a causeway over the water, the Miners Track then follows the N shore past ruined mine workings. Some distance short of the head of the lake the track begins a steady ascent, passing a waterfall and soon meeting the foaming stream that cascades out of Glaslyn, the highest lake in the Horseshoe. The slabs of Y Gribin are now obvious on the left. Ford the stream at the outflow from Glaslyn (take care when the river's in spate) and begin scrambling straight away.

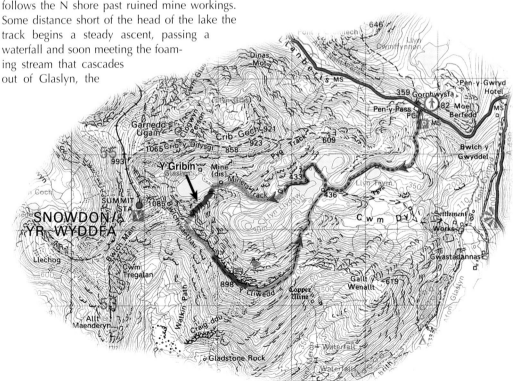

CLIMB

Y Gribin, grade 1

A path skirts right of the first crag but the route is too short as it is, and these clean lower rocks give scrambling as good as anything higher up. Above the entry slabs cross a level section past a big boulder to reach the steeper rock of the ridge proper. Now climb a series of little easy angled rock steps, following water worn grooves (streaming gutters in the rain) and helpful lines of handholds. The flanks on either side are loose and unpleasant, so stick with the rounded crest where the exact line can be varied depending how interesting you want to make it. Just as you're getting into the swing of things it's all over, the ridge opening onto a plateau-like neck. Climb SSW onto the broad saddle of Bwlch y Saethau. Turn left and scramble easily onto the summit of Lliwedd as for route 33.

DESCENT

See route 33.

Lliwedd and Llyn Llydaw from Crib Goch (Route 33)

Grade	250m Difficult
Distance	7km
Ascent	600m
Time	6½ hours
Start/finish	Pen-y-Pass pay and display car park (SH647556); this is expensive, and fills up quickly at weekends. If full, consider the tougher walk in from Nantgwynant via the Watkin Path and a scrambling descent of Y Gribin ridge (see route 36). Alternatively park further afield (Llanberis, say) and catch a bus.
Maps	OS Landranger (1:50000) 115; OS Explorer (1:25000) OL17; Harvey British Mountain Map (1:40000) Snowdonia
Accommodation	See route 33
Sleeping out	See route 33
Public transport	See route 33
Seasonal notes	Despite dank appearances Lliwedd doesn't take much drainage and decent winter conditions are rare. Ridge Route has a different persona in winter – for some unaccountable reason appearing as the route Cold Water Sandwich (240m IV). The grade assumes the unlikely scenario of true winter nick; a splatter of slush doesn't really count. It is exposed to the elements at any time of year, and wouldn't be hugely pleasant in the wet, even though it would be more amenable than most Lliwedd climbs.

Getting into the groove on pitch 4

Awesome situations, a variety of tricky pitches and a big traditional feel make this an experience to savour. Who cares if the only distinctively ridge-like section is a fraction of the total route length? Don't be misled by the relatively modest rating – in this case Difficult means just that, and calling Ridge Route the most beginner-friendly line on the crag really isn't saying much. The spiritual home of grand old-fashioned Welsh mountaineering, Lliwedd is the country's largest cliff, a sprawling sea of grey and green that makes a mockery of the notion of climbing wall-tidy grades. Essentials here include route-finding savvy, a helmet and a grade or two in hand; as well, of course, as a sense of adventure. Pipe and breeches are optional.

APPROACH

Follow route 36 on the Miners Track as far as Llyn Llydaw. (You could use a bike to save time on this bit.) Ahead, the leviathan scale of Lliwedd's north face becomes increasingly apparent. Dropping from the mountain's twin summits are the two main buttresses, East and West. Slanting Buttress is slightly further right, and from here looks like an insignificant adjunct to the main story. Visible from afar, two giant quartz Ss mark the start of Ridge Route.

Don't cross the Llydaw causeway, but stay left of the lake to follow a flagstone-paved path

that climbs towards Lliwedd's east shoulder. Continue on this to roughly the 600m contour, then split right to traverse the hillside over boggy patches. The path, such as it is, seems to fade in and out of existence at random, but the general gist is obvious. Now feeling dwarfed by the full expanse of the looming precipice, pass craggy hummocks to reach a scree slope beneath the baffling spread of the West Buttress. A rough path crosses the scree, then makes a rising traverse over steep vegetation and scrambly ground to the foot of Slanting Buttress. Its apparent insignificance was misleading; the scale of even this relatively minor wing is more Scottish than Snowdonian. Gear up on the scree, where the lower quartz S meets the ground.

CLIMB

Ridge Route, 250m Difficult

Pitch 1, 40m
Climb easy-angled rock just left of the quartz S. It's better than it looks from below, although the runners are well spaced. Belay from blocks on a little stance just below a grass ledge.

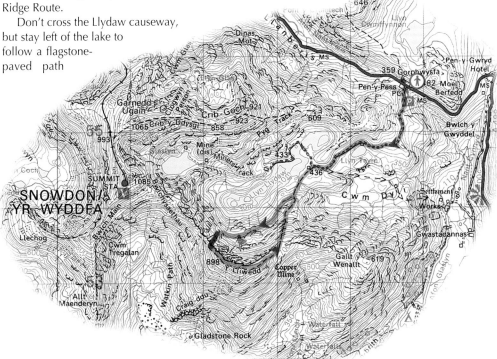

187

37 Ridge Route
A Slanting Buttress
B West Buttress
C East Buttress

Pitch 3, 35m
Climb the slab, moving slightly left to reach a generous grass floored alcove in the base of the left-hand corner (a possible alternative belay). Exit the alcove via an obvious line of weakness in its left wall, steep flakes leading to an awkward top-out. Cross the grass ledge above, and climb left over big blocks to reach a magnificent stance on the arete overlooking Slanting Gully. Above, steep lichenous ground doesn't invite a direct assault.

Pitch 2, 40m
More of the same; make towards a chunky steepening up high and slightly left. This is cleaved by two prominent deep corners. Belay on a ledge by a short slab, just below the right hand corner.

Llyn Llydaw from the ridge on pitch 5

The superb corner of pitch 7

Pitch 4, 12m

Sidle left to enter a steep shiny groove above a lot of empty air. Hard at first, it soon eases into a slabby gangway; exit this right to an even more atmospheric stance on the arete.

Pitch 5, 45m

Ahead is a short wall split into three parallel sloping grooves. The middle one is yours, and proves unexpectedly troublesome. Footing is tricky, and positive holds notable by their scarcity; soloists and wet weather climbers might have an unhappy moment here. It's possible to belay on a ledge just above the groove, but careful rope work permits another 35m of climbing with minimal drag. Move right onto the extremely exposed arete, and pick gingerly up its stacked flakes (not all entirely immobile) to a tremendous photogenic climax on a short level crest. Belay where the ridge meets the mountainside.

Pitch 6, 28m

This needs a steady head. Move right along a short scrappy ledge, then climb an excitingly steep blocky quartz-streaked section to reach a reassuring belay ledge at the foot of a pronounced slabby corner.

Pitch 7, 20m

Bridge up the corner, with more interest and excitement than might have been anticipated. Once a few metres above a spiked block move right awkwardly to win a spacious ledge. By now you may be questioning Ridge Route's decidedly traditional grade – but be a good sport.

Pitch 8, 30m

Above, slabby ground leads up to a square-cut overhang, which you'll pass on the left. Follow the slabs, then move left around a little rib to enter a groove, the continuation of the corner of pitch 7. This leads easily to level ground on Lliwedd's summit ridge.

DESCENT

A pleasant scrambly walk over Lliwedd's summit, as for route 33.

Route 38 – Nantlle Ridge

Grade	1 (easier, if you must)
Distance	13km
Ascent	1120m
Time	6½ hours
Start/finish	Rhyd-Ddu station (SH572525), or the pay and display car park next door on the A4085
Maps	OS Landranger (1:50000) 115; OS Explorer (1:25000) OL17; Harvey British Mountain Map (1:40000) Snowdonia
Accommodation	Snowdon Ranger Youth Hostel 0845 371 9659; Craflwyn bunkhouse, Nantgwynant (National Trust) 01766 510120; campsite in Dyffryn Nantlle; Snowdon Inn bunkhouse (owned by the Cwellyn Arms pub in Rhyd-Ddu, which also offers B&B accommodation) 01766 890321
Sleeping out	The lonely little cwms on either side of the main ridge would suit seekers of solitude, but access from above could be an effort.
Public transport	Regular buses from Caernarfon and Beddgelert to Rhyd-Ddu, including a Snowdon Sherpa service. Or for something a bit quirkier, try the Welsh Highland Railway, an Ifor the Engine-style narrow gauge tourist steam train that connects Caernarfon to Rhyd-Ddu, and is eventually promised to link up with Beddgelert and Porthmadog. Linear walkers might appreciate the Nantlle Ridge Taxi Service, which connects Talysarn at the Western end with Rhyd-Ddu in the east (01286 676767).
Seasonal notes	Low altitude and maritime position aren't generally the hallmarks of reliable winter hills, but in a rare snowy cold snap this would make a quality winter tramp spiced with the odd passage of scrambly grade I.

Y Garn (left) and Mynydd Mawr (Route 39) from Rhyd Ddu

THE CRAG-GIRT GRANDEUR of Snowdonia's giants is compressed into a small corner of the national park – along with most of the crowds. And now for something subtly different. The adjacent Nantlle hills feel very much a backwater, neglected by most; they have other charms too. A grassy stride along elegant curved aretes, the traverse of the main ridge linking all the summits in the range is one of the highlights of Welsh walking, with a rare sense of peace and spacious seaward views. Mildly scrambly moments are spread out along the way, and although pleasant enough they're unlikely to tax even the most nervous hillwalker.

Mynydd Drws-y-Coed (left) and Trum y Ddysgl from Y Garn

APPROACH

Cross the road and follow a marked path W over the valley flats, looping around a private house to cross the Afon Gwyrfai before following a track (signed) to the B4418. Leave the roadside straight away on another track heading SW, then branch off right on a little path that zigzags steeply up the E flank of Y Garn – the day's only unadulterated slog. Once the angle begins to relent bear right to reach the summit cairn on the lip of the N face.

RIDGE WALK

A broad grassy ridge now leads SSW towards Mynydd Drws-y-coed, which from this angle is an impressive shark's fin. The route up its sharp crest looks daunting from below, but resolves into an easy scramble. Paths skirt just left of the good stuff, but naturally it's better to stay right, on the edge of a very abrupt drop. Clamber over a rocky bump, then continue up a series of blocky, mossy steps – slippery when wet – passing close to a little detached pinnacle to reach the summit. Stay on the airy ridge to descend to a col, from where scrappy scrambling leads up to Trum y Ddysgl.

Here the ridge briefly changes mood, becoming a soft grassy whaleback above a sweeping concave slope. An easy descent W leads to an abrupt narrowing, where the cwms flanking either side of the mountain pinch tight to form an unusual green gangway – no real scrambling here, unfortunately. A gentle climb beside an old wall then gains the broad top of Mynydd Tal-y-mignedd, crowned with an odd square-cut obelisk. Cross boggy ground SSW before making an unpleasant steep descent on eroded ground to a low col. From here it's a respectable climb to the day's last summit, Craig Cwm Silyn. A wall runs into a tier of scrappy crags, perched scree and ample vegetation. Taken direct it might warrant a grade 2, and needs careful handling. There's an easier line just right of the wall. Easier still is to loop quite far right to avoid the scramble

Scrambling near the summit of Mynydd Drws-y-Coed

Moel Hebog from Craig Cwm Silyn

altogether; the various alternatives soon meet above the crag to continue up the northeast ridge. Beyond a short series of grassy 'pinnacles' (minimal scrambling opportunities) the path passes a boulder field to reach the stone-walled summit wind break. Keen walkers could continue SW over Carnedd Goch to the outlying Mynydd Graig Goch, but this only takes you further from your starting point.

DESCENT

The single drawback of this linear ridge walk now becomes apparent. If you haven't arranged transport from Nantlle back to Rhyd-Ddu then the best option is to retrace your steps. Climb back over Mynydd Tal-y-mignedd, cross the grassy gangway and climb steeply to reach the SW end of Trum y Ddysgl's summit ridge. To inject a bit of variation here turn hard right (care needed in mist) to descend the mountain's long rounded south-southeast ridge. This easy descent above the dense forestry of Cwm Du leads to the rugged pass of Bwlch-y-ddwy-elor. From here the route to Rhyd-Ddu descends through pine woods on a series of tracks, sometimes boggy, then crosses open hillside below Mynydd Drws-y-coed and Y Garn to rejoin the approach route.

Route 39 – Sentries' Ridge, Mynydd Mawr

Yr Aran from the lower pinnacles

Grade	3
Distance	6.5km
Ascent	500m
Time	4 hours
Start/finish	Rhyd-Ddu station (SH572525), or the pay and display car park next door on the A4085
Maps	OS Landranger (1:50000) 115; OS Explorer (1:25000) OL17; Harvey British Mountain Map (1:40000) Snowdonia
Accommodation	See route 38
Sleeping out	There's nowhere suitable, and nothing to be gained from it.
Public transport	See route 38
Seasonal notes	South-facing and low, this would need an exceptionally cold and snowy spell to come into winter nick; grade III seems likely.

THE HARDEST – many would say the best – of the grade 3 routes described in this book, Sentries' Ridge has the scale and atmosphere of a true classic. The only popular line on the tremendous tottering precipice of Craig y Bera, it illustrates perfectly the futility of trying to define scrambling and climbing as distinct activities, and the limits of accurate grading. Though there are few technical moves the exposure is awesome, and the rock suspiciously wobbly throughout the route's considerable length. Sentries' Ridge is certainly more serious than many Moderate and Difficult climbs, and can only sensibly be recommended to competent mountaineers. Caveats aside, it is terrific. The name strictly refers only to the lower third of the route as climbed in 1910, but the upper sections flow naturally on from this.

APPROACH

Walk N through Rhyd-Ddu village, turning left past the Cwellyn Arms on the road signed for Nantlle. At the edge of the village turn right onto a forestry track. Follow this through the pines for a little over 1km; when above the SE end of Llyn Cwellyn take a waymarked footpath on the left. This ascends through an old clear-felled area to the forest boundary fence at Bwlch y Moch

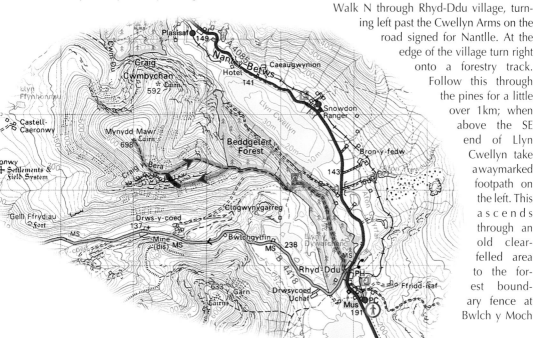

(not named on 1:50000 map); the view of Snowdon's quiet side is tremendous from here. Cross a ladder stile and follow a grassy ascent path alongside the forest fence. Climb another stile to reach the highest corner of the woods on a shoulder of Mynydd Mawr's broad east ridge.

Leave the main trail here, turning left onto a faint traverse route across the steep grass of the mountain's southern flank, staying just above a fence line. The bristling pinnacles of Craig y Bera soon hove into view. The distinctive chunky tower is part of Pinnacle Ridge, a rarely climbed Diff – Sentries' Ridge is nearer and less prominent. Cross a double stile over a parallel fence and wall, then pick across the swathes of scree below the crag that attest to its unfortunate instability. Sentries' Ridge is the second buttress along, bounded on both sides by scree gullies and with its base set higher than that of the adjacent Pinnacle Ridge. Its heather and broken rocks look inauspicious from below, but things soon improve higher up.

CLIMB

Sentries' Ridge, c250m, grade 3

Skirt right of the sheer lowest wall to follow a line of wear up heather and scrappy rock steps, bearing right of a slabby section and trending back left above it to reach the base of a marked steepening. It may be worth roping up here. Climb a short vague groove to reach the airy ridge crest. Pick along the pinnacles, handling the rock with care, to reach a more massive and arresting gendarme straddling the crest – this is the technical crux. Climb a little cracked slab to reach a sharp spike beneath the mossy top of the gendarme. A sling around this spike protects a reachy move rightwards across the right flank, with a long step onto a block in a tight notch beyond. Pop over the next easy pinnacle to reach the heather slopes that mark the top of the lower ridge.

The continuation ridge is slightly offset, a soaring rock crest with a perpendicular left face and a heathery depression running along its right side. It is possible to walk all the way up this depression,

On the arresting gendarme

(Left) Ascending the soaring crest

but that'd be a waste of a good scramble. Far better is to stick to the crest with little difficulty but a lot of exposure, only feinting right to avoid the forbidding final few metres. At a little col beyond the soaring crest step right to regain easier rock, soon reaching another notch in the ridge with a deep hole down to its right.

The steep rock mass above the notch is as intimidating as it looks. It could be avoided on the right but is best taken direct with care. The holds are good, but not all of them are attached, and it's a long way to fall. The subsequent section is climbed via a vague left-slanting groove. Three squat rubbly-looking gendarmes are all that remain. Skirt left of the unstable first two to tackle the final one head-on. The ridge now merges into the slopes above Craig y Bera.

Gain the main path on Mynydd Mawr's east ridge, first heading W along the edge of the crags, then curving N up the grassy ridge to reach the mountain's domed summit. With a sweeping panorama over the sea, the Lleyn Peninsular, Snowdon, the Moelwynion and Nantlle hills, this is a good place to take a break.

DESCENT

Return down the ridge path, continuing E past the top of Craig y Bera. A steep grassy descent at the end of the ridge brings you back to the forest edge and the Rhyd-Ddu path. It's worth stopping for a fine ale at the olde worlde Cwellyn Arms en route.

The pinnacles of Craig y Bera from Llechog (Snowdon)

Grade	160m Severe
Distance	7km
Ascent	550m
Time	5½ hours
Start/finish	End of the Cwm Nantcol road close to Maes y Garnedd farm – pay a modest parking fee at the farmhouse (SH642270)
Maps	OS Landranger (1:50000) 124; OS Explorer (1:25000) OL18; Harvey Superwalker (1:25000) Rhinogs
Accommodation	Kings Youth Hostel, near Dolgellau 0845 371 9327; campsite in lower Cwm Nantcol
Sleeping out	The crinkled Rhinogau could have been made with the camp-climb combination in mind. The flat – if slightly soggy – plot on the north bank of Llyn Hywel is a well-known and atmospheric site, and ideally placed for the ridge. There are many more original options too.
Public transport	A bus or train will get you to Llanbedr on the coastal strip at the mouth of Cwm Nantcol; from there you're on your own, and it's a 7km walk-in to the start of the route described.
Seasonal notes	Although it must happen occasionally, this south-facing arete is unlikely to offer reliable winter climbing; avoid the main difficulties and you'd have a snowy scramble of about grade II.

The South Ridge seen in profile from Llyn Hywel

THE RHINOGAU (also known as 'Rhinogydd' in Welsh; usually anglicised to Rhinogs) are the bull terrier of Snowdonian mountain groups – small in stature, but 'rruff'. This rugged sprawl is as untamed as anywhere south of Galloway. Indeed, the heather-choked hollows and crazily tiered outcrops of the impenetrable interior give the hills a certain Caledonian character, backed by sweeping views over a glinting sea to a frieze of distant peaks. For lovers of obscure facts (to say nothing of obscure routes) Rhinog Fach's South Ridge is the only gritstone climb in this book. But Stanage this ain't; in the Rhinogau crowds are conspicuous only by their absence. The route is discontinuous and escapable, but fun in detail and attractive for its esoteric novelty. What's more it tops out on a fine remote summit at the heart of this little Welsh wilderness.

On the steep rib of pitch 3

Llyn Hywel, Y Llethr and distant Cadair Idris (Route 41) from the top of pitch 4

APPROACH

Maes y garnedd farm, at the start of this route, was the family estate of John Jones, a bigwig in the English Civil War's military and political circles and a signatory to the death warrant of Charles I. The surging stream of events has moved on since, leaving beautiful Cwm Nantcol as a quiet backwater. From the layby at the road-end a sign points to a path laid with flagstones, leading NE through rough boggy pastures at the head of the valley. Follow this gradually uphill beneath rambling little outcrops towards the impressively rugged Bwlch Drws Ardudwy, an historic through-route. As you enter the jaws of the pass the path descends slightly towards a boggy level; branch right here, crossing a stream and a stile over a drystone wall. Now take a rougher path uphill through heather and rocks, following a shallow valley S where a stream can be heard murmuring beneath the scree. Branch left at a junction,

ascending under the rambling chaos of Rhinog Fach to reach Llyn Hywel, a haunt, it was once claimed, of one-eyed fish.

Rhinog Fach's stepped South Ridge can now be seen on the hillside above, running from a swathe of scree to the mountain's summit. Pick carefully up heather and scree to the foot of the ridge; bear right to miss out the lowest tottery-looking rib, and start climbing at a little steep wall just beyond.

CLIMB

South Ridge, 160m Severe

It's possible to make a scrambling ascent of the South Ridge, avoiding any tricky bits – or even the entire climb – by slinking left onto scree and heather at opportune moments. But why?

Pitch 1, 15m

Ascend the wall to the broad ridge crest, continuing up heather to reach the next clean rock.

Pitch 2, 15m
Climb to a block, the front face of which is cleft by a zigzag crack; go up this (or cop out to the right) then continue up a further rock step to a good belay ledge.

Pitch 3, 15m
Climb a steep rib (care with gear) to reach a small ledge; step up and left to belay at a more spacious stance.

Pitch 4, 45m
Scramble fairly easily up the crest on heathery ledges and short rock steps to reach a level terrace below a substantial rock wall that overlooks a gully on the right flank of the ridge.

Pitch 5, 20m
The crux is hard and exposed; a pair of ropes is invaluable. Climb a short tricky groove to a good runner and holds just below a little overhang. Move right, crossing a grass patch to reach a big square-cut block above a by-now-formidable drop – a very long sling around this gives welcome reassurance. Step nervously onto the top of the block. Take time to place another runner here (a medium cam is useful); it's the last easily-found protection. Now commit to the steep wall just right of the arete, with some loose holds and much excitement. Pull with relief onto a flat ledge on top, and a sound thread belay.

Pitch 6, 50m
Another long scramble up the crest brings you to within a short stumble of the summit.

On a clear afternoon the view spans much of Snowdonia, from Cadair Idris and the Arans in the south to the desolate grass humps eastward and the crowded northern skyline...and let's not forget Trawsfynydd nuclear power station. There's a sense of being at the hub of it all, yet subtly removed – and that's the magic of the Rhinogau.

DESCENT

Hardy folk could head N, making a direct descent to Bwlch Drws Ardudwy and a long rough ascent over Rhinog Fawr. However this may seem a bit keen with a bag full of gear. A descent SSE parallel to the South Ridge soon runs into nasty scree. It's more canny to drop E along a wall before turning S beside another one to reach a low col above Llyn Hywel. Now cut back NNW, skirting the top of a smooth grassy slab to meet the lake shore before returning to Cwm Nantcol the way you came.

Llyn Hywel from the tremendously airy pitch 5

Moody Cyfrwy Arete from the north

Grade	200m Difficult
Distance	7km
Ascent	800m
Time	5½ hours
Start/finish	Pay and display car park on the minor road that runs from Dolgellau along the northern foot of the mountain (SH697152)
Maps	OS Landranger (1:50000) 124; OS Explorer (1:25000) OL23
Accommodation	Braich Goch bunkhouse and Inn, Corris – the best backpacking accommodation around (though a 20min drive from the north side of Cadair) 01654 761229 www.braichgoch.co.uk Kings Youth Hostel, near Dolgellau 0845 371 9327; bunkhouses exist more locally, but availability is sporadic. There are two rustic campsites near the start of the walk, but since the only facilities are at the National Park car park, it doesn't seem worth paying to camp.
Sleeping out	The neighbourhood of Llyn y Gadair is the obvious wild camp site – and very impressive it'd be too, with a grandstand view of the morning light seeping down the Arete. The pokey hut on the summit of Penygadair is a high level alternative if you don't mind risking the legend that anyone who spends the night on Cadair's slopes will descend either a bard or a basket case.
Public transport	There'll be a fair walk or a hitchhike, whichever transport option you take. The nearest train station is Morfa Mawddach on the coastal line connecting Machynlleth, Barmouth and Porthmadog. Abergwynant on the A493 down in the Mawddach valley is the nearest bus stop; Dolgellau itself isn't much further.
Seasonal notes	The route is reasonably high by Welsh standards, and has plenty of north in its aspect – but that nearby sea is not liable to improve the winter climbing prospects. A true winter ascent of Table Direct might be unlikely, but given a good snowfall there's no reason not to have a look at Cyfrwy Arete itself, which is grade II if you skirt the main difficulties.

CADAIR IDRIS LOOMS domineeringly over a tableau of woods, pastures and the sandy Mawddach estuary – a softer setting than the northern Snowdonian valleys, and arguably the most postcard-pretty part of the national park. Still, Cadair itself is all mountain, with a stern precipitousness to equal anything in the country. Cyfrwy Arete lives up to the grand *ambience* of this seat of legendary giants – a mountaineering route par excellence, exposed but never desperate. A hearty starter up Table Direct gives you roughly 200m of top-quality climbing in total. Traditionally this optional start has been graded VDiff, while the continuation up Cyfrwy Arete is considered Moderate. There's certainly a difference in ambience between the sweeping lower walls and the more broken upper ridge, but move for move the climbing is of a

pretty consistent standard. Difficult seems a fair grade for both.

APPROACH

From the car park walk briefly SW along the minor road, then turn left on a track past Ty-nant farmhouse (bunkhouse accommodation occasionally available). This is the popular Pony Path, perhaps the easiest plod to the main summit Penygadair. The path starts uphill along a wooded stream bank before bearing right over meadows, climbing quite steeply to reach a gate through a drystone wall. Beyond the gate leave the Pony Track, heading diagonally leftwards uphill, picking out a path that climbs quite gently through grassy hummocks. Ahead Cyfrwy Arete looks increasingly imposing, a toothed crest buttressing the eastern end of a great broken wall of crags. On reaching a rubbly moraine, head roughly E, then climb a grassy rib SE to reach the shore of Llyn y Gadair, nested in its rugged cirque. Now climb unstable scree, making towards the base of the huge conical tower at the foot of Cyfrwy Arete – this is Table Buttress, home to Table Direct. Cyfrwy Arete proper starts above the steep lower walls of Table Buttress; the quickest approach to it skirts left up broken ground before moving back right on a terrace. But unless pushed for time it'd be a wasted opportunity not to start direct.

CLIMB

Table Direct, 50m Difficult

'Table Direct' is doubly a misnomer since the line dodges the issue of the steep upper walls and doesn't even lead all the way to the Table – which is actually found some way higher up Cyfrwy Arete; nevertheless it's a superb few pitches. Although it looks steep from a distance – and certainly feels it – the route is endowed with generous holds, and well suited to climbing in big boots if that's your thing. Make towards the bottom right of Table Buttress. Two pinnacled ribs cut down slightly lower than the main crag; climb scrappy ground between these to reach a well-trodden ledge on the left beside a square-cut block that leans against the face.

The groovy corner pitch on Table Direct

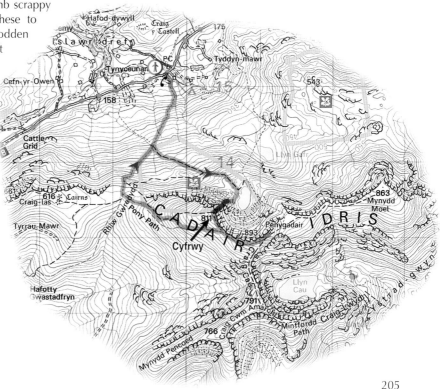

Descending from The Table

Pitch 1, 25m

Starting immediately right of the leaning block, climb a short steep corner (which seeps after rain), then bear easily right along an ascending series of little platforms. Once these fade into greenery head straight up a wall just left of an obvious groove; it looks quite blank, but excellent holds are hiding. Belay on a spacious ledge directly below a defined corner.

Pitch 2, 15m

Climb this corner in spectacular fashion; blocks and spikes provide convenient holds and runners. At the top of the corner move carefully over poised blocks to belay on an airy little ledge.

Pitch 3, 10m

Move to the right end of the ledge overlooking a deep green gully. Climb questionable flakes on the crest to reach a terrace at the foot of a final steep tier.

Ignoring this upper wall, walk about 10m down the mucky ledge to reach a gearing-up spot at the base of Cyfrwy Arete, where the initials CA are scratched unnecessarily into a rock.

CLIMB

Cyfrwy Arete, 150m Difficult

Pitch 1, 40m

Climb a clean rib above the stance – quite tricky to start – then move slightly right to enter and ascend an easy corner, leading to the pinnacled arete. Consider belaying here if rope drag is an issue. Thread a way up the crest (some wobbly spikes) to reach the dramatic tilted top of the Table, a detached mini-summit separated from the main ridge by a breezy gap.

Pitch 2, 15m

Downclimb into the gap from the far right end of the Table; easier than it looks. A small nut at the lip of the downclimb protects the second in descent, and can be removed from the security of jugs below. If the second isn't confident it may be wise

41 Table Direct and Cyfrwy Arête
A Table Buttress
B Cyfrwy Arête upper section

CONTINUATION

Turn left, walking around the rim of the cwm to rejoin the well-scuffed Pony Path. From here it'd be daft not to make the short ascent to the summit of Penygadair, marked by a substantial cairn and a historic old shelter.

DESCENT

The obvious circuit down the Fox's Path to Llyn y Gadair looks tempting on paper, but the section above the lake is relentlessly steep and horribly eroded. For once being sensible will win you friends; stick with the Pony Path all the way back down. First returning to the Cyfrwy-Penygadair saddle the route then cuts over the S slopes of Cyfrwy to reach the low col of Rhiw Gwerdydd. From here it drops N down a little series of zig-zags, before bearing right over Cadair's lower slopes to regain the road by Ty-nant farm.

Llyn y Gadair from the upper ridge

to split this pitch, belaying just below the down-climb. Briefly descend a grubby gully on the left side of the gap to gain an obvious line of weakness that leads up and left to a big spike belay.

Pitch 3, 15m
This pitch is as demanding as anything on Table Direct, but it can be avoided using insecure grassy ground on the left. Climb the steep wall directly above the big spike; holds and runners do materialise but the exposure is considerable. Gain a small ledge at 10m, then climb a further 5m to a bigger ledge and block belay.

Pitch 4, 20m
Easy scrambling up the crest leads to a steep triangular wall. A left-leaning gangway is the obvious way to go, requiring a couple of medium wires and a can-do attitude. Above is another block belay.

Scramble, 60m
From here it's moving together or unroped scrambling ground, with some wonderfully airy ridge-crest positions. The ridge gradually eases into scrappy grass and then quite suddenly you're on top of Cyfrwy.

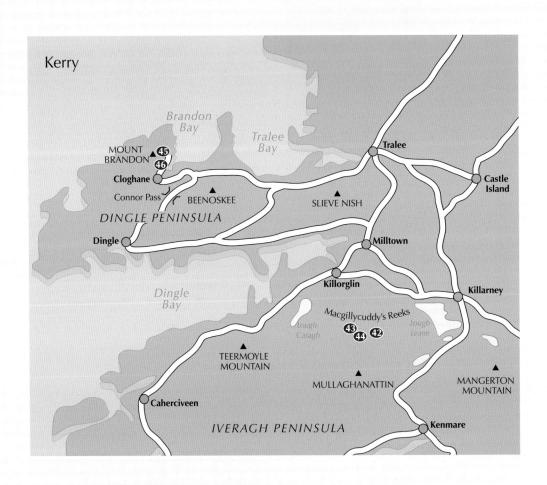

Kerry

Brandon
Bay

Tralee
Bay

MOUNT
BRANDON ▲ 45
46

Cloghane

Connor Pass

BEENOSKEE

DINGLE PENINSULA

SLIEVE NISH

Tralee

Castle
Island

Dingle

Milltown

Killorglin

Dingle
Bay

Macgillycuddy's Reeks

Lough
Caragh

43
44 42

Lough
Leane

Killarney

TEERMOYLE
MOUNTAIN

MULLAGHANATTIN

MANGERTON
MOUNTAIN

Caherciveen

IVERAGH PENINSULA

Kenmare

IRELAND

Ireland's most interesting mountains are scattered along its coastal fringes. From the ragged wastes of Connemara to the imposing architecture of Kerry's sandstone giants, these are some of the grandest landscapes to feature in this book. Lovers of wild scenery and hard walking will be in their element; the hills are generally emptier than those of England and Wales, with clear paths and amenities much thinner on the ground. It feels like a scaled-down Scottish Highlands, only warmer. These are distinctly maritime mountains; whether it's the tang of a salty sea breeze, the lash of rain or the squelch of bog, water is the dominant element. Geology and the moist temperate weather conspire to rob Ireland of the expanses of quality mountain rock climbing found in Snowdonia or the Lakes; big inland crags here are generally broken and vegetated. Nevertheless the mountaineering routes detailed in this book are of a scale and quality to match the best elsewhere, their challenge only increased by occasional loose rock, greenery and a faint air of neglect.

Carrauntoohil NE face (Route 44) and Stumpa (Route 43) from Lough Gouragh   209

Route 42 – MacGillycuddy's Reeks Ridge Traverse

Grade	2 as described (easier options are available)
Distance	14km (if starting from Alohart)
Ascent	1650m (if starting from Alohart)
Time	7 hours
Start	The quieter option is from the end of the minor road at Alohart (V849872) – parking is limited, so please don't block the farmer's gates. The much busier alternative is the big car park at the cheesy tourist trap of Kate Kearney's Cottage (V881888) which adds some ascent and distance to the day.
Finish	Gate where the 'Hydro Road' track meets the Glencar to Killorglin road (V772871); parking is difficult here, but there is a car park 1km SW along the tarmac road.
Maps	Harvey Superwalker (1:30000) MacGillycuddy's Reeks is the best and clearest; OSI Discovery (1:50000) sheet 78 will do, though it lacks important details such as cliffs, paths and some major hill names. It is also worth noting the OSI's inconsistent dual use of Gaelic and Anglicised place names, which confusingly try to say both 'potato' and 'potahto' at the same time. A recent addition is the OSI Leisure map (1:25000) to MacGillycuddy's Reeks, printed on waterproof paper.
Accommodation	Several campsites and hostels in Killarney including Killarney International Hostel (IYHA) 00 353 (0)64 31240; Black Valley hostel (IYHA) 00 353 (0)64 34712 – remote but stunning location; the Climber's Inn, Glencar 00 353 (0)66 9760101; self-catering holiday cottage in Alohart owned by Mary and Mike O'Connor 00 353 (0)86 3739513
Sleeping out	The many idyllic coums and loughs sheltered beneath the ridge provide more wild camping opportunities than you can shake a tent pole at.

Cruach Mhor (left), Carrauntoohil and Beenkeragh from Cnoc na Bhraca

Public transport	Not great hereabouts. Killarney to Killorglin buses ply the N72; alight at Beaufort and walk several km into the Gap of Dunloe to reach the E end of the ridge. As this is a linear route drivers either need to leave a car at each end before starting, or arrange an evening pick up. Alternatively chance your arm hitching, a good option in laid-back Kerry – or it would be if there were more traffic.
Seasonal notes	Given the Reeks' southerly latitude and exposure to balmy Atlantic winds, cold snaps here rarely last long enough to create névé, ice and frozen turf. That said, a fresh heavy snowfall would be sufficient to give this traverse an Alpine feel. In decent conditions the scrambling skyline route between Cruach Mhor and Cnoc na Peiste must be at least grade I/II.

IRELAND'S HIGHEST MOUNTAINS cluster in a tight huddle, as distinctive and dramatic a range as any in these islands. The contrast between this great green wall and the rolling farmland at its northern foot is striking; it's almost as if a cutting of high Kintail had been transplanted into the soft Kerry soil. Although days start and finish in the rich pastures of this gentle southerly clime, the interior feels very West Highlands. Indeed, a full traverse of the main ridge is the best walk of its type described in this book, and compares favourably with Scottish equivalents. Multiple Munro-sized summits, narrow grassy crests and a short burst of superb easy scrambling make this a real treat for hillwalking connoisseurs. If it were Snowdonia or the Lakes the paths would be mobbed, but in the Reeks midweek your only company is likely to be on top of Carrauntoohil.

APPROACH

Walking the route east to west means the best bits of scrambling are done in ascent. Ballagh Pass is your first objective, gained either by a stony zigzagging track up its E flank starting from the road S of Kate Kearney's in the Gap of Dunloe, or via a less obvious route from Alohart to the W of the pass. As the latter is slightly shorter it is described here.

From the end of the single track road head E through one gate and then another, before following a sketchy path leftwards along the

The Big Gun from Cruach Mhor

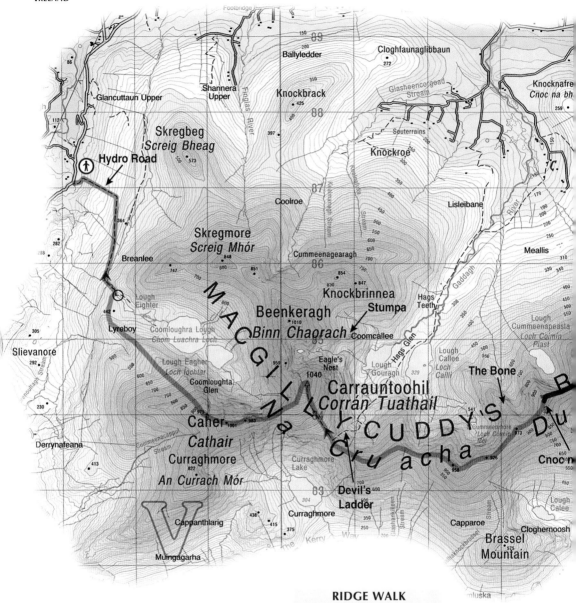

RIDGE WALK

fence line separating the valley pastures from the rough common grazing of the hill. This bisects an old track at approximately V855873, which ascends onto the pass. Routes from either side of the pass meet on the broad and more or less pathless peat hags up on top; head S to pick up a steep well-trodden line up heathery slopes onto the summit of Cnoc na Bhráca. If you spot a contouring path at about the 550m mark then give it a miss; it's not the easier option it purports to be.

From Cnoc na Bhráca cross a subsidiary peak to a saddle (spot height 635m on the Harvey map) which bounds the head of a tight rocky coum dropping towards Alohart. This is a more direct and brutal way onto the Reeks ridge. The rough path then continues up the long E ridge of Cruach Mhor, first of many Munro-sized summits to come; some limited scrambling can be contrived by sticking religiously to the crest. As you climb, the toothed arete linking Cruach Mhor to The Big Gun begins to look very promising.

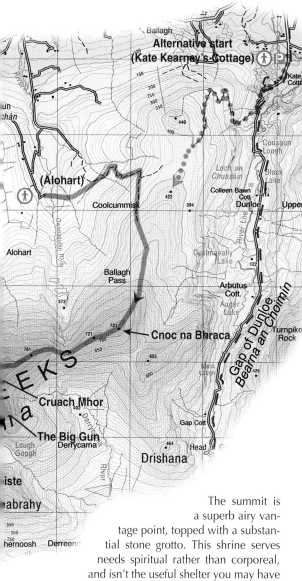

where a series of slightly friable slabby steps above big drops can be a touch dicey in high wind. The well-named Big Gun is the rockiest major peak in the range. Descend the short steep SW ridge, scrambly and loose in places, avoiding the shallow gully just right of the crest. From the next col the ridge onward to Cnoc na Peiste is a rising series of rocky steps. It is quite exposed, giving short bursts of scrambling if you stick to the crest; an inferior easier path stays on the left flank.

Cnoc na Peiste to Carrauntoohil

That's the scrambling done with. Beyond the fine vantage of Cnoc na Peiste it's grassy striding almost all the way and speedy progress can be made. The next few peaks are quite similar in character, but as you're hoofing it along a narrow turfy ridge above dramatically steep faces, with huge views over hills, dales and sea, then what's not to like? At Maolán Bui a get-out option down the NW ridge The Bone might appeal in poor weather, or when the clear blue loughs below are too inviting to resist. If you're made of sterner stuff continue over a minor bump to Cnoc an Chuillinn, from where a steep descent leads to a lower saddle-shaped hill. Drop down the far end of this to the major col at the top of the hellish Devil's Ladder, the eroded scree chute on one of the popular walks up Carrauntoohil (see route 43), which now looms above.

Join the stony tourist track for an unmitigated slog to the cross-crowned monarch of Ireland. It is a genuinely majestic mountain, and this is pretty much its only pedestrian approach (a fact worth bearing in mind in descent).

DESCENT

Carrauntoohil

Note that there are no safe descents from Carrauntoohil's summit from N through E to SE, as this way lies a big cliff. If you're stubborn enough to try returning to Alohart under your own steam it'd be possible to reverse route 43 along the scrambly NW ridge to Beenkeragh, from where a long gruelling descent over Knockbrinnea would eventually get you home. It's customary

The summit is a superb airy vantage point, topped with a substantial stone grotto. This shrine serves needs spiritual rather than corporeal, and isn't the useful shelter you may have hoped for from a distance. It does have one use for the secularist, however, acting as a prominent landmark from which to gauge your progress (or lack thereof) throughout the day.

Cruach Mhor–Big Gun–Cnoc na Peiste, grade 2

Head S onto the narrow block-heaped crest, which soon breaks into a row of shattered little pinnacles. A path slinks along the right flank missing most of the scrambling (grade 1). Going direct is much more engaging; just pick a line weaving through or clambering over the teeth, and test every hold for looseness. Things get more interesting as you approach The Big Gun, to complete the Reeks as a linear route, however, which means giving Beenkeragh a miss and descending on a path around the head of cavernous Coomloughra instead; in poor visibility the Kerry Mountain Rescue Team advise following a magnetic bearing of 230° for about 50m from the summit cross, and then 195° for roughly another 200m. As you lose height the ground pinches in to form an unmistakeable narrow ridge.

From a small col the onward route over the shark's fin of Caher looks imposing, but unfortunately the traverse of Ireland's third highest peak turns out to be a sheep in wolf's clothing. There's no real scrambling but the position above a huge rambling face is magnificent. From the main summit continue to the smaller West Top.

FINAL DESCENT

A clear path descends the NW shoulder, steep and rocky at first and soggy lower down. Height loss is rapid and you'll soon be hopping the bogs to Lough Iochtair (OSI call it Lough Eighter) in the mouth of Coomloughra Glen (aka Coomloughta Glen); bear a little left to avoid the worst of it before looping back to the lake's outflow. Here, pick up a 4WD track known as the Hydro Road. This cuts N across the lower slopes of Cnoc Iochtair (not even named on the OSI's 1:50000 map), and then after just over 1km swings left and descends steeply to the public road not far NE of Lough Acoose. Now you've just got to get home again – with luck you'll have thought this through beforehand.

Cruach Mhor (left) and The Big Gun from Cnoc na Peiste

Grade	Difficult (easier variations are possible)
Distance	11km
Ascent	1050m
Time	7 hours
Start/finish	Cronin's Yard paying car park (V836873) or the nearby car park at Lislebane (V827873)
Maps	See route 42
Accommodation	See route 42
Sleeping out	There are excellent pitches by the shore of Lough Gouragh, and higher up the coum beneath Carrauntoohil's NE face.
Public transport	Killarney to Killorglin buses stop at Beaufort on the N72, about 8km from either start point.
Seasonal notes	This being subtropical Kerry, Stumpa an tSaimh is probably too low ever to offer genuine winter climbing. However, the lofty spine between Beenkeragh and Carrauntoohil would be fantastic under snow – grade I seems a fair guesstimate. The sandstone can be pretty slippery when wet, and the Gaddagh River is sometimes hard to cross safely in spate; save this one for a dry day.

Stumpa looking sinister above Lough Gouragh

THE PEAKS flanking the western side of Hag's Glen are the most impressive in Kerry – and that's no faint praise. Enclosing the ice-gouged hanging corrie of Cummeeneighter (not named on the maps) is a ragged cirque, starting low down with the remarkable jutting peak of Stumpa an tSaimh ('stump of sorrel'). Above 'Stumpa', a pinnacled crest leads to the lofty dome of Beenkeragh, the country's second highest summit; from here another rocky ridge sweeps on around the head of the coum to Carrauntoohil itself, a pyramid point crowning a rambling Alpine-scale face with few equals in the British Isles. Following the skyline gives Ireland's best and longest scramble; an optional direct start up the menacing Stumpa nudges the grade into easy rock climbing, adding a mountaineering flavour to the day. Whether or not you accept this challenge, here's a route to savour.

NB If you're discussing plans with other climbers, or locations with the mountain rescue, it's worth noting a naming ambiguity. Stumpa an tSaimh is often erroneously referred to as the Hag's Tooth. Though Stumpa may suit its misnomer admirably, the real Hag's Tooth is actually a prominent crag a little down the

valley. As if to pile on more layers of confusion, the maps label a smaller crag even further down as the Hag's Teeth. In fact the true Hag's Teeth are the pinnacles on the ridge linking Stumpa to Beenkeragh; this ridge might be commonly (and correctly) referred to as the Hag's Tooth Ridge, but I've declined to do so in case it compounds the confusion.

APPROACH

From the Lislebane car park follow the obvious stony 4WD track up Hags Glen. The alternative path from Cronin's Yard is signed for Carrauntoohil; after just over 1km this route fords the Gaddagh River to join the Lislebane track. Another ford is reached 2km from Lislebane. Branch right just before this river crossing, taking a sketchy path

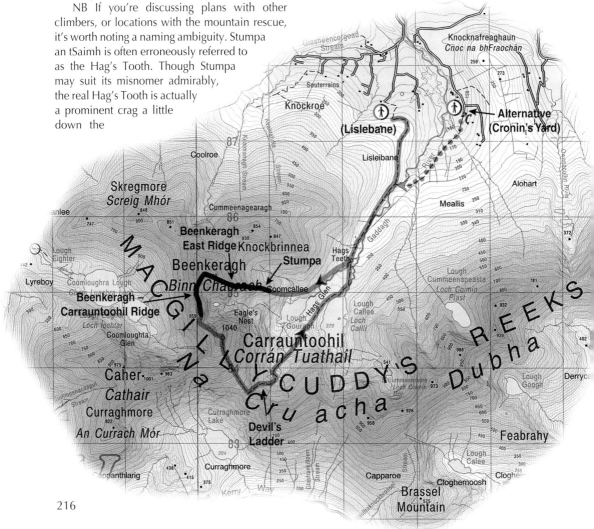

along the W side of the stream draining Lough Gouragh. Ahead, Carrauntoohil emphatically dominates the glen, while the brooding presence of Stumpa on the right adds an air of melodrama – fear not, the direct route isn't as monstrous as it looks from below. The path makes a rising traverse between mucky crag tiers above the lough, heading for the NE face of Carrauntoohil (see route 44). Stay with it only long enough to reach a shallow scree-filled gully that cuts up through the crags towards the base of Stumpa.

NON-CLIMBING ALTERNATIVE

The most enjoyable rope-free option for those avoiding the direct route up Stumpa is to enter this gully briefly, and then move right along an obvious grassy terrace; from here climb ledges and craggy walls that provide excellent (avoidable) scrambling pitches. Now outflank Stumpa on bouldery slopes to its right; seen from this angle it turns out to be an extended crest rather than the sheer tower it appeared from below. Surprisingly, the highest point can actually be gained with nothing harder than a bit of scrappy scrambling – a well-scuffed grassy gully is the key, and also constitutes the only safe descent. Once behind Stumpa, the East Ridge of Beenkeragh is easily reached at a little col.

CLIMB

Stumpa an tSaimh, Difficult

Although technically straightforward this is every inch a mountain route, with copious loose rock and a general air of seriousness; it is best done in four or five fairly short pitches, and is not suitable for beginners at the grade.

Climbers should ascend the scree gully to reach a vague Y-shaped junction. Move about 10m left here, then climb the rambling go-anywhere ground below the base of the pinnacle proper, weaving up a succession of rock tiers and grass ledges. It's a fairly mild scramble at first, but as the rocks get steeper and more continuous most people will appreciate a rope. You're aiming for the jutting serrated prow that guards the obvious crest – the base of this can be reached in one long pitch, although rope drag and the possibility of the rope knocking stones onto the second might mean you prefer to do it in two; there are several potential belay ledges.

Starting up Stumpa

- **A** Stumpa an tSaimh
- **B** Lower Tiers
- **C** Access Gully
- **D** Walkers' route bypassing Stumpa an tSaimh

Stay left of the prow, climbing steps and ledges to enter a corner; carry on up this until it's possible to swing right onto a little hanging slab, and so gain the grassy crest above the prow. A steep exposed wall bars onward progress; climb it direct on good holds, with a high step-up to reach the next grassy crest – a good place to belay. Scrappy scrambling leads to another steep impasse; from the right, step left onto a ledge, then make a hard airy move onto a sharp crest that seems to consist entirely of wobbly flakes. It's worth setting up a belay straight away to best safeguard your second on the hard bit. Stumpa's summit is now visible, and won by an easy pitch of grassy scrambling.

It's possible to descend the far side of the pinnacle and then cross the top of a drunkenly tilted slab to reach Beenkeragh's East Ridge, but the first few metres are dangerously shattered; better to descend the short grassy gully on the N flank, then regain the crest at the little col mentioned above.

CLIMB

Beenkeragh East Ridge, grade 2

The grade assumes you take a fairly direct line, but with no heroics – it's possible to make things easier or a lot harder by weaving around.

A series of short rock steps and little level crests, the ridge beyond the col offers some lovely scrambling on rough sandstone (though look out for the occasional wobbly bit, as ever with the Kerry mountains). The difficulties can mostly be skirted, but really needn't be. After a while the ridge crest splits into two roughly parallel lines of buttresses, the right side sporting an impressive tiered pinnacle that can be climbed from behind with care. Either of these rows can be scrambled; taken direct some of the bigger buttresses are hard enough to be considered proper climbing. Most people seem content to plod up the scree slope between the buttresses to the point at which they re-merge; above this there's more enjoyable blocky scrambling. The difficulties gradually ease until you're just walking up the long rock-and-grass crest that leads eventually to the summit cairn of Beenkeragh.

CLIMB

Beenkeragh–Carrauntoohil ridge, grade 1

The onward route is a narrow ridge curving over two steep-sided minor summits, with plenty of optional scrambling. It's easy enough, but the position is dramatic. This also happens to be part of the famous Coomloughra horseshoe, a circuit over Beenkeragh, Carrauntoohil and Caher. Although this is a deservedly popular walk it isn't described in detail in this book. The best sections of it are split between this route and route 42.

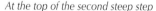

At the top of the second steep step

Carrauntoohil from Beenkeragh

Ignoring the obvious flanking path, the initial descent from Beenkeragh down a slabby crest is quite entertaining. From the col beneath, the first minor summit is quickly reached; again a flanking path avoids the difficulties while the crest is better. The second minor summit has the best of the scrambling – rather more than expected if you stick with the skyline.

A low col beneath the NW flank of Carrauntoohil marks the end of the hands-on stuff. From here it's possible to descend steeply N down Brother O'Shea's Gully, a scree path zigzagging into the depths of the coum. Otherwise it's a scrappy stony slog onto the summit of Ireland.

DESCENT

As noted in route 42 descent from Carrauntoohil needs careful navigation in a pea souper; to reach Hags Glen without simply falling into it,

follow a magnetic bearing of 192° until there's no doubt that you're on the very well-scuffed tourist path. From about the 900m contour this path then descends SE to reach the low col at the head of the scree gully known (deservingly) as the Devil's Ladder. Although this is the quickest way to the valley floor, and a popular route used daily by many inexperienced people, it is highly eroded and could be dangerous, with a risk of knocking loose boulders down onto fellow mountaineers. The ground eventually eases, the path leading quickly back down the Hags Glen.

A more imaginative descent option from just above the col at the top of the Devil's Ladder is the narrow path that traverses the breakneck (not literally, we hope) east face. If you can locate the top of this – not easy – you'll be able to descend via the divine Heavenly Gates (see route 44) to regain the approach path that passes below Stumpa, as described earlier in this chapter. The Harvey map indicates the rough course of this path.

Route 44 – Howling Ridge, Carrauntoohil

Grade	c300m VDiff
Distance	9km
Ascent	850m
Time	6–8 hours
Start/finish	Cronin's Yard paying car park (V836873) or the nearby car park at Lislebane (V827873)
Maps	See route 42
Accommodation	See route 42
Sleeping out	Camping for a couple of nights in the corrie below the face would be a good way to get a number of Carrauntoohil's ridges climbed. The emergency shelter marked on the Harvey map (V808846) is a bit pokey for a planned stay.
Public transport	Killarney to Killorglin buses stop at Beaufort on the N72, about 8km from either start point.
Seasonal notes	The 1987 first ascent of Howling Ridge was in full-on winter conditions; it's said to be grade III/IV. Although Reeks winter climbing is now a rare event there's no question that it would be one of the best routes of its type in the British Isles. Given the altitude and aspect, optimistic parties might still get lucky occasionally. Howling Ridge in the rain is best left to experienced masochists.

It's hard to pinpoint your chosen route on Carrauntoohil's daunting north and east flank.

On the right, Stumpa sticks out like a sore thumb

MATCHLESS LOCATION, high mountain drama, absorbing climbing – and plenty of it; this is the figurehead mountaineering route on the country's biggest peak, Ireland's emphatic answer to Tower Ridge. The huge rambling spread of Carrauntoohil's North and East faces is both baffling and daunting on first acquaintance. Howling Ridge is just one of several ribs known as The Bones, and from a distance its precise line tends to merge into the mass of tottering pinnacles, gullies and buttresses that scatter the mountain.

Luckily the starting point is unambiguous; so too is route finding once underway. Although it's not a particularly technical ascent for the grade, the serious positions, quasi-Alpine scale and difficulty of retreat make this unsuitable as a first big VDiff. Familiarity with questionable rock is useful, as is smooth switching between fixed pitches and running belays. This is the most amenable and popular of Carrauntoohil's ridge climbs – see Appendix 1 for the others.

On pitch 1 above the Heavenly Gates

APPROACH

Follow route 43 as far as the path beneath Stumpa an tSaimh. Then, instead of turning off this path, stay with it to climb through the crags above Lough Gouragh and enter the lowest tier of the hanging corrie beneath Carrauntoohil, which from here looks very imposing. Where the path for Brother O'Shea's Gully continues up the corrie branch left, climbing a spur known as the Eagle's Nest and passing a small emergency shelter. Above is the steep rock of Primroses, the mountain's true northeast ridge; Howling Ridge begins a long way left of this, but the two routes join together much higher up the mountain. Bear left to climb steep scree at the foot of the face, soon reaching the unmistakeable notch of the Heavenly Gates, a gap between the mountain and a blunt pinnacle. Howling Ridge starts here (while the path continues its spectacular traverse to meet the busy tourist route on the col above the Devil's Ladder).

CLIMB

Howling Ridge, c300m VDiff

This popular route may have been picked fairly clean, but loose material still remains. Stonefall inevitably rakes the Heavenly Gates path; it'd be a shame to take out an unsuspecting walker through simple carelessness. Retreat can be contrived at some points by moving into Collins' Gully, which bounds the left side of the ridge, but the descent of this is far from unproblematic, and the best escape option is to keep climbing. Some sections can be scrambled unroped or climbed with running belays, while the upper reaches around The Tower and The Finger are perhaps best tackled with fixed belays. Pitching the whole thing is also an option – it'll take at least eight belays.

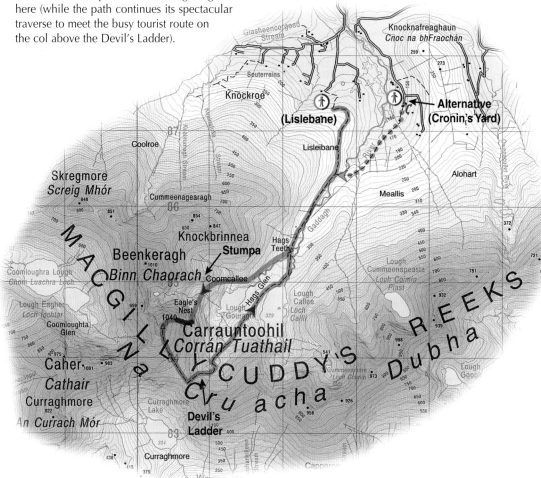

Sunset on the pinnacles; Stumpa (Route 43) lurks in the mist below

Start on the broad buttress immediately above the Heavenly Gates, which turns out to be more exposed than it looks. The best line is well-trodden and obvious, weaving direct up a series of ledges and slabby walls – Mod/Diff on superb rough sandstone. Further right is an easy grassier line; but why bother? Fifty metres of great climbing brings you to a broad ledge, the First Plateau. A grassy crest now leads to a short rock step where the strata slope awkwardly leftwards; above this is the Second Plateau. Beyond is the Overhanging Prow, which does what it says on the tin. It is said to be VS if taken direct, though

44 Howling Ridge
A Heavenly Gates
B Primroses
C Pippet's Ridge
D Carrauntoohil summit

almost everyone declines the offer, outflanking it on the right on grassy ground before climbing to the Third Plateau via a short groove with some questionable rock.

If a rope hasn't yet seemed necessary the Third Plateau might be the place to get it out. A steep groove and short tricky wall gain the easier crest above, leading in about 20m to the Fourth Plateau. You're now at the base of the exposed 25m pitch known as The Tower, which is arguably the route's crux. Follow good clean rock up a 'ladder' of horizontal breaks to reach a little notch just right of the top of the tower; pass right along this, crossing a short airy slab with some loose bits on the N flank of the tower to belay at a neck just beyond it – care is needed with rope drag on this pitch.

Next comes The Finger, another steep pitch of about 20m; go straight up the crest in a magnificent position to belay on top. Howling Ridge now lurches radically rightwards, joined to the upper section of Primroses by an unusual slabby knife edge, The Bridge. This is just a walk – but don't trip. From the far end of The Bridge it's said to be possible to skirt the top section of the ridge by moving left into the mucky trough of Collins' Gully, but the remainder of Howling Ridge is fairly amenable and very spectacular. Two exposed Moderate pitches lead up and over a rank of blocky pinnacles; not all of the rock is above suspicion, and it needs a light touch. Beyond a final level toothed crest the ground eases into scrambling, and then just rough walking. A stony 100m ascent up the last section of the Northeast Ridge brings you out on the summit of Carrauntoohil.

DESCENT

See route 43.

The eastern Reeks from the Fourth Plateau

The slabby knife edge and the top section of Faha Ridge

Grade	1/2 minimum; harder variations are also described in the text
Distance	7.5km
Ascent	940m
Time	4½ hours
Start/finish	Car park at Faha (or An Fhaiche), the end of the minor road from Cloghane (Q493120)
Maps	OSI Discovery (1:50000) sheet 70 is pretty poor – it doesn't even mark the major path up Mount Brandon from Faha; with luck, the new OSI Leisure map (1:25000) Brandon Mountain will be better.
Accommodation	Mount Brandon hostel in Cloghane www.mountbrandonhostel.com 00 353 (0)66 7138299
Sleeping out	A wild camp amongst the rocks and tarns of Brandon's superb eastern corrie complex would be very special, but best out of sight of the busy path.
Public transport	Not a great option, but possible; bus 273 links Cloghane with the town of Tralee.
Seasonal notes	As the most maritime and westerly of 3000ft-ers, Mount Brandon isn't ideally suited to winter climbing – it's a shame, as the seeping vegetated crag tiers of its east face are vaguely reminiscent of Beinn Bhan of Applecross, and would have provided superb ice climbs when mammoths last tramped the earth. The high-level Faha Ridge must still occasionally hold enough snow for proper winter fun and looks like it would make a superb grade I/II traverse.

WITH THE ROLLING OCEAN on three sides there's almost an island feel to Mount Brandon (the maps have it as Brandon Mountain but locals say Mount Brandon, which is good enough for me). Too often the Atlantic sends armadas of rain and mist to dash themselves on the summit reefs, but on a clear day the sea also makes the most spectacular of backdrops for one of Ireland's great mountains. Rearing from the beach to a weathered crest several kilometres long, the craggy multi-topped profile of Dingle's holy mountain dominates the sandy sweep of Brandon Bay and the scatter of rural villages at its foot. This eastern aspect is the massif's trump card, a row of deep-scooped corries, huge headwalls of layered sandstone backing a string of blue pools, the Paternoster Lakes. The intervening ribs between the hollows provide enjoyable routes to the summits on the main ridge; Faha Ridge is justifiably the most famous of these. The mountain is named after the 6th-century saint Brendan the Navigator who is said to have spotted America from the summit, and sailed off into the sunset to 'discover' the New World 1000 years before Columbus. With Paradise on his doorstep you wonder why he bothered.

APPROACH

From the car park a track heads roughly W past a house. Beyond a gate turn slightly uphill to a well-tended gated grotto. The path now continues on a rising traverse across the hillside some way below the grassy crest at the eastern end of the Faha Ridge. It's a popular walker's route to the summit, well-scuffed and marked by occasional posts. Stay with the path for about 2km until it reaches a high point before descending into Mount Brandon's eastern coum. From here head NW, climbing fairly steeply to the ridge crest. Turn left onto an 822m summit, unnamed on the OSI map but known locally as Binn na Port. This is the site of a remarkable promontory fort, said to date from the Iron Age; they couldn't have picked a better spot. Despite the weatherbeaten position the two rows of stone ramparts are still formidably well preserved.

Looking west along the Faha Ridge

227

CLIMB

Faha Ridge, 1/2

It's a tricky route to grade. Taken direct there are short sections of Moderate and Difficult climbing; despite their brevity a fall from these could well be fatal. Teams determined to stick to the skyline will have to choose between lightweight and bold, or lugging a rope all day for a total of about 25m climbing. These short cruxes can easily be skirted – but avoid too much of the steep stuff and you're barely scrambling at all.

Continuing W towards a small col, the ridge narrows into a pronounced rock and grass crest, with an exciting rooftop feel and inspiring perspectives over the nearby crags and corries. There is a path of sorts, but as so often on the Irish hills it's nothing like the eroded motorways of Snowdonia and the Lakes; the Faha Ridge may be superb, but few people seem to have cottoned on. Bursts of easy scrambling on rough sandstone blocks and airy grassy walking bring you to another minor summit. Descend carefully from this to reach a rocky neck at the base of a promontory formed by a huge tilted slab. From here the grade 1/2 option descends briefly rightwards, where a rough walk leads beneath the N side of the promontory to reach a broad bouldery col at the point that the Faha Ridge meets the craggy east spur of Coimin na gCnamh.

Optional climb, Moderate

The braver skyline alternative leads out along the rock arete formed by the upper edge of the tilted slab. It's an easy scramble to the sharp tip, but slipping is inadvisable. The onward route to the bouldery col is less straightforward, as it's barred by a sheer rock step at least 15m high. The only feasible way down is to bear ever so slightly right (facing out) from the tip of the slab, grassy steps leading to a short steep rock groove with reachy moves between the best holds. This Moderate pitch is best avoided in the wet.

Beyond the col the spur presents a number of options. Its left flank may be a sizeable crag, but the rough slopes to its right offer a route to the top of Coimin na gCnamh with nothing harder than a bit of hands-on walking. If this seems an

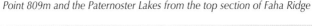

Point 809m and the Paternoster Lakes from the top section of Faha Ridge

Brandon Peak (Route 46) from Faha Ridge

anti-climax then you may prefer a more head-on way up the spur.

Optional climb, Moderate/Difficult

From the col walk up to the first rock tier on the crest, the lowest point of which is a square-cut prow about 7m high; it's possible to climb this via an obvious groove at about Difficult, but the final moves are quite mucky. Alternatively move up and left, climbing a short steep wall and a grassy trough, before stepping right along a ledge some way above the top of the square-cut prow. The spur now continues as a series of short steep steps and intervening grassy ledges. Taken direct the first step offers some quite tricky climbing, with occasional wobbly blocks and the added bonus of a vegetated top-out. You may notice the scale of the crag below to the left. The whole step can be turned on the right.

Easier scrambly ground now leads up the crest of the spur to the summit. Head S around the rim of the coum, joining the popular Faha path for the final climb to the cross marking the top of Mount Brandon. A small ruin here is said to be the site of St Brendan's oratory.

DESCENT

Return N, then take the main path E into the coum. It's quite steep and stony as it descends through the crag tiers, but you're soon down among the ice-scoured outcrops and clear pools of the corrie floor. After crossing a stream the path then climbs briefly around the south flank of the Faha Ridge to reach the high point as described in the approach section. An easy 2km descent brings you back to Faha.

Route 46 – East Ridge, Brandon Peak

Grade	Moderate (maximum) or 1/2 (minimum)
Distance	7km
Ascent	800m
Time	4 hours
Start/finish	Layby near a bridge on the dead-end road from Cloghane, beside the turn-off to a farm (Q491084)
Maps	See route 45
Accommodation	See route 45
Sleeping out	The shores of Loch Cruite may look a nice camp site on the map, but the ground is actually pretty rough; perhaps the best bet for a flat pitch is the SE side.
Public transport	See route 45
Seasonal notes	Unlike the Faha Ridge this route isn't a long elevated crest; with its low start and steep profile, only the short easier upper section is likely to hold much snow – grade I, at a guess. By avoiding the optional hard pitches the ridge should be OK in the wet.

Brandon Peak from the Connor Pass road; the shadowed East Ridge slants from right to left

THE THIRD HIGHEST SUMMIT in the Brandon chain is a charismatic peak in its own right, more prominent from some angles than its bigger neighbours. Dividing two rugged corries, its precipitous East Ridge is an obvious and attractive line. The twisting Connor Pass road provides perhaps the most informative distant view of the route. From here it's clearly a game of two halves, the precipitous pinnacled terminal nose leading to a more laid-back upper crest. True to its appearance the bulk of the scrambling comes in a burst low down on the route, where sound, rough sandstone, bird's eye exposure and some excellent (but avoidable) challenges provide a winning combination. Above this it's just a rough ridge walk, but still airy and superb. A grassier descent via yet more sharp-edged ridges concludes this photogenic half-day horseshoe.

APPROACH

Turn right off the road and follow a track through the farmyard. The track goes straight on uphill to reach little Loch an Mhónáin in its heathery cirque. Just before the lake turn right, contouring the rough and almost pathless hillside along the line of a fence for a few hundred metres, before bearing slightly uphill to reach the southern end of Loch Cruite. Wade through the boulders and heather above its west shore. The steep and rocky lower section of the East Ridge dominates the skyline; accessing it will clearly be hard work. At about grid reference Q483095 turn left, scrabbling up the mucky bed of a broad ill-defined heathery gully. Once above the lowest scrappy crags at about the 400m contour, follow a line of weakness rightwards to reach the base of a row of clean buttresses.

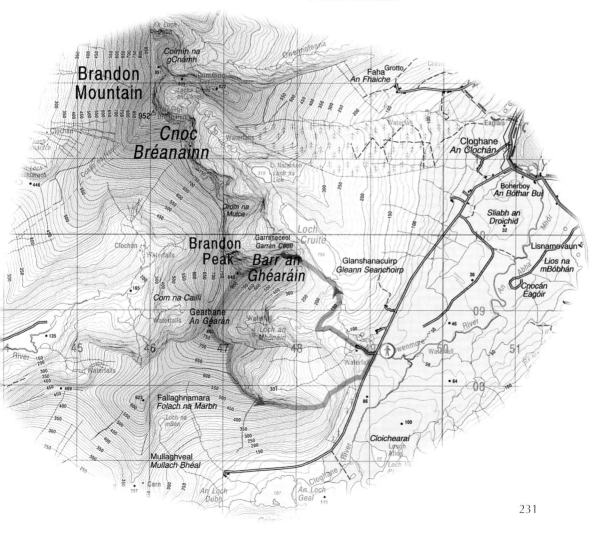

231

Approaching the overhanging wall...

CLIMB

East Ridge, Moderate
(could be made much easier)

The lower ridge isn't a defined arete but rather a series of compact buttresses and bouldery sections scattered up a broad heather-clad crest. Excitement is there to be sought, with some excellent stretches of hard scrambling and Moderate climbing above heady drops. Although it may sound a bit unorthodox, the rounded sandstone suits rock shoes better than walking boots. If that's a bit too much like real climbing then rest assured that the bold bits are all entirely optional; judicious weaving around keeps the difficulty level low.

The first tier is beyond the scope of scrambling grades. If you're not feeling brave it can be avoided by skirting left on scrambly ground, before returning rightwards to the blocky crest. However those with sufficient nerve might prefer a more direct approach. A number of possibilities exist, some of which look fairly hard. For a really outstanding 15m Moderate pitch just follow your nose to the obvious wide rounded

crack running straight up the weathered slab. A rope might be welcome, indeed worth its weight in gold if it means not missing out on the excitement; but given dry rock and the necessary competence this is a friendly solo with no nasty surprises.

Above a bouldery ledge is the next notable obstacle, a short steep wall above a considerable drop. Again this can be avoided with a quick scramble to the left, but the holds on the wall are good. Continue scrambling on go-anywhere ground. Beyond a bouldery section is the second meaty pitch, a slabby rib just right of the main crest that provides a good 15m of delicate Moderate climbing with butterfly-inducing exposure; again, simply by staying left this can be entirely avoided. A while later the crest is barred by a short vertical step where various bold lines await the adventurous; unsurprisingly, this too can be outflanked with a leftward feint. Beyond a final short sharp rock crest the scrambling peters out into strenuous bouldery walking.

Ironically this is just the point at which the route becomes really narrow and ridge-like for

...and taking in the view from the top!

the first time. A rough path treads the sharp upper crest in spectacular fashion, expansive views over Brandon Bay opening out behind. As if to add a last note of drama the ridge leads over a huge overhanging prow (a potential new route?) before continuing its airy course to the elegant summit of Brandon Peak.

DESCENT

You are now on the main spine of the Brandon massif, a graceful ridge walk in its own right. Although it is tempting to continue N over Mount Brandon to make a descent of the Faha Ridge (route 45) before walking out via the Paternoster Lakes, this best-of-Brandon enchainment is quite taxing. The rather quicker and less rigorous way back to the car is not without charms of its own. Head SSW around the rim of the Loch an Mhónáin corrie, where a narrow grassy arete leads to the minor peak of An Géarán overlooking the Connor Pass hills. Though it seems a likely descent line the mountain's east ridge is actually pretty steep. It's better to stick with gentle SSE slopes, where a path (of sorts) picks up a fence line leading out onto the southeast ridge. The crest soon swings E, offering a quick (if rough) descent towards the road. Not far from the bottom bear NE to avoid steep slopes, reaching the road just N of a small forestry plantation, a short walk from the layby.

Brandon Bay from high on the ridge

Grade	c370m Difficult
Distance	8km
Ascent	500m
Time	6 hours
Start/finish	Private track turnoff for Gleninagh (L820562); the nearest available car parking is some distance along the public road.
Maps	Harvey Superwalker (1:30000) Connemara is the best; OSI Discovery (1:50000) sheet 37 is less clear and comprehensive
Accommodation	Local hostels include: Harbour House, Rossroe 00 353 (0)43 933 – the austere philosopher Wittgenstein used to live next door, and it's still an inspiringly back-to-basics sort of place; Letterfrack Lodge 00 353 (0)95 41222; Sleepzone, Leenaun 00 353 (0)95 42929
Sleeping out	Gleninagh may look suitable on paper, but the entire valley is a sponge and the chances of finding a pleasant pitch are slim.
Public transport	Bus 419 runs from Galway bus station to Leenaun, then along the N59 to Clifden. The crossroads just E of Kylemore would be your closest stop; from here it's a long walk along the R344 minor road to the Gleninagh turn-off.
Seasonal notes	Carrot Ridge is too low and too slabby to make a good winter route; given the lack of positive holds and general boldness it's best saved for a dry day.

Approaching Bencorr through the bogs of Gleninagh 235

RISING FORBIDDINGLY out of the bleak Connemara landscape, the Twelve Bens (aka Pins) are as rugged as any massif in the west of Ireland – which is to say, very. For hills this rocky it's surprising at close quarters to discover that in between acres of quartzite the range is one giant sponge. Indeed the peat bogs and their guardian midge hordes are practically of a Caledonian ferocity. The same can be said for the hills, of which Bencorr is both beauty and the beast. Among so much exposed stone, Carrot Ridge is the stand-out line, visible from afar and irresistible in its obviousness. Appearances are auspicious, and the climb does not disappoint. Quality quartzite, grand slabby situations and a setting and scale worthy of the Scottish Highlands make this one of the very finest routes of its grade in the British Isles.

but first you've got to park. Space is extremely limited along the public road; there's room for a couple of cars some way NW of the turn-off, and also a tiny layby fitting one vehicle several hundred metres SE near a bridge over the Tooreenacoona River. The track is signed as private property, but there's no other practical route over the extensive bogs of the lower valley so just be unobtrusive and hope for the best. After 1km pass (quietly) through a group of farm buildings, beyond which the private road becomes a footpath. A further 1.5km along the floor of Gleninagh brings you to an old sheep fold. Carrot Ridge already looks appetising; from this angle its gentle curve is actually more reminiscent of a banana. It stands proud of the hillside, bounding the left edge of Bencorr's huge quartzite wall and starting a lot higher than the main crag; the base is a distinctive pale slab.

APPROACH

The walk up Gleninagh starts on a private track that branches off the Recess to Kylemore road at L820562;

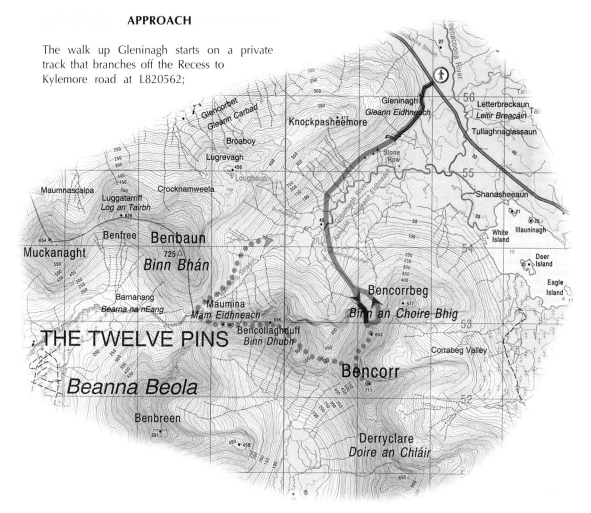

Gleninagh and distant Mweelrea (Route 48) from pitch 6

Under the Second Step

Crossing a stream, head roughly S to ford the Gleninagh River at some stony shallows. Now make a beeline for Carrot Ridge, sploshing through the waterlogged flats before a long trudge up a sponge-and-scree slope to reach the foot of the climb.

CLIMB

Carrot Ridge, c370m Difficult

Although technically straightforward, the climbing is excitingly run out, and positive holds are notable for their scarcity. The route is marred only by its escapability leftwards at three key

points: the top of pitch 2; the top of pitch 3 and the slabby ledge below pitch 7. Start at the toe of the pale slab.

Pitch 1, 25m

Climb the slab close to its left edge to a little stance on the blunt arete, below a steepening.

Pitch 2, 25m

Step right to ascend a short groove – place runners here as there are few higher up. Continue straight up the rounded crest on small holds to belay on a big ledge.

47 Carrot Ridge
A The pale slab
B main crag

Pitch 4, 30m
The menacing wall of the First Step looms some way above; luckily it is skirted rather than being taken head on. Make a short sharp pull from the ledge, and then bear right to gain and follow a vague groove leading up to an obvious recess on the right flank of the Step – excellent climbing and protection. Belay at a little stance just right of the recess.

Pitch 3, 30m
Easy ground leads to a steep step – the rock is sounder than it looks. Belay at a wide gravel-floored ledge.

Pitch 5, 15m
Traverse easily left to the corner in the back of the recess, which is climbed quite steeply for a few

At the top of the Second Step, with plenty of scrambling still to come

metres until it's possible to pull left onto a ledge on the ridge crest.

Pitch 6, 15m
Walk left again to enter a little chimney/corner which leads with interest to another well-positioned stance.

Scramble, c90m
Pleasant padding leads on up the slabby ridge crest – if dry it should be OK to proceed unroped. On nearing the distinctive Second Step the ridge narrows briefly before reaching a little col. Continue up an easy slab at the base of the Second Step to belay just under a short steep wall.

Pitch 7, 44m
This pitch might be split into two, although there aren't so many runners that drag becomes an issue. Breach the wall at its lowest point, then move rightwards over a little slab to gain a slabby groove running up the ridge just right of centre. This leads easily but magnificently to gentler ground at the top of the Second Step.

Scramble, c100m
A superb easy clamber up the clean slabby upper crest soon leads to the top of Carrot Ridge.

Optional continuation
The minor top of Binn an tSaighdiúra is a stiff uphill hike away, and the main summit of Bencorr further still. This latter would be well worth visiting if time allows. From Bencorr there are three main descent options. The obvious route to the road would appear to be a descent via Bencorrbeg, fine but for the murky mires and meandering river at its foot. The distinct east ridge of Bencorr is a pleasant scrambly ascent, but getting safely off the end of it is problematic in descent. All things considered it might be preferable to continue the round over Bencollaghduff before descending to Maumina pass, where a good path into Gleninagh is met.

DESCENT

Alternatively, it's a lot quicker to descend directly from the top of the climb. To do so, first ascend briefly to pick up a clear traverse path that heads left over the scree slope flanking the E side of Carrot Ridge. Pick a way down this slope with care – it's a lengthy descent on unpleasant ground, and would not be amusing after dark. Re-cross boggy Gleninagh and its river to regain the valley-bottom approach path at the sheep fold.

High on pitch 7

Grade	1
Distance	16km (including detour to Mweelrea summit)
Ascent	1230m (including summit)
Time	8 hours (including summit)
Start/finish	Layby on the R335 just NW of Doo Lough (L827696)
Maps	OSI Discovery (1:50000) sheet 37
Accommodation	See route 47; also Delphi Mountain Resort, a luxurious outdoor centre at the foot of Mweelrea 00 353 (0)95 42208
Sleeping out	The depths of Glencullin would be an atmospheric setting for a wild camp, but the ground is unremittingly bumpy and boggy – likewise the two remote coums below the main peak of Mweelrea.
Public transport	Leenaun is the closest you'll get by bus. The 419 runs from Galway bus station to Leenaun.
Seasonal notes	Despite the warming sea that laps Mweelrea's toes, the upper section of Ben Bury's East Ridge is high enough to be worth a look in a cold snowy spell – likely to be grade I/II. Further along the circuit, the airy summit ridge of Ben Lugmore would prove an exciting mountaineering-style winter walk, possibly with some interesting cornices overhanging Glencullin if you've really lucked out with the snow. Incidentally, Ben Bury's huge botanically burgeoning northern wall has tremendous scope for winter climbing, although the chances of good winter conditions are sadly slim.

Mweelrea from near Clifden

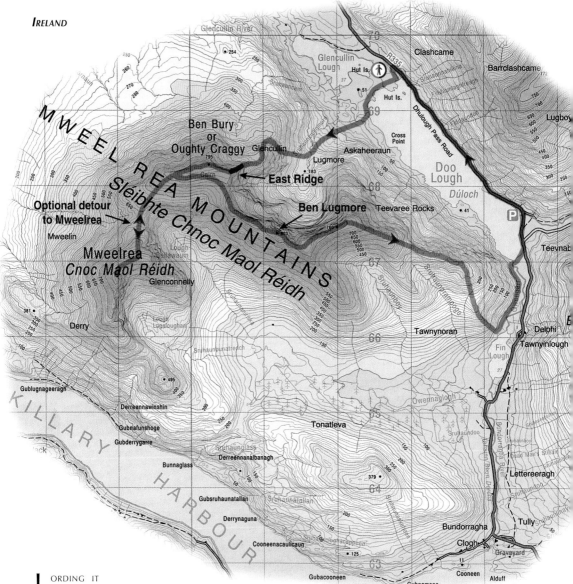

Lording it

over the deep ocean trench of Killary Harbour, often touted as Ireland's only fjord, Mweelrea is the highest massif in the province of Connacht. A crown of bold summits and sharp ridges enclosing ice-gouged hollows of striated sandstone where clouds boil as if in giant cauldrons, the mountain truly befits its local translation 'bald king'. The classic walking circuit from Delphi takes in all the main summits but involves negligible scrambling; a slightly more exacting route ascends via the short steep East Ridge of Ben Bury. The demands here are modest, and the pleasure is really in nifty routefinding through intimidating and little-trod terrain. Nevertheless it's a grand start to one of the great hillwalks of Ireland. From Ben Bury a there-and-back detour bags Mweelrea's 814m high point; the circuit then concludes in stirring style over the multi-topped and narrow-spined Ben Lugmore.

APPROACH

A track runs from the roadside to the shore of Doo Lough, which it then follows W to ford a little river. Continue along the shingly beach to Sruhauncullinmore stream, and take a vague, easily-missed path into the lower reaches of

Glencullin, a dramatic hollow backed by dour, dripping precipices. Ascend briefly in the bed of the coum, then bear right over rough pathless ground, crossing the stream and heading for the grassy spur at the bottom of Ben Bury's East Ridge. An obvious ledge cuts across the lower reaches of the slope below a line of overgrown outcrops; walk rightwards along this and then, when opportunity affords, go straight up on grass and through rocky patches, including a curious row of boulders, to make towards a blunt mini-summit.

CLIMB

Ben Bury East Ridge, grade 1

The highest rocks of the mini-summit form a gently sloping tier of excellent rough sandstone – an enjoyable scramble, though brief and easily avoided. From the mini-summit descend slightly, then continue up the now better-defined crest dividing the depths of Glencullin from the shallower rock-walled corrie to the right.

The ridge soon rears into a marked prow. Two adjacent grooves run up the front of this; although grades are hard to estimate they'd certainly be worth a look for teams equipped with gear. From the scree band at the foot of the steep rocks the unroped scrambler's alternative cunningly avoids the obstacle by walking briefly left to overlook Glencullin, then climbing back rightwards up a pale rocky depression. At the top of this, traverse right across a grassy bay to gain the crest directly above the rock prow. Signs of passing feet – hardly a path – now weave up the ragged grassy ridge, via a couple of little rock steps and short airy aretes formed by tilting slabs that shelve off into the coum. This is satisfying scrambling, but not at all difficult. Too soon the ridge debouches onto the gently sloping top of Ben Bury. Head roughly W to the summit cairn.

Detour

The optional round trip from here to the peak of Mweelrea itself will take about 1½ hours and needs a bit of attention in poor visibility; an easy stony descent W and then SW leads to a low and slightly soggy saddle above remote Lough Gellawaum. A steepening climb S from here then brings you to a cliff top, with the main summit located a little way right around the edge. Return the same way, perhaps skirting just right of the summit of Ben Bury to save on ascent.

Mweelrea from near Lough Fee – peat cutting in progress

The Sheeffry Hills from rock step below the mini summit

CONTINUATION

Heading SE from Ben Bury, a short descent gains a little col where a cairn marks the top of the popular path that climbs out of Glencullin via a ramp on the craggy headwall. This would be a good place to bail if the weather has turned. Otherwise continue uphill around the edge of the Glencullin cliffs, a giddying sweep of vertical vegetable and tottering sandstone. Any crowds will likely be left behind at the col, and the path leading on along the narrowing grassy arete has a less trodden feel. With a gulf of space to your left and steep slopes on the right this is ridge walking at its finest; a pity there's no scrambling to speak of. Of several high points strung along the ridge the official summit of Ben Lugmore is the third, marked as spot height 803m on the OSI Discovery map (but unaccountably anonymous). Beyond the main peak is a broader boulder-topped summit; swing left here, hugging the edge where pleasant airy strolling leads to the high ground at the top of the steep ridge that forms the E arm of Glencullin (just past spot height 760m as marked on the map). Although it may be feasible to descend this subsidiary spur with care, a better option is to stay with the main ridge as it swings ESE.

DESCENT

Still narrow and at times rocky the ridge steadily drops towards Delphi, with some fairly steep sections but no real difficulty. Attention is split between the hulking form of Ben Creggan dead ahead and birds-eye views of miniature cars speeding silently along the Dhulough Pass Road far below. Beyond a little saddle at a height of about 450m a short climb gains an elongated minor summit dotted with boggy sloughs and slabby outcrops. The latter offer enjoyable scrambling and bouldering if you've still got the oomph. Descend from the far end of the minor summit until it's possible to see down the craggy slopes leading to the roadside. A direct descent runs into potentially treacherous terrain, requiring both reasonable visibility and a degree of mountain savvy. Easier going is found by bearing right, almost S, making towards the far end of Fin Lough. Once safely in the valley head towards Doo Lough, following a fence line across the rough slopes just W of the Owengarr River to reach a sluice gate at the Doo Lough outflow. Cross this to regain the road. The 30min march back to the car might be avoidable by hitchhiking.

(Above) Glencullin cliffs from Ben Bury's upper ridge
(Below) Doo Lough and the Sheeffry Hills from high on the East Ridge

ROUTE SUMMARY TABLE

In ascending order of route difficulty

Route	Chapter	Type	Grade	Distance	Ascent	Page
Nantlle Ridge	38	Walk/Scramble	1	13km	1120m	190
Daear Ddu	32	Scramble	1	8km	780m	164
Crib Lem	22	Scramble	1	14km	1100m	124
Sharp Edge and Hallsfell Ridge	1	Scramble	1	7km	680m	30
Lliwedd via Y Gribin	36	Scramble	1	8km	650m	182
Mweelrea Circuit	48	Scramble	1	16km	1230m	241
Cwm Bochlwyd Horseshoe	31	Scramble	1	6km	900m	160
Faha Ridge	45	Scramble	1/2	7.5km	940m	225
Yewbarrow Traverse	9	Scramble	2	5km	620m	64
MacGillycuddy's Reeks Ridge Traverse	42	Scramble	2	14km	1650m	210
Sphinx Ridge	10	Scramble	2	8km	830m	68
Langdale Pikes ridges	6	Scramble	2/3	5km	750m	51
East Ridge, Y Garn	26	Scramble	2/3	4.5km	650m	140
Pinnacle Ridge, St Sunday Crag	4	Scramble	3	12km	700m	42
Cam Crag Ridge and Intake Ridge	15	Scramble	3	9km	650m	89
Sentries' Ridge	39	Scramble	3	6.5km	500m	194
East Ridge, Brandon Peak	46	Scramble/ Climb	Mod (optional)	7km	800m	230
Needle's Eye Arete	25	Scramble/Climb	Mod	4km	620m	136
Dolmen Ridge	29	Scramble/Climb	Mod	5.5km	700m	152
East Gully Arete	30	Climb	Diff	5.5km	700m	156
Crenation Ridge	7	Climb	Diff	7km	920m	55
Ridges of Winnats Pass	17	Climb	Diff	1.5km	150m	100
Clogwyn y Person Arete	34	Climb	Diff	8km	850m	173
Stumpa an tSaimh	43	Climb	Diff	11km	1050m	215
Carrot Ridge	47	Climb	Diff	8km	500m	235
Cyfrwy Arete	41	Climb	Diff	7km	800m	203
Slanting Buttress	37	Climb	Diff	7km	600m	185
The Claw	19	Climb	Diff	4km	200m	109
Pinnacle Ridge, Braich Ty Du	24	Climb	VDiff	1km	150m	133
Amphitheatre Buttress	21	Climb	VDiff	8km	650m	120
Sub Cneifion Rib and Cneifion Arete	28	Climb	VDiff	4km	500m	148
Arrowhead Ridge	11	Climb	VDiff	7.5km	830m	73
Howling Ridge	44	Climb	VDiff	9km	850m	220
Commando Ridge	20	Climb	VDiff	1km	140m	114
Central Arete, Glyder Fawr	27	Climb	VDiff	5km	700m	144
Grey Crag Linkup	16	Climb	Mild Severe	6km	760m	93
South Ridge, Rhinog Fach	40	Climb	Severe	7km	550m	199
Westmorland's Route	5	Climb	Severe	8km	720m	46
Pikes Crag Ridge	8	Climb	Severe	7km	920m	60
Napes Needle and Needle Ridge	13	Climb	HS	8km	830m	80
Eagle's Nest Ridge	12	Climb	MildVS	8km	830m	76
Skeleton Ridge	18	Climb	HVS	3km	150m	104
East Ridges of Nethermost and Dollywagon Pikes	3	Winter	I (barely)	11km	800m	38
Striding and Swirral Edges	2	Winter	I	10km	840m	34
Circuit of the Southern Carneddau	23	Winter	I	15km	1030m	128
Snowdon Horseshoe	33	Winter	I	11km	1060m	167
Gyrn Lâs Ridge	35	Winter	Easy II	7km	900m	178
Pinnacle Ridge, Gable Crag	14	Winter	III	9km	730m	84

APPENDIX 1
FURTHER ADVENTURES...

Most of the best and all of the most famous ridges have been described here but the selection in this book is not exhaustive. Those of an exploratory persuasion might find this list of also-rans helpful.

THE LAKE DISTRICT

The paucity of Cumbrian winter routes covered in the book says more about the quality of recent seasons than it does about the omitted climbs; a deep freeze is required, since these are generally turfy:

- Great Doup Buttress, Pillar, 120m II
- Serendipity Ridge, Scoat Fell Crag, 115m III
- Juniper Ridge, Wasdale Screes, 130m I/II
- Pendulum Ridge, Scrubby Crag, 120m III
- South Pinnacle Ridge, Rampsgill Head, 90m IV
- Central Ridge, Rampsgill Head, 90m IV.

The adventurous might also explore the north and northeast side of Lingmell in summer or winter.

THE REST OF ENGLAND

The ridge-climbing potential of the Exmoor coast has not yet been fully worked out; prospective explorers would have to be experienced with crumbling shale, steep vegetation and tidal issues.

WALES

Several historic Snowdonian ridge routes have lapsed into botanical obscurity, and are due a gardening renaissance. These include:

- Central Arete, Creigiau Gleision, Foel Goch, c100m VDiff
- The Great Ridge, Creigiau Gleision, Foel Goch, c130m Severe
- The Tower, Creigiau Gleision, Foel Goch, VDiff

- West Ridge, Creigiau Gleision, Foel Goch, VDiff
- Cannon Ridge, Tryfan West Face, c150m Severe
- Pinnacle Ridge, Craig y Bera, Mynydd Mawr, at least Difficult (some say substantially harder) – there's more to go at hereabouts too, but if you thought Sentries' Ridge was wobbly...

Less obscure but no less worthwhile are:
- Mallory's Ridge, Y Garn (Nantlle), 115m VS 4c
- Eastern Arete, Y Garn (Nantlle), 140m VDiff
- Llechog Ridge, Snowdon, 1/2
- Seniors' Ridge, Glyder Fawr 1
- Main Gully ridge, Glyder Fach, 2/3
- Pinnacle Rib Route, Tryfan East Face, 175m VDiff
- Overlapping Ridge Route, Tryfan East Face, 185m Severe
- Gashed Crag, Tryfan East Face, 170m VDiff
- Eastern Arete, Ysgolion Duon, 200m II/III

And finally...
- Yr Esgair, Foel Goch, 180m II/III
  The most compelling ridge line in North Wales, this should only be considered in winter – and even then only with sound névé/frozen turf. Being suicidally unstable in summer it is one to avoid unless you're that way inclined too.

IRELAND

While the unmissable Irish classics have all been described, several other Kerry ridges would also be worth a look for cool-headed types not averse to loose rock and greenery:
- Pippet's Ridge, Carrauntoohil, Severe
- Primroses, Carrauntoohil, HVS
- Curved Gully Ridge, Carrauntoohil, VDiff/Severe
- Northeast ridge, Caher, VDiff
- Mystic Ridge, Mount Brandon, Severe
- East Ridge, Knocknagantee, 3
- Southwest Ridge, Hungry Hill, 1 (minimum)
- Grey Soldier Ridge, Ballydavid Head, Severe.

APPENDIX 2
FURTHER READING

For those picking up hill skills these text books come highly recommended.

The Hillwalker's Guide to Mountaineering
  Terry Adby and Stuart Johnston
  (Cicerone 2003)
  Clear and helpful skills advice for budding mountaineers on the classic hard scrambles.

Rock Climbing
  Pete Hill (Cicerone 2008)
  For when the going gets tougher.

Avalanche!
  Robert Bolognesi (Cicerone 2007)
  Pocket guide to avalanche prediction, which is after all useful for avalanche avoidance.

Mountain Weather: Understanding Britain's mountain weather
  David Pedgley (Cicerone 2006)
  Learn how weather maps translate on the ground, and how to work with conditions to maximise the chances of a successful trip.

While a comprehensive list of the climbing and walking guidebooks covering every area touched on in this book would require a second volume in itself, a small clutch of recommendations might be handy:

North Wales Rock
  Simon Panton (Ground Up 2006)

Scrambles in Snowdonia
  Steve Ashton (Cicerone 2007)

Welsh Winter Climbs
  Malcolm Campbell and Andy Newton
  (Cicerone 2008)

Lake District Rock (FRCC 2003)

Scrambles in the Lake District, Volume 1: Southern Lakes
  Brian Evans (Cicerone 2007)

Scrambles in the Lake District, Volume 2: Northern Lakes
  Brian Evans (Cicerone 2007)

Lake District Winter Climbs
  Brian Davison (Cicerone and FRCC 2006)

Munster's Mountains, 30 Walking, Scrambling and Climbing Routes
  Denis Lynch (Collins Press 2001)

USEFUL CONTACTS AND WEBSITES

TRANSPORT

Traveline gives transport options, suggested routes and timetables for any journey in the UK – www.traveline.org.uk.

For comprehensive public transport info and route maps in the Lake District visit the **Cumbria County Council** website – www.cumbria.gov.uk.

For information on **Snowdon Sherpa** bus services in the north of Snowdonia see www.snowdoniagreenkey.co.uk.

For **Irish bus** information see www.buseireann.ie.

WEATHER FORECASTS AND CONDITIONS REPORTS

The **Met Office** website offers dedicated mountain area forecasts – www.metoffice.gov.uk.

The **Mountain Weather Information Service** is funded by the Scottish government, but still provides good mountain-top forecasts for Snowdonia, the Lakes and the Pennines as well as links to mountain webcams – www.mwis.org.uk.

The Lake District National Park **Weatherline** offers a mountain weather forecast, links to webcams around the park and daily fell-top conditions reports from Helvellyn (particularly useful in winter, although they err on the side of alarmist at times) – www.lake-district.gov.uk/weatherline.

Snowdonia National Park runs a similar service with local forecasts and a Snowdon webcam, but without the on-the-ground detail – www.eryri-npa.co.uk.

Met Éireann is the Irish meteorological service online – www.met.ie.

Reports on Snowdonian winter climbing conditions are sometimes posted at www.snowdonia-adventures.co.uk.

Lakes-based winter climber Steve Ashworth has a blog with regular winter conditions reports at www.mixedmaster.blogspot.com.

As the de facto national climbing forum and the biggest single source of live info www.ukclimbing.com can be a good place to pick up tips on winter conditions. Given the volume of traffic on this site, if someone suggests that a particular venue is in good condition it would be wise to predict queues there the following day; the wily won't treat it as gospel, but use the information as a guide to what might also be possible at quieter venues nearby.

TIDE TABLES

For tide information in Britain and Ireland your first port of call could be the Admiralty's online **Easy Tide** service http://.easytide.ukho.gov.uk. Remember that tide times are generally quoted in GMT, so allowances have to be made during British Summer Time (BST).

Swell forecasts and live weather buoy data are available on a number of websites including www.magicseaweed.com.

ACCOMMODATION

The **Youth Hostel Association of England and Wales** has the most extensive network of affordable accommodation in rural areas – www.yha.org.uk.

The Irish counterpart to the YHA, **An Óige**, runs a smaller network – www.anoige.ie.

There are also many independently-run hostels and bunkhouses throughout Britain and Ireland, details of which can be found at www.independenthostelguide.co.uk.

OTHER ORGANISATIONS

The **British Mountaineering Council** (BMC) is the representative body for climbers and hillwalkers in England and Wales. It seeks to protect the hill environment, promote our interests, and to serve as an umbrella organisation to which hundreds of clubs are affiliated – www.thebmc.co.uk.

The **Mountaineering Council of Ireland** (MCI) performs a similar function to the BMC in the Republic of Ireland – www.mountaineering.ie.

The **Ramblers Association** tend to represent more earthbound hillgoers – www.ramblers.org.uk.

As the largest single landowner of coasts and hills, and an organisation with a generally enlightened attitude to conservation-weighted land management and public access, it can be worth keeping abreast of developments at the **The National Trust** – www.nationaltrust.org.uk.

The **Campaign for National Parks** is a charity that seeks to protect our most highly-prized landscapes, acting as an umbrella organisation for a large number of smaller environmental and amenity groups across England and Wales – www.cnp.org.uk.

As the national coordinating body for the many local volunteer mountain rescue teams the **Mountain Rescue Council of England and Wales** deserves our support – www.mountain.rescue.org.uk.

GUIDES AND INSTRUCTORS

Whether you're building the skills and confidence to tackle the harder ridges independently or just fancy a supervised day out doing something you normally wouldn't, professional supervision might be an attractive option.

As the National Mountain Centre for England and Wales, **Plas y Brenin** runs some of the best courses anywhere – www.pyb.co.uk.

The Scottish equivalent to Plas y Brenin, offering mountain training in the Cairngorms, is **Glenmore Lodge** – www.glenmorelodge.org.uk.

The **Association of Mountaineering Instructors** holds a region-by-region list of qualified freelance instructors on its website – www.ami.org.uk.

FURTHER INFORMATION

www.ukscrambles.com offers an online forum and route information for British scrambles.

www.ukclimbing.com has a database of crags and routes, and its forums can be a valuable source of information for summer climbs as well as winter conditions.

If this book's brief delve into the Exmoor coast has kindled an intrepid spark then the website detailing the awesome looking Coast Traverse will stoke the fire – see www.exmoor92.fsnet.co.uk.

APPENDIX 4
GLOSSARY OF CLIMBING JARGON

You need more than a command of the language to tackle a technical climb, but just in case you're wondering what your climbing chums are on about…

abseil　Technique for descending ropes. Best performed gingerly rather than in flamboyant SAS style; abseiling accidents are far too common.

abseil tat　An anchor of sling or cord on which to set up an abseil. Treat the strength and reliability of any in situ tat you come across with great suspicion, as your life will depend on it. Sensible climbers carry their own supply.

à cheval　Astraddle, as on horseback. A common manoeuvre on narrow airy ridge crests.

arete　A well-defined narrow ridge. Also used to describe smaller outward-pointing features on crags (the opposite of corners).

balancey　Said of a passage of climbing that requires a delicate and well-honed sense of balance. The holds will be small.

to belay　To protect a partner from falling (or at least, from falling too far) using a rope controlled with techniques or devices that create friction. *Belay* as a noun refers to the arrangement of anchors set up to secure the belayer.

bridging　Spreadeagling one's legs between widely spaced holds set on slightly different planes – the opposite walls of a chimney or corner, for instance. Americans call this *stemming*, though its connection to flower arranging is not obvious.

cam　aka Friend (a brand name that has become generic in the mould of Hoover). A spring-loaded protection device designed to fit a range of crack sizes.

chimney　A fissure in a crag, usually noisome, more or less parallel-sided and wide enough to get into – if you insist. Chimneys tend to be climbed with a mixture of bridging, inelegant grunting and the dreaded back-and-foot technique (about which the less said the better).

chossy　Dirty, loose or overgrown. Too often all three at once.

corner　The point of convergence between two planes (of rock, in our case); often ideal places to practise one's bridging.

crux　The hardest pitch or move on a route; make sure your mate gets to lead this bit unless you are the hero.

to flank (vb)　To go around an obstacle (as in, to outflank it).

foot traverse　A traverse in which the holds are best placed to be used by the feet – there won't be much to hold onto.

gendarme　A distinct pinnacle on a ridge.

groove　Like a corner, only less pronounced and of wider angle. Not deep enough to be called a crack.

hand traverse　A traverse that is all on your hands. There isn't a lot to stand on – only smears, perhaps.

hex　*aka* chock. An irregularly shaped hexagonal nut, often slung with cord or tape, sometimes wire. Usually carried in bigger sizes to supplement one's (smaller) nuts.

jamming　The black art of ascending steep cracks by wedging hands, feet or fingers inside, rather than actually holding onto anything.

jugs	Generous handle-like holds, often met with the expression 'Thank God'.
mantle	A tricky technique to mount a ledge devoid of anything worthy of the name 'hold'. Needs practice.
moving together	Two or more people climbing simultaneously, but roped together and using runners. Very easy to get wrong with potentially disastrous consequences.
neck	A pronounced narrow bit joining two broader bits – on a ridge perhaps. Also the thing one tries not to break.
névé	Hard frozen snow – a delight to climb if you've remembered to bring ice axe and crampons; very dangerous if you haven't.
niche	An alcove in the rock, too shallow to be a cave.
nut	A metal wedge, usually slung with wire, that is inserted into cracks and fissures to provide protection. Nuts tend to be carried in smaller sizes than hexes.
offwidth	A deep fissure that is too narrow to enter bodily, but too wide to climb by jamming hands and feet inside it. Offwidths are almost invariably slimy and polished, and always best avoided.
protection	Nuts, chocks, cams, pegs, bolts, threads, slings, ice screws, warthogs, frozen Mars Bars hammered optimistically into fissures – anything the leader clips to the rope in order to minimise the length and undesirable consequences of a fall.
runner	A piece of protection placed by the leader to safeguard a fall.
runout	An unusually long distance between places where protection can be found. (As an adjective, 'run out', can used to describe a passage of climbing on which there is an unusually long distance between places where protection can be found.)
slab	An area of rock inclined on the friendly side of vertical. That's not to say all slabs are easy, however. They often lack generous holds, in which case ascent may require delicate, balancey padding, smearing and a lot of faith in friction.
sloper	A hold which slopes, rather than a positive incut.
smearing	Using the friction of sole rubber on rock, in the absence of any actual foothold.
smears	Placements for the feet that rely on the friction of sole rubber on rock.
spike	*aka* bollard. A pointy bit of rock. A sling draped over a spike might provide very quick-to-place protection, but not all spikes are firmly attached to the mountain.
thrutch	Can be said of the ascent of jamming cracks, offwidths and chimneys by a variety of freestyle techniques. Inelegant and exhausting, and you'll know it when you see it.
thuggy	A strenuous passage that succumbs to a powerful unsubtle technique – overhanging but well endowed with jugs, perhaps.
traverse	Going across something rather than up it. One can 'traverse', rock walls, ridge crests and even steep slopes. But not roads. (As an adjective, 'traversey' may be used to describe a passage of climbing that involves a lot of going across.)
turf	A mixture of soil and plant matter – when frozen solid this is a lovely medium for winter climbers; when unfrozen it really isn't.
wall	A more or less flat vertical bit of rock; steeper than a slab, but not generally overhanging.
zawn	*aka* geo. A deep inlet in a tidal sea cliff, like a cave but with no roof.

LISTING OF CICERONE GUIDES

For full and up-to-date information
on our ever-expanding list of guides,
please visit our website:
www.cicerone.co.uk.

Cicerone's mission is to inform and inspire by providing the best guides to exploring the world

Since its foundation 40 years ago, Cicerone has specialised in publishing guidebooks and has built a reputation for quality and reliability. It now publishes nearly 300 guides to the major destinations for outdoor enthusiasts, including Europe, UK and the rest of the world.

Written by leading and committed specialists, Cicerone guides are recognised as the most authoritative. They are full of information, maps and illustrations so that the user can plan and complete a successful and safe trip or expedition – be it a long face climb, a walk over Lakeland fells, an alpine cycling tour, a Himalayan trek or a ramble in the countryside.

With a thorough introduction to assist planning, clear diagrams, maps and colour photographs to illustrate the terrain and route, and accurate and detailed text, Cicerone guides are designed for ease of use and access to the information.

If the facts on the ground change, or there is any aspect of a guide that you think we can improve, we are always delighted to hear from you.

Cicerone Press
2 Police Square Milnthorpe Cumbria LA7 7PY
Tel: 015395 62069 Fax: 015395 63417
info@cicerone.co.uk www.cicerone.co.uk

CICERONE